The Politics of Unfunded Mandates

BUSINESS/SCIENCE/TECHNOLOGY DIVISION
CHICAGO PUBLIC LIBRARY
400 SOUTH STATE STREET
CHICAGO, IL 60605

American Governance and Public Policy

A SERIES EDITED BY

Barry Rabe and John Tierney

This series examines a broad range of public policy issues and their relationship to all levels of government in the United States. The editors welcome serious scholarly studies and seek to publish books that appeal to both academic and professional audiences. The series showcases studies that illuminate the successes, as well as the problems, of policy formulation and implementation.

The Politics of Unfunded Mandates

Whither Federalism?

Paul L. Posner

GEORGETOWN UNIVERSITY PRESS / WASHINGTON, D.C.

Georgetown University Press, Washington, D.C. 20007
© 1998 by Georgetown University Press. All rights reserved.

10   9   8   7   6   5   4   3   2   1   1998

THIS VOLUME IS PRINTED ON ACID-FREE ⊚ OFFSET BOOK PAPER

Library of Congress Cataloging-in-Publication Data

Posner, Paul L.
   The politics of unfunded mandates : whither federalism? / Paul L.
Posner.
     p.   cm. — (American governance and public policy)
   Includes index.
   ISBN 0-87840-708-1 (cloth).—ISBN 0-87840-709-X (pbk.)
   1. Unfunded mandates—United States. 2. Intergovernmental fiscal
relations—United States. 3. Fiscal policy—United States.
I. Title.   II. Series.
HJ275.5.P67   1998
336.73—dc21   98-16020

R0456042240

CHICAGO PUBLIC LIBRARY

to Arlene and Jennie

CHICAGO PUBLIC LIBRARY

Contents

List of Tables   xi

Preface   xiii

Acknowledgments   xv

1 **Introduction**   1
MANDATES: THE EVOLUTION OF FEDERAL CONSTRAINTS 3,
THE MANDATE DIALECTIC 5,   ADDRESSING THE POLITICS OF MANDATES:
THE FOCUS OF THE BOOK 10,   NOTES 17

2 **Evolving Models of the Policymaking Process for Our
Federal System**   20
CLASSIC VIEWS OF POLICYMAKING 20,   EMERGENCE OF DYNAMIC
MODELS OF NATIONAL POLICYMAKING 23,   SHIFTING MODELS OF
THE FEDERAL SYSTEM 28,   IMPLICATIONS FOR THE POLITICS OF
MANDATES 30,   NOTES 32

3 **Federal Mandates: Congressional Alignments**   36
ROLL CALL VOTING ON FEDERALISM ISSUES 36,   MANDATE ROLL CALLS:
98TH THROUGH 101ST CONGRESSES 39,   IMPLICATIONS 54,
NOTES 54

4 **The Rush Toward Consensus**   57
INVENTORY OF SIGNIFICANT MANDATES, 1983–1990 57,
SIGNIFICANT MANDATES PASSED WITH BROAD SUPPORT 58,
MANDATES IN THE 99TH CONGRESS 60,   IMPETUS FOR THE
MANDATES OF THE 99TH CONGRESS 61,   CONSENSUS EXPLAINED:
DISARMING THE CONSTRAINORS 66,   IMPLICATIONS 74,
NOTES 74

5 **State and Local Government Interest Group Behavior   78**

STATE AND LOCAL GOVERNMENT OPPOSITION 78,   STATE AND LOCAL
GROUPS MIXED VIEWS ON MANDATES 81,   SOURCES OF STATE AND
LOCAL AMBIVALENCE 83,   FEATURES OF MANDATES THAT LIMIT STATE
AND LOCAL INFLUENCE 86,   IMPLICATIONS 89,   NOTES 91

6 **Asbestos and the Politics of Consensus   94**

THE POLITICAL EXTRAPOLATION OF SCIENCE 95,   THE SCHOOLS:
TARGET FOR REGULATORY EXPANSION 96,   EARLY FEDERAL POLICY
ACTION FOLLOWS THE INCREMENTAL MODEL 97,   REGULATION
BEGETS REGULATION 101,   MANY ROADS LEAD TO WASHINGTON 102,
A NEW CONGRESSIONAL CHAMPION EMERGES 105,   THE POLITICS OF
UNANIMITY 107,   THE AMBIVALENT POSITION OF THE SCHOOLS 111,
A REPUBLICAN SENATE ENACTS A STRONGER BILL 113,   HOUSE-SENATE
NEGOTIATIONS 115,   A LEGISLATIVE POSTCRIPT ON COSTS 117,
IMPLICATIONS 118,   NOTES 120

7 **Education for Preschool Handicapped Children   126**

THE GROWTH OF THE FEDERAL PRESENCE IN SPECIAL EDUCATION 127,
PASSAGE OF THE 1975 MANDATE 130,   CONSENSUS DISSOLVES
DURING IMPLEMENTATION 131,   PRESCHOOL HANDICAPPED COVERAGE
MAKES THE AGENDA 133,   THE SENATE PASSES A PRESCHOOL
MANDATE 138,   THE BILL BREAKS THROUGH TO THE HOUSE
AGENDA 144,   THE SCHOOLS AWAKEN TO THE COST IMPACTS OF THE
SENATE BILL 147,   THE HOUSE BILL: THE POLITICS OF CONSENSUS 150,
THE POISONED CARROT? 153,   IMPLICATIONS 154,   NOTES 155

8 **The Politics of Mandate Reform   160**

MANDATE REFORM ACHIEVES AGENDA STATUS 160,   ACTION IN
CONGRESS 168,   IMPLICATIONS 175,   NOTES 176

9 **The Impact of Mandate Reform   180**

OVERVIEW OF MANDATES ENACTED IN 1996 181,   MANDATE
RESTRAINT AND MODIFICATION 182,   THE MARCH OF MANDATES
CONTINUES 185,   MANDATE ROLLBACKS 187,   THE POLITICS OF
FEDERAL MANDATES REVISITED 189,   OTHER INSTITUTIONAL
DEVELOPMENTS 202,   IMPLICATIONS 206,   NOTES 207

10 Conclusions   211
IMPLICATIONS OF THE NEW POLICYMAKING PROCESS 211,
STATE AND LOCAL GOVERNMENTS AND MANDATES 215,
WHITHER FEDERALISM? 222,   NOTES 229

Appendix 1: Major Mandate Legislation,
**   98th–101st Congresses   233**
Index   239

List of Tables

3-1 Mandate Support Scores by Congress and Party   42

3-2 Mandate Support by Area   44

3-3 Administrations' Mandate Support by Area, 1983–1990   46

3-4 Regression of Overall Mandate Index on Independent Variables   48

3-5 Regression Results for Six Mandate Dimensions, Senate   50

3-6 Regression Results for Six Mandate Dimensions, House   52

4-1 Features of Major Mandate Legislation, 98th–101st Congresses   58

4-2 Floor Conflict over Significant Mandates   59

4-3 Mandate Support by Party, 99th Congress   70

9-1 Congressional Budget Office Mandate Statements, 1996   181

9-2 Party Support for Mandates by Policy Dimension   192

9-3 Senate Voting Model for Mandates   194

9-4 House Voting Model Mandates   196

9-5 Influence of Party on Mandate Scores   197

Preface

The idea for this book really began in the 1980s—a time when federalism leapt from the pages of academic journals and books to the front pages of newspapers and talk shows. I well remember a *Washington Post* article prompted by President Reagan's daunting federalism initiatives of the early 1980s that gave instant fame and recognition to what it considered to be abstract concepts pursued by a handful of academics and an obscure federal body known as the Advisory Commission on Intergovernmental Relations. It turns out that, although serious reform proposals met with little success, federalism was to enjoy more than its fifteen minutes of fame. In fact, conflict over the federal role in domestic policy emerged to become a salient feature of our contemporary political debate, as it had in previous eras of our political history.

Much of the conflict from the early 1980s through the mid-1990s centered on federal grant programs—should they be devolved to the states and under what conditions? Starting with the Reagan block grants of 1981 and carrying through to the welfare reform block grant of 1996, considerable political rhetoric and academic research alike focused on the impacts of shifting power for making decisions about major programs from the federal government to the states.

Yet, while the devolution debate raged, the federal government found a new set of tools to carry out national domestic policies implicating states and localities—the federal mandate in its numerous forms. Research showed that this tool attracted wide support, even during supposedly conservative eras when federal power had gone out of fashion. It became apparent that the fiscal and programmatic impact of these new centralizing tools was every bit as significant, if not more so, than the much touted block grants of the Reagan era. These new regulatory initiatives prompted major intergovernmental conflict, as the intensity of fiscal fears expressed by state and local officials was matched by the hopes and expectations of beneficiaries of these programs.

As high as the stakes were, the research on the politics that gave rise to these new tools of federal power was surprisingly sparse. As interest in mandate relief and reform picked up in the 1990s, a systematic study of the political roots of mandates became even more essential to understand what interests and needs they satisfied and whether mandate reform could be expected to significantly alter the use of these tools. It is my hope that this book will fill that gap in our collective understanding, answering many questions and raising others for future research and puzzlement as well.

Acknowledgments

A book like this is a major project that could not have been done without the encouragement, technical guidance, and emotional support from several important people and institutions in my life. The research for this began as a doctoral dissertation in political science at Columbia University. The encouragement and advice of Professor Demetrios Caraley was of great importance, and his generous sharing of his perspectives helped me mold my methodology and approach. Professor Richard Pious was also a key player, offering encouragement and sage advice as a contemporary; the time he spent coaching me and his detailed comments on earlier drafts were particularly helpful.

The intellectual foundation for my interest and many of my ideas on intergovernmental regulation is perhaps most directly attributable to several federalism scholars who had served with distinction as staff with the Advisory Commission on Intergovernmental Relations (ACIR). David Beam, who now directs the public administration program at the Illinois Institute of Technology, spent countless hours in selfless devotion to seeing this project through to successful completion. His insights and ideas were not only stimulative, but formative to the framework and approach of this book. Any study of mandates must start with his pathbreaking work directing ACIR's studies of intergovernmental regulation in the 1980s. Timothy Conlan, now with George Mason University, was also an erstwhile advisor whose analytical insights were always interesting. His generous participation as a reader of early drafts and his encouragement and assistance in bringing this book to publication have been invaluable. David Walker, now of the University of Connecticut, contributed sage comments and a lifetime of work that influenced much of my thinking on federalism; his comments on an earlier draft helped sharpen the message considerably. Margaret Wrightson, a colleague now with the U.S. General Accounting Office, also helped with advice and suggestions, particularly on methodology and regression analysis.

I reaped the benefits of two statistically gifted professionals in completing the regression models of mandate roll call voting. Gregory Dybalski, a stastical expert with the U.S. General Accounting Office, and

Patrick Brogan, actively worked with me to set up and run innumerable regressions on mandate roll calls and generally upgraded my statistics knowledge tenfold.

I must also express my gratitude to some important people at my primary place of employment, the U.S. General Accounting Office (GAO), where I currently serve as Director of Federal Budget Issues. Doing this book was a project separate and apart from my GAO job and accordingly finishing the book at times came to be as demanding as a second job. I appreciated the support, and forbearance given by colleagues and supervisors alike, including Bill Gadsby, Gene Dodaro, Jennie Stathis, and Susan Irving, among many others. These are but a few of the many wonderful people at GAO, top to bottom, that make it such an excellent place to develop public policy analysis that makes a difference. Needless to say, the views expressed in this book are entirely my own and do not represent those of the U.S. General Accounting Office.

The support and patience of the editorial staff of Georgetown University Press have also been critical to bringing this book to publication. In particular, I must express my gratitude to John Samples, my editor, whose painstaking attention to detail and quality made the book so much better and readable, and whose patience gave me the time I needed to prepare a manuscript that both he and I liked.

Finally, a journey like this does not conclude without the emotional support of several significant people in one's life. First and foremost is my wife of twenty-nine years, Arlene. She was with me at the start, when I first entered graduate school in 1969 and, sometimes to my surprise, hung in there with me through numerous lost weekends till the end of this project today. Her patience, active encouragement, and persistent belief in my ability to finish helped drown the many moments, hours, and days of self-doubt that raised their ugly heads during this project. My daughter Jennie, a graduate of the University of Virginia, practically grew up with this project. She helped by being herself—kind, caring, fun, and supportive; she also entered roll call data on Lotus spreadsheets, albeit for a small fee! Many friends were coconspirators as well, helping with good cheer and encouragement, beginning with Gary Dwoskin, who has served as ex-officio brother for forty-seven years. I want to thank my parents, Bernard and Bess Posner, who gave me a lively interest in public life and policy and a desire to make a mark in that world. Finally, a warm and everlasting tribute goes to Alex Halperin, a wise and valued person in my life.

1

Introduction

Anyone familiar with the American political dialogue in the post–World War II era learned that national policymakers were grappling with issues of vital importance to the whole nation, and increasingly the entire planet. The federal government, after all, had weapons of mass destruction sufficient to obliterate human existence. When not gripped by the drama of war and peace, national leaders were, among many other things, preoccupied with managing the nation's economy, guaranteeing economic security to the elderly and the poor, improving the educational opportunities of our children, and underwriting the financing for much of our nation's infrastructure. The public learned to train many of their personal hopes and frustrations on leaders and institutions in Washington, with the encouragement of a nationalized media and the leaders themselves.

For most of the postwar period, it appeared that state and local governments, those governments "closest to the people," had become the farthest thing from their minds. It appeared, indeed, that these governments were, if anything, stumbling blocks to achieving goals and services valued by an increasingly cohesive national community. Federalism was relegated to academic journals and cocktail parties, of seeming irrelevance to leaders intent on achieving great national goals in Washington.

The dialogue now seems to be changing. Beginning in the 1980s and increasing in the 1990s, federalism reemerged as a value of some consequence. Even if state and local governments were not the lead item on the evening news, recognition grew that they were the critical "middlepersons" responsible for implementing many of those bold new federal initiatives and that their performance had a critical bearing on national goals and values. Moreover, as national leaders wrestled with fiscal limitations and public qualms and concerns about an overextended federal presence, state and local governments were rediscovered by right and left alike. Having undergone extensive administrative, fiscal, and political modernization, state and local

1

governments were ready to take on new challenges that were brought to them in an era of federal constraints.[1]

In this new environment, the health of our federal system became a legitimate policy issue at the national level. Many worried that the proliferation of national initiatives had come to jeopardize the diversity and responsiveness of state and local governments to unique and differing needs and interests. In brief, federal programs were alleged to have prompted an overcentralized, inefficient, and unaccountable system of government. In the guise of helping citizens to solve their private troubles, the federal government was said to have sapped the vitality from states and localities by cajoling, enticing, and then ordering them to carry out federal goals and objectives.

Mandates and other forms of federal regulation epitomized the lack of balance and accountability in our federal system. Experiencing the joy of creating new benefits while passing down the pain of paying for them, federal officials had seemingly little discipline in foisting new responsibilities on the state and local sector. Although state and local costs were not visible at the federal level, these mandated programs at some point threatened to undermine the capacity of state and local governments to respond to the unique needs of their publics.

Devolution and mandate reform came to be new watchwords in the national debate. Some want to return power to the states and swear off using mandates, reflecting traditional values in our system and a new awareness of the strength of state and local governments as partners in public service. Passage of the welfare reform block grant in 1996 reflects this renewed commitment to restoring states' authority in our system. Passage of the Unfunded Mandates Reform Act of 1995 signals recognition of the need to hold federal officials more accountable for the intergovernmental consequences of national actions.

Others, however, view devolution and mandate reform with some regret and concern, aware that a national community will continue to hold national officials accountable for addressing problems and values of national consequence.[2] Shifting the locus of decisionmaking for public programs is not a politically or policy-neutral action, since it vitally affects who gets what, where, when, and how. Groups enjoy differential access and influence at different levels of government, and governmental officials at different levels face differing incentives and constraints as well. Some have argued, for instance, that states' competition for economic resources makes them poor custodians for redistributive or environmental programs since their public policies will be too sensitive to business and middle-income taxpayers at the expense of other constituencies and values.[3]

MANDATES: THE EVOLUTION OF FEDERAL CONSTRAINTS

The foregoing suggests that the stakes of this federalism debate are significant, as they have been at other times in our history. Woodrow Wilson once observed that the relation of states to the federal government is the cardinal question of our constitutional system. He also advised that the balance is destined to be redefined by each generation, for "it is the life of the nation itself."[4]

In the postwar years, that relationship became increasingly volatile, as shifting national political and economic forces challenged traditional definitions of federal, state, and local roles in our system. During this era, the federal government expanded its role in domestic policy not by employing legions of federal employees to implement new national programs in such areas as education, mental health, or environmental protection. Rather, to legitimize the growing federal presence and limit federal fiscal liabilities, various tools were deployed to leverage the involvement of nonfederal actors—principally state and local governments—to serve as federal policy intermediaries and implementors.[5] Through the late 1970s, federal grants were the principal tool used to gain state and local participation, and federal assistance grew to comprise over 25 percent of state and local budgets.

The highly restrictive nature of the over 500 grant programs accompanied by prescriptive administrative conditions prompted intergovernmental concerns; one scholar noted that the seemingly incessant "intergovernmentalization" of domestic policy undermined the effectiveness and responsiveness of our system.[6] In spite of these concerns, the system could nonetheless be characterized by many as cooperative in its emphasis on sharing responsibilities and compensating state and local governments for their participation in federal programs.[7]

In fact, some scholars noted that the federal need for states as partners conferred political resources on the states that limited the federal role and introduced a decentralizing bias into federal program design and implementation.[8] Spurning a view of a hierarchical relationship with the federal government at the top, these observers suggested that bargaining between federal and state partners, both equipped with substantial leverage and political resources, more aptly characterized cooperative grant programs. Though federal agencies are armed with money and rules, they must rely on the voluntary cooperation of states, who have the option of not participating in the program. Indeed, federal agencies seeking to enforce federal rules on recalcitrant states frequently backed down in the face of angry congressional delegations and threats by states to leave the program, stranding beneficiaries in need of federally funded services.

The 1970s are now agreed to have marked the recognition of a new, more coercive era in our federal system, during which mandates and other forms of federal regulation vied with grants as a major domestic policy tool of the federal government. The first careful study charting these trends was done by the Advisory Commission on Intergovernmental Relations (ACIR), which observed that federal legislation in the 1970s increasingly relied on compulsory approaches to implement domestic policy goals.[9] John Kincaid observed that the emerging federal deficit was clearly one factor but that, ironically, cooperative federalism had paved the way for coercion because it lowered the constitutional and political barriers to federal involvement and created heightened expectations for national policy outcomes.[10] Having initiated federal involvement with grants, it is almost as if national policymakers reached for a more certain and direct form of leverage over states, one that not coincidentally appeared to be cheaper as well.

"Mandates" is a broad term that actually covers several distinctly different tools used to regulate states and localities. Most people would think of mandates as direct orders imposed by the federal government on the states or local governments to carry out federal policies or programs. This is clearly included in the definition, but so are conditions of grants received by states and localities. Technically, states or localities can refuse a grant, but this is unlikely, particularly for the larger grants such as for highways or Medicaid. Moreover, conditions have become increasingly compulsory, as Congress has extended certain requirements to all grants ("crosscutting requirements") or linked compliance with conditions in smaller programs to the continued receipt of larger pots of federal money ("crossover sanctions"). Finally, preemptions of state and local authority and programs also fall under the mandate rubric. Although technically not a positive command, preemptions prompt similar issues and effects on state and local resources and flexibility. A more extensive discussion of the definitional issues of mandates appears later in this chapter.

Systematic inventories of mandates are hard to come by—the National Conference of State Legislatures identified 185 mandates in 1993.[11] An ACIR study of federal preemptions alone identified 439 statutes enacted since 1789 that displaced state and local authority.[12] Of the 439 preemption statutes tracked by ACIR, over half have been enacted since the 1970s. Figure 1.1 shows the quickening pace in statutory activities for four other major forms of intergovernmental regulation: crosscutting requirements, partial preemptions, crossover sanctions, and direct orders.

When the entire spectrum of federal intergovernmental regulations is examined, it is difficult to identify a major state or local service that

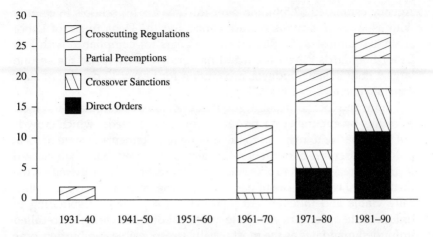

Figure 1.1: *The Growth of Federal Mandates, 1931–1990*

Source: Advisory Commission on Intergovernmental Relations, Federal Regulation of State and Local Governments: The Mixed Record of the 1980's, A-126 (Washington, D.C.: ACIR, 1993), p. 46.

has not been touched by one or more federal mandates. Significant federal mandate areas include air and water pollution, equal employment and service access to protected minorities, wage and hour standards, educational opportunities for the handicapped and women, criminal justice, and transportation policy.

THE MANDATE DIALECTIC

Mandates raise important issues, both fiscal and nonfiscal, for state and local governments, as well as for the federal government. On the fiscal front, earlier studies by the Urban Institute and by Catherine Lovell at the University of California at Riverside were the first to document the fiscal impact on states and localities.[13] A more recent study by Price Waterhouse that was sponsored by the National Association of Counties found that counties spent $4.8 billion in fiscal year 1993 for twelve unfunded federal mandates, or over 12 percent of locally raised revenues.[14] Methodological concerns have been raised about these estimates, notably that they include costs that would have been paid anyway under state and local laws, but it is difficult to deny their significance.

Estimates developed by federal agencies for specific program mandates have been particularly alarming: the Environmental Protection

Agency estimated $2.5 billion over thirty years for schools to comply with asbestos in schools requirements, and the Department of Labor estimated almost $1.5 billion over ten years for compliance with Fair Labor Standards.[15] And Medicaid has grown to comprise the second largest item in state budgets, accounting for nearly 13 percent of state general revenues in 1993.[16]

State and local officials argue that mandates distort state and local priorities by encumbering resources for federal needs, which crowds out the capacity to respond to the unique requirements of state or local publics. Observers of our federal system are worried that when viewed in the aggregate, the proliferation of federal mandates threatens the institutional capacity of subnational governments to survive as politically viable and independent jurisdictions capable of responding to unique state or local needs. State and local officials view the so-called unfunded mandates as the most fiscally irresponsible and burdensome federal actions, although mandates funded fully or partially by the federal government may also distort state and local priorities toward serving federally aided programs.

Mandates carry nonfiscal implications for states and localities as well. The preemption of state or local authority to impose their own laws in such areas as occupational safety and health and surface mining reclamation undermines their capacity to respond to diverse needs in flexible ways.[17] Federal rules implementing mandates often impose a "one-size-fits-all" set of uniform procedures and service delivery approaches that are not tailored to diverse situations throughout the country. The initiative of state and local governments to pioneer innovative approaches is undermined as a result.

Perhaps most important, mandates can serve to undermine accountability in our intergovernmental system. At the federal level, the link between the joy of enacting benefits and the pain of paying for them is broken, removing an important discipline on the creation of public programs. In a sense, state and local costs are perceived as "free" at the federal level, thus increasing federal incentives to literally pass the buck when federal budgetary constraints tighten.

Is the distortion of state and local priorities that is brought on by mandates desirable? Proponents of national regulatory programs in such areas as environmental pollution or handicapped education argue that state and local governments, if left to their own devices, would not provide sufficient resources or protection for programs of national priority and significance. In the view of economists, federal grants or mandates are required to overcome the distortions in public services for programs whose benefits or costs cannot be fully captured by individual states or localities. These jurisdictions have incentives to provide too few services for programs like higher education whose benefits spill over jurisdictional boundaries. They are tempted to export costs to other jurisdictions for problems like wastewater that literally spill over intergovernmental boundaries.

Differing state standards can be viewed as inefficient for a national economy dominated by large national or multinational firms. National mandates, then, help to ensure a uniform level of services throughout what has become a national community with increasingly common expectations for benefits.

Cycles of Mandates

From the time the mandate issue burst onto the policy agenda in the 1970s, these issues have been debated, and the nation's policymakers have proved receptive to mandate advocates and state and local interests in waves or cycles.[18] The first bow wave of major mandates was passed in the 1960s and 1970s, covering such important areas as civil rights, education, and the environment. This major regulatory spike in turn prompted state and local concern that corresponded with a decline in the real value of federal grant funds in the late 1970s. New York's mayor Edward Koch expressed early outrage in a seminal 1980 article, acknowledging his complicity as a congressman in voting for many mandates that subsequently saddled him with large fiscal "millstones" as mayor of New York City.[19]

The advent of the Reagan Administration appeared to mark a turning point on the issue, as the executive branch, if not Congress with a newly elected Republican Senate, had pledged to exercise restraint in the regulatory arena. The regulatory relief task force, headed by Vice President Bush, claimed to save $6 billion in state and local capital costs and about $2 billion in annual recurring costs as a result of reducing regulations in such areas as handicapped transit, bilingual education, and wage standards for federally aided projects.[20] Although Reagan's regulatory relief program was primarily geared toward reducing burdens on business, state and local governments also benefited from such reforms as Executive Order 12291, requiring all major proposed agency regulations to undergo cost-benefit analysis and to be cleared by the Office of Management and Budget. Congress responded to intergovernmental concerns as well by passing the State and Local Cost Estimate Act of 1981, requiring the Congressional Budget Office to quantify the state and local cost impacts of proposed federal legislation as it moves through Congress.[21]

State and local concerns about mandates appeared to ebb with these reforms. David Beam and Timothy Conlan suggest that the 1980s became an "interregnum" during which intergovernmental interests turned their attention to other issues.[22] Accompanied by a new wave of block grants ushered in by the Reagan Administration, it indeed appeared as if the mandate problem had been vanquished. Yet, just as state and local interests were looking the other way, mandates reared their head once more. The ACIR documented that more major intergovernmental regulatory programs were enacted by Congress in the 1980s than in the 1970s.[23]

In an almost predictable fashion, the bow wave of mandates enacted in the 1980s and early 1990s eventually inspired renewed state and local protest. Major state and local interest groups sponsored a National Unfunded Mandates Day in October 1993, including press conferences and visits to their congressional delegations to ask for mandate relief. Congress responded by passing unfunded mandate reform legislation in early 1995, signed by the president.[24] Going beyond the 1981 cost estimation approach, this new process enabled opponents of mandates to raise a point of order in either house of Congress that would require a majority of the body to override.[25]

It is a function of the coalition-building process that modest legislation such as mandate reform is sold with high expectations, suggesting that Congress has solved the mandate problem once and for all. Passage of the new procedural protections for state and local interests may well change the outcome, for it may signal a resurgence of state and local influence within Congress. But it may also suffer the fate of comparable protections for local governments against state mandates, where state legislative officials have continued to pass mandates when compelling state interests are at stake.[26]

Role of the Court

Throughout these years, Congress itself has been the predominant source of most mandates.[27] This assessment is consistent with those of other students of federalism, who argue that Congress is the architect of our system of federalism.[28] Nonetheless, the Supreme Court sets the parameters that define boundaries for congressional actions and, more broadly, the federal government's role in our system.

The Court has become engaged in the mandate dialectic in recent years also, and its views have shifted as well. Until recently, the Court was generally permissive in legitimizing the broad authority of the national government to regulate state and local governments. With the New Deal the Court began to use an expansive view of the interstate commerce clause and the 14th Amendment, among other provisions, to justify the unprecedented growth of the federal role in our system that has taken place over the past sixty years.

One 1976 case did overturn a congressional statute extending federal wage and hour protections to state and local governments, breathing new life into the 10th Amendment, which reserves powers not otherwise delegated to the federal government for the states and the people.[29] However, in a key 1985 ruling—*Garcia v. San Antonio Metropolitan Transit Authority*—the Court reversed the 1976 precedent and reaffirmed the authority of the federal government to directly regulate the affairs of state and local governments. Speaking for the majority, Justice Blackmun indicated that state and local governments must rely on the national political process, not the courts or the Constitution, for protections against federal mandates. The Court expressed its view that states and localities have sufficient political resources to defend themselves against mandates in Congress.[30]

In the following eleven years, however, the Court has changed its view by ruling that the Constitution does provide protection for states and localities against certain direct-order mandates. In several recent cases, the Court essentially has held that Congress may not "commandeer" and compel state or local officials to enforce federal regulatory programs. In a 1992 case, *New York v. United States*, the Court struck down a federal law regulating disposal of low-level radioactive waste that required states to either provide for its disposal or take title to the waste generated within its borders, using the 10th Amendment as its rationale.[31] In a 1995 case, *United States v. Lopez*, the Court constrained the application of the interstate commerce clause to justify federal regulatory interventions by concluding that a law banning guns at public schools lacked sufficient connection to commerce across state boundaries.[32]

In perhaps the most significant ruling, in *Printz v. United States*, the Court overturned the mandate on local police to perform background checks on prospective gun purchasers that was included in the Brady Handgun Violence Prevention Act of 1993. The Court reaffirmed its earlier decision in *New York* by ruling that such commandeering of local officials violated the system of "dual sovereignty" undergirding our Constitution.[33]

The implications of the Court's recent rulings are still unclear. While it appears to have prohibited direct-order mandates that command state and local officials to enforce federal regulatory programs, the Court's rulings do not address the mandate tools most commonly deployed at the federal level—grant conditions, crosscutting requirements, crossover sanctions, partial preemptions, and total preemptions. Consistent with a long line of Court decisions, the *Printz* decision suggests that these approaches do not violate federalism principles because participation by the states is voluntary, at least technically. Thus, it would appear that Congress retains considerable flexibility in mandating new responsibilities and preempting old ones, maintaining its status as the linchpin of our federal system.

ADDRESSING THE POLITICS OF MANDATES: THE FOCUS OF THE BOOK

As the recent history just recounted indicates, federal mandates have proven to be resilient, surviving previous waves of reforms designed to curb their use. This suggests that mandates are the product of deeply rooted political forces in our system. The persistence of reform initiatives, however, also suggests that federalism arguments and state and local interests at least periodically force their way onto the federal agenda as well. This illustrates that congressional decisions on mandates are the product of a swirl of powerful and potentially conflicting forces.

The purpose of this book is to examine the political forces behind the adoption of federal mandates over the years and the political prospects for initiatives that seek to restrain the use of mandates. A comprehensive assessment of the politics of federal mandates should ultimately help us to understand whether mandates are destined to continue as a principal tool of federal action. Assessing the sustainability of mandate reform, then, requires an understanding of the sustainability of mandates themselves as tools of federal action.

With all the controversy mandates provoke, it would be expected that a considerable body of analysis would already be available to address the questions raised earlier. Excellent studies have, in fact, been done to inventory and categorize federal mandates and discuss their consequences for federalism and program outcomes. Most notably, the Advisory Commission on Intergovernmental Relations has done the pathbreaking work pinpointing definitional boundaries and charting trends and federalism implications.[34] However, comparatively little work has been done to systematically analyze the politics of mandates.[35]

The relative dearth of political analysis reflects an observation made by Samuel Beer in 1978 that the political relations between mayors and members of Congress were one of the great unexplored mysteries.[36] Since then, the political questions surrounding congressional passage of mandates have remained largely unexplored in political science. Although considerable scholarship has focused on legal issues and consequences of Supreme Court rulings on federalism questions, comparatively little analysis has addressed how effective states are in using the political process to deflect federal mandates and constraints.[37] This book, then, is intended to fill this gap in our collective understanding of the political forces influencing the evolution of our federal system.

A key assumption underlying the analysis here is that mandates call forth distinct political patterns that transcend the particular substantive policy objectives they implement. The politics of mandates are most assuredly influenced by the policy area involved, such as the environment or handicapped access. However, this book will focus on the unique or distinctive political patterns prompted by the characteristics of mandates as tools of government.

The view that different types of government policies elicit their own unique politics was first articulated many years ago by Theodore Lowi to refer to the different political responses prompted by distributive, regulatory, and redistributive policies.[38] Subsequently, other political scientists such as Lester Salamon concluded that the different tools used by government to implement public policy—e.g., grants, loans, tax expenditures, and regulations—have their own unique set of characteristics, actors, and "political economies" that make a difference for program outcomes and for the politics involved with their creation and implementation.[39]

Key Questions and Focus

This book will address the following key questions that are critical to assessing the politics of federal mandates:

- What political forces prompted the growing reliance on mandates as a policy instrument? What role have changes in our party system, interest group organization, congressional policymaking, and ideas played in this process?
- What political variables are most important in explaining support for mandates within Congress? Do mandates serve as a predictable basis for partisan division within Congress, that is, is any one party a reliable ally of state and local governments on these issues? What role do other factors such as ideology play in influencing congressional decisions to adopt mandates?
- To what extent have state and local governments become effective in constraining congressional activity on mandates? Do they have sufficient intensity, resources, and support to become a restraint on national encroachment? Under what conditions are they likely to gain influence over the mandating process, and what does this suggest for their future strategies?
- To what extent can mandate reform be expected to reduce the federal reliance on mandates and types of mandates chosen?

A definition of mandates is needed to guide the discussion, for the term can potentially apply to a wide range of policy actions. Some researchers, such as Catherine Lovell and her associates, have defined mandates broadly as "any responsibility, action procedure, or anything else that is imposed by constitutional, administrative, executive, or judicial action as a direct order or that is required as a condition of aid."[40] In a more recent study, ACIR coined the term "federally induced costs" to refer to nine types of federal activities that expose state and local governments to additional costs.[41] Although traditional mandates and preemptions enacted by Congress are included, so are federal limitations on state and local taxing authority that arise from tax-exempt bond restrictions, federal administrative actions that impose costs, and the intergovernmental implications of other federal policies such as immigration reform.

This book will focus exclusively on federal mandates themselves, but this still calls for further specification. Mandates could consist of either an affirmative obligation to take action on a policy problem such as treating municipal sewage or a constraint or prohibition on taking action such as preempting state and local laws that require retirement at age fifty-five. Although they appear to be different, in fact the inter-governmental issues raised are similar. For example, preemptions of state revenue sources or standards in such areas as mandatory retire-ment can have just as much state and local fiscal impact as federal actions that mandate new responsibilities.

Mandates involving state and local governments can also reach the private sector, for example, minimum wage requirements, or they can apply uniquely to state or local functions, for example, regulating asbestos in schools. A hybrid mandate applies equally to state and local governments and private entities but imposes unique roles for state and local governments to enforce the federal standards on private entities, such as with occupational safety and health. In these cases, state and local governments are both mandate target and mandate enforcer. For the purposes of better targeting the analysis to the political response by Congress to the intergovernmental mandate issue, this book primarily focuses on those programs that mandate actions or constraints unique to state and local governments.

An additional definitional issue must be resolved. Though federal actions directly ordering affirmative actions or preempting state laws or programs are clearly mandates, what are conditions of aid? The courts have traditionally not viewed grant conditions as mandates, reasoning that state and local governments voluntarily accept the grant.[42] However, grants often require major commitments of state resources, changes in state laws, and even constitutional provisions to conform to a host of federal policy and administrative requirements.[43] As Zimmerman acknowledges, the conditions for some programs must be regarded as mandates when the federal grant program is too large for state and local governments to voluntarily turn down, or when new and onerous conditions are added some time after state and local governments have become dependent on the program.[44] Were it otherwise, recent laws requiring states to extend Medicaid to newly eligible groups—a $3 billion state price tag makes it among the most fiscally burdensome of contemporary mandates—would have to be excluded from our definition due to the technically voluntary nature of the Medicaid program.[45]

Expanding on a typology first introduced by ACIR, this study will encompass six forms of mandates used to regulate states and localities:

- *Direct orders.* The most coercive type of mandate involves federal direction of policy or program to state and local government, typically with criminal or civil sanctions. Examples include federal clean water standards and fair labor standards pertaining to minimum wage and overtime pay.
- *Crosscutting requirements.* Technically conditions of grants, these policies cut across all or most grants received by state and local governments. OMB catalogued over sixty of these requirements, including handicapped access to federally funded facilities and environmental review requirements.
- *Crossover sanctions.* These mandates are sanctioned by withdrawal of all or a portion of a different federal assistance program. An example is the twenty-one-year-old drinking age, which triggers withholding of a portion of a state's highway allotment if violated.
- *Partial preemption.* These mandates preempt state enforcement of standards, typically on private-sector activities, but permit states to participate in enforcement under federal delegation and control. Through those programs, states can implement their own standards, but they typically must be at least equal to federal standards and procedures. Examples include the occupational safety and health program and many environmental programs.
- *Total preemptions.* These are federal laws that preempt state or local laws completely in an area. Unlike mandates that generally compel state or local governments to take some policy action or observe federal goals when pursuing their own policies, total preemptions prevent state and local officials from implementing their own programs in a policy area. Examples include preemption of state and local restrictions on cigarette advertising and preemption of state and local pesticides laws.[46]
- *Major program-specific grant conditions.* These are requirements that are attached to major federal assistance programs that demand significant fiscal and policy actions by states and local

government recipients. Examples include mandates for extending Medicaid coverage to new groups of poor children and mothers and requirements to provide a free appropriate education for all handicapped children.

Furthermore, this book will focus more specifically on congressionally enacted mandates. Although mandates can be imposed by the courts and the executive branch agencies, Congress is acknowledged to be the central actor and originator of the most significant mandates, earning it the dubious distinction of being "mother of mandates."[47]

Research Strategy

This work examines congressional consideration of mandates from the 1980s through the end of 1996. It will analyze the political forces prompting congressional mandates and mandate reform using a multidimensional approach to ensure coverage of the broad sweep of congressional actions, and to give an in-depth treatment of the variables responsible for mandate decisions. Moreover, the evolution of the issue from the 1980s through 1996 requires an approach that captures the policymaking process over a period of time to understand the extent to which the political forces and outcomes have changed.

The analysis first examined mandating during the 1983–1990 period (the 98th through the 101st Congresses). The patterns and conclusions from this period were then compared with mandates considered during 1996—the first year of congressional experience with the Unfunded Mandates Reform Act (passed by the 104th Congress). This permitted us to assess continuities and changes across the two periods and also enabled us to reach some conclusions about the impact of mandate reform on mandate politics at the federal level.

Several specific analytic approaches or "slices" were used to illuminate political patterns. First, congressional voting behavior was analyzed through a roll call analysis of all House and Senate votes on mandates from 1983–1990 and 1996. Such an analysis can help us to understand the variables associated with mandate support or opposition. Most important, roll call analysis can help us to assess the extent to which mandate voting is a distinct voting dimension, affected by predictable and systematic political forces. The presence or absence of such a dimension will go a long way toward an understanding of whether federalism is a stable or consistent basis underlying congressional choices or mandate voting is a function of support for the substantive policy issues supported by the mandate.

However, roll call analysis can capture only those issues that prompt voting conflict on the floor. In fact, a separate analysis showed that the most important and costly mandates enacted during this period were passed without divisive roll call votes and often by unanimous consent—a political outcome that must be explained through more qualitative research. Moreover, roll call analysis does not help explain significant aspects of the political story behind mandates: how they reached agenda status and were defined. One of the most important parts of the analysis is understanding the role played by state and local governments in lobbying on mandate issues.

To address these issues, a more qualititative approach was adopted to better understand the conflicts and eventual consensus reached in many cases. The twelve most significant mandate actions were selected from the 99th Congress—a Congress that passed a large number of important and costly mandates. Selecting one Congress permitted a comparison and contrast of the twelve measures against the backdrop of a single Congress, which controls for other variables such as overall leadership, political climate, and partisan composition of the Congress. The forces providing the impetus for these mandates to attain agenda status were summarized; the approaches used by mandate advocates to mollify potential opponents were assessed; and the positions and roles of the two parties were analyzed. Special analysis was done to explain why conservatives who might otherwise be expected to block or mobilize opposition to mandates failed to do so in these cases. The key mandates passed in 1996 were assessed using a similar qualitative framework.

State and local interest group positions and behavior were defined and categorized for legislation during these periods. Assessments were made of the extent to which the various state and local organizations were unified or divided on mandate bills and of their ability to form alliances with other groups in the process. Particular attention was paid to explaining instances when state and local behavior appeared to be counterintuitive, that is, when these organizations either failed to mobilize or actually supported a federal mandate.

To gain a more in-depth understanding of the variables affecting mandate outcomes, two case studies were conducted to address the politics underlying the passage of two mandates with very different outcomes in the same program area—the asbestos in schools mandate and the extension of special education mandate. The advantage of this selection is that both mandates principally affect the schools, but Congress responded with different outcomes in the two cases—passing a major mandate on asbestos with few concessions made for the schools, but converting a mandate into a grant program for preschool education of handicapped children. As such, these two cases should further illuminate the variables influencing congressional responses to mandates and the conditions under which state and local interests can influence mandate decisions.

Finally, the forces that led to the passage of the Unfunded Mandates Reform Act of 1995 were analyzed to assess how reform reached agenda status and why Congress decided to take on mandate reform at that time. The book then concludes with an analysis of congressional decisions on mandates in 1996—the first year the new mandate reform procedures were in effect. Armed with a new law and a Republican Congress dedicated to restoring federalism, at least in principle, it could be expected that congressional behavior would follow a different course than it had in earlier years. The analysis here explores changes as well as continuities in congressional mandate decisions by comparing the 1996 experience with the earlier period studied.

Quantitative data on roll calls was drawn from *Congressional Quarterly*'s roll calls reported at the end of the year. Qualititative research was based on the review of documents such as congressional hearings, committee reports, floor debates, interest group statements, and various academic and journalistic reports. Interviews were done with over ninety congressional, interest group, academic, and federal agency officials on the mandate issue in general as well as on specific programs reviewed.

The chapters in this book, in effect, peel back the layers of the politics of mandating. Chapter 2 discusses various models of the policymaking process that provide the context for mandate decisionmaking and helps set the stage to understand the empirical presentations that follow. Chapter 3 presents the analysis of congressional roll calls on mandates during the 1980s that reveal the underlying dimensions shaping congressional decisions. Chapter 4 explores the most important mandates enacted in the 99th Congress in 1986 and provides an understanding of the forces responsible for their broad support and enactment. Chapter 5 analyzes the positions and influence of state and local government interest groups—potentially key actors in mandate decisions. Chapter 6 provides the first case study that describes in depth the politics behind the passage of the asbestos in schools mandate in 1986, and Chapter 7 provides a similar case study on the passage of the mandate extending federal handicapped education requirements to preschool children. Chapter 8 discusses the forces that brought mandate reform to the federal agenda in the 1990s and led to the passage of the 1995 reform legislation. Chapter 9 analyzes the influence the Unfunded Mandates Reform Act had on mandate decisions in 1996.

And finally, Chapter 10 draws conclusions on the implications of these findings for both our national policymaking process and our federal system.

NOTES TO CHAPTER 1

1. Richard Nathan coined the term "devolution revolution" to refer to the restoration of states' roles in our system. Richard Nathan, "The Role of the States in American Federalism," in *The State of the States*, 3rd edition, ed. Carl E. Van Horn (Washington, DC: Congressional Quarterly Press, 1996), pp. 13–32.

2. John D. Donahue, *Disunited States* (New York: Basic Books, 1997).

3. Paul Peterson, *The Price of Federalism* (Washington, DC: Brookings Institution, 1995).

4. Woodrow Wilson, *Constitutional Government in the United States* (New York: Columbia University Press, 1921), p. 173.

5. Lester Salamon, ed., *Beyond Privatization: The Tools of Government Action* (Washington, D.C.: Urban Institute Press, 1989), pp. 3–22.

6. David B. Walker, *Toward a Functioning Federalism* (Cambridge, Mass.: Winthrop, 1981), p. 219.

7. John Kincaid, "From Cooperative to Coercive Federalism," *Annals* 509 (May, 1990), pp. 139–152.

8. Richard Nathan, "State and Local Governments under Federal Grants," *Political Science Quarterly* 98 (Spring, 1983); Martha Derthick, *The Influence of Federal Grants* (Cambridge, Mass.: Harvard University Press, 1970). Another excellent presentation of the bargaining perspective is Helen Ingram, "Policy Implementation through Bargaining: The Case of Federal Grants-in-Aid," *Public Policy* 25 (Fall, 1977).

9. Advisory Commission on Intergovernmental Relations, *Regulatory Federalism: Policy, Progress, Impact and Reform*, A–95 (Washington, DC: U.S. Government Printing Office, 1984).

10. John Kincaid, "From Cooperative to Coercive Federalism."

11. National Conference of State Legislatures, *Mandate Catalogue* (Washington, D.C., December, 1993).

12. Advisory Commission on Intergovernmental Relations, *Federal Statutory Preemptions of State and Local Authority: History, Inventory, and Issues*, A–121 (Washington, DC: ACIR, 1992), p. iii.

13. Catherine Lovell, *Federal and State Mandating on Local Governments: An Exploration of Issues and Impacts* (Riverside, Ca.: University of California, Graduate School of Management, 1979); also Thomas Muller and Michael Fix, "Federal Solicitude, Local Costs: The Impact of Federal Regulations on Municipal Finances," *Regulation* (July / August, 1980).

14. Price Waterhouse letter to the Honorable Barbara Sheen Todd, National Association of Counties, 25 October 1993.

15. Estimates cited in ACIR, *Federally Induced Costs Affecting State and Local Governments* (Washington, DC: ACIR, 1995), p. 12.

16. Jocelyn M. Johnston, "The Medicaid Mandates of the 1980's: An Intergovernmental Perspective," *Public Budgeting and Finance* (Spring, 1997), pp. 3–34.

17. Jerome Hanus has characterized the legal preemption as "authority costs"; see Jerome Hanus, ed., *The Nationalization of State Government* (Lexington, Mass.: D.C. Heath, 1981).

18. See David R. Beam and Timothy J. Conlan, "The 1995 Unfunded Mandates Reform Act: The Politics of Federal Mandating Meets the Politics of Reform," *Journal of Public Budgeting and Financial Management* 7(3), pp. 355–386.

19. Edward Koch, "The Mandate Millstone," *Public Interest* (Summer, 1980).

20. Presidential Task Force on Regulatory Relief, *Reagan Administration Achievements in Regulatory Relief for State and Local Governments: A Progress Report* (Washington, DC: Executive Office of the President, 1982).

21. Public Law 97–108.

22. David R. Beam and Timothy J. Conlan, "The 1995 Unfunded Mandates Reform Act: The Politics of Federal Mandating Meets the Politics of Reform," p. 5.

23. Advisory Commission on Intergovernmental Relations, *Federal Regulation of State and Local Governments: The Mixed Record of the 1980's*, A–126 (Washington, DC: ACIR, 1993).

24. Public Law 104–4, 109 Stat. 48.

25. This legislation would exclude many major mandates from coverage by the new point of order process, including mandates enforcing civil rights such as disability protections, as well as mandates accompanying most large grant programs such as special education. See Committee on Governmental Affairs, U. S. Senate, *Report on the Unfunded Mandate Reform Act of 1995 (S1)*, Report No. 104–1, 11 January 1995.

26. U.S. General Accounting Office, *Legislative Mandates: State Experiences Offer Insights for Federal Action* (Washington, DC: U.S. General Accounting Office, September, 1988).

27. Advisory Commission on Intergovernmental Relations, *Regulatory Federalism: Policy, Process, Impact and Reform*, A–95 (Washington, DC: U.S. Government Printing Office, 1984), p. 5.

28. David Walker, *Toward a Functioning Federalism* (Cambridge, Mass.: Winthrop, 1981), p. 107. Also see Timothy Conlan, "Congress and the Contemporary Intergovernmental System," in Robert Digler, ed., *American Intergovernmental Relations Today: Perspectives and Controversies* (Englewood Cliffs, N.J.: Prentice-Hall, 1986), p. 89.

29. *National League of Cities v. Usery*, 426 U.S. 833 (1976).

30. *Garcia v. San Antonio Metropolitan Transit Authority*, 105 S. Ct. 1005 (1985).

31. *New York v. United States*, 505 U.S. 144 (1992).

32. *United States v. Lopez*, 514 U.S. 549 (1995).

33. Printz, Sheriff/Coroner, Ravalli County, *Montana v. United States* (1997).

34. Advisory Commission on Intergovernmental Relations, *Regulatory Federalism: Policy, Process, Impact and Reform* (1984); *Federal Regulation of State and Local Governments: The Mixed Record of the 1980's* (1993); *Federally Induced Costs Affecting State and Local Governments* (1994).

35. Political scientists have examined the politics surrounding the passage and implementation of specific mandates. See, for example, Norman J. Vig and Michael E. Kraft, *Environmental Policy in the 1990's* (Washington, DC: Congressional Quarterly Press, 1990). An informative study of the politics of the 1995 mandate reform legislation is David R. Beam and Timothy J. Conlan, "The 1995 Unfunded Mandates Reform Act: The Politics of Federal Mandating Meets the Politics of Reform."

36. Samuel Beer, "Federalism, Nationalism, and Democracy in America," *American Political Science Review* 72 (1978), pp. 9–21.

37. John C. Pittenger, "Garcia and the Political Safeguards of Federalism: Is There a Better Solution to the Conundrum of the Tenth Amendment?" *Publius: The Journal of Federalism* 22, No. 1 (1992), pp. 1–20.

38. Theodore Lowi, "American Business, Public Policy, Case-Studies and Political Theory," *World Politics* 16 (July, 1964), pp. 677–715.

39. Lester M. Salamon, ed., *Beyond Privatization: The Tools of Government Action* (Washington, DC: Urban Institute Press, 1989), p. 8.

40. Catherine H. Lovell, Max Neiman, Robert Kneisel, Adam Rose, and Charles Tobin, *Federal and State Mandating on Local Governments: Report to the National Science Foundation* (Riverside: University of California, June, 1979), p. 32.

41. Advisory Commission on Intergovernmental Relations, *Federally Induced Costs Affecting State and Local Governments*, M–193 (Washington, DC: ACIR, 1994).

42. Even the Supreme Court decision overturning federal direct order mandates over state and local pay decisions on 10th Amendment grounds in *National League of Cities v. Usery* acknowledged that requirements attached to the voluntary offer of financial assistance would be viewed differently. 426 U.S. 833 (1976).

43. Charles H. Levine and Paul L. Posner, "The Centralizing Effects of Austerity on the Intergovernmental System," *Political Science Quarterly* 96, No. 1 (1981), pp. 67–87. See also Administrative Conference of the United States, *Drafting Federal Grant Statutes*, (Washington, DC: ACUS, 1988).

44. Joseph K. Zimmerman, "Federally Induced State and Local Governmental Costs" (paper delivered at the 1991 Annual Meeting of the American Political Science Association, Washington, D.C., 1 September 1991), p. 4.

45. Julie Rovner, "Governors Ask Congress for Relief from Burdensome Medicaid Mandates," *Congressional Quarterly Weekly Report*, 16 February 1991, p. 417.

46. See Joseph K. Zimmerman, *Federal Preemption: The Silent Revolution.*

47. David Walker, "Evolving Devolution, Continuing Centralization, and a Resulting Conflicted and Dysfunctional Federalism" (paper presented at USIS Germany-Sponsored Lectures, 13–20 June 1997), p. 12.

2

Evolving Models of the Policymaking Process for Our Federal System

The dearth of empirical studies of the politics of mandates in particular does not mean we are without intellectual benchmarks to guide our analysis. Several broader views of the policymaking process and federalism provide ideas and models to help explain the politics of federal mandates and the outlook for reform. Each of these theories aids in defining mandate politics at various times and stages in our recent history. No one model or approach may exclusively explain the trends at any one time. Rather, ideas from several different models may be necessary to fully capture the outcomes of mandate policymaking.

CLASSIC VIEWS OF POLICYMAKING

Classic, traditional models of policymaking in our federal system suggest that Congress would show considerable restraint in passing mandates applying to the state and local sector. The policymaking process itself is characterized as being incremental in nature, channeling new claims into small, step-by-step departures from current policy. This tradition would predict that new demands for federal action might take the form of familiar federal assistance programs rather than new mandates imposed on the state and local sector.[1] Consistent with our Madisonian system, new government programs are difficult to enact in our multiple-veto, pluralistic system. David Truman voiced the conventional wisdom when he wrote that defensive groups opposed to new policies such as mandates, for example, have an advantage because the deck is stacked against new government action.[2]

The interest group system was also said to be biased against government action. Schattschneider notes that, classically, pressure group politics is a selective process that represents small groups with intensely felt, exclusive interests but does not serve diffuse interests articulating more broadly shared values.[3] More recent theories suggest that groups representing narrower interests of producers affected by new regulatory proposals, such as state and local governments, have greater incen-

20

tives to organize and pursue intense political action than groups purporting to represent broader publics benefiting from such programs.

Mancur Olson discusses the free-rider problem that afflicts broader groups trying to marshall political action: Since all can benefit from the pursuit of a broad group's interests, such groups will have difficulty forming and sustaining a dedicated membership base.[4] James Q. Wilson similarly observes that broader interests standing to gain from federal regulatory programs will not have the level of intensity that those who must pay the costs will have for such programs.[5] Truman's notion that disturbances are at the root of interest group formation also suggests that groups like state and local governments aggrieved by governmental actions would be more likely to organize and mount political campaigns to defend their interests.

The party system in general was said to offer the greatest protection for states and localities against federal intrusion. Although parties were not acknowledged in the early history of the republic, *The Federalist Papers* recognized that the state role in selecting national officials would ensure that "a local spirit will prevail" in Congress.[6] As late as 1960, Morton Grodzins noted that the party system was decentralized, with its power base concentrated at the state and local level. National office holders, whether they be presidents or congressmen, owed their nominations to state and local party leaders—typically governors or mayors. Accordingly, they would have to be sensitive to the prerogatives of these officials when formulating national policy.[7] As Banfield and Wilson observed in their classic 1963 study of city politics, congressmen and senators are essentially local politicians, and those who forget it soon cease to be politicians at all.[8] David Truman noted that the dominance of congressional nominations by state and local party leaders ensures that congressional decisions will defer to state and local interests: "If a legislator's risks are localized, he will look in that direction when making difficult choices on matters of public policy."[9]

The cleavages defining the party system, at least since the 1930s, could be expected to at minimum prompt a healthy debate over mandates expanding the federal role. More specifically, one of the defining principles of the Republican Party was preserving federalism and constraining the growth of federal power.[10] The Republican occupancy of the presidency during much of the 1970s and 1980s, as well as their control of the Senate between 1981 and 1986 and the entire Congress since 1995, could be expected to ensure significant federal restraint on mandates during these times.

The growing organizational presence of state and local governments as interest groups in Washington might also be expected to stem the tide of federal mandates. Organizations including the National

Governors Association, National Conference of State Legislatures, National Association of Counties, National League of Cities, and the U.S. Conference of Mayors grew to become major lobbies in Washington, with highly professional staffs dedicated to advancing state and local positions on pending legislation. Samuel Beer, coining the term "topocrats", suggested that these organizations bring a major decentralizing influence to bear on the design and administration of federal programs.[11]

At an early time, these traditional notions of constraints may indeed have accurately described congressional policy. Prior to the 1960s, in fact, it appears that a presumption against coercive federal mandates on the state and local sector had been accepted as one of the rules of the game by all actors in the system.

It is of some interest that the classic models of policymaking served as the underpinning for the Supreme Court's seminal *Garcia* ruling. The Court's view that state and local governments should rely on the political process to protect their interests was premised on the classic models' assertions of the institutional limits to national power, as articulated by such legal scholars as Herbert Wechsler and Jesse Choper.[12] Choper argued that state interests are protected by such institutions as the influence of state and local parties on national office holders, prior state and local positions held by congressmen, the growing presence of state and local lobbies, and the numerous veto points by which proposed mandate legislation can be blocked by state and local officials and their congressional allies.

Observers of federalism note that Congress did show the kind of restraint commensurate with a cooperative system of federalism prior to the 1960s. For example, the Kestnbaum Commission—a 1955 commission convened by the Eisenhower Administration to study the status of intergovernmental relations—asserted that federal regulation of state and local government was not even an appropriate federal policy agenda item, noting that the national government is generally not allowed to impose mandatory duties on states and localities.[13] As recently as 1961, M. J. C. Vile, an English observer, characterized congressional views on federal-state relations as a legislative body of local politicians defending state power.[14]

American experts on federalism viewed the system in similar terms before the great outpouring of national legislation in the 1960s. Daniel Elazar writes that until the 1960s, the political influence of states meant that Congress would favor and protect states in federal legislation.[15] The Advisory Commission on Intergovernmental Relations reported that, prior to the 1970s, landmark federal regulatory statutes such as the Fair Labor Standards Act, the Social Security Act, and Title VII of the Civil Rights Act of 1964, which barred racial and sexual discrimination in employment, exempted state and local governments from their regulatory nets in deference to federalism values.[16] David Vogel argues that support for American business at one time also attained the status of a widely shared rule that was subscribed to by all political actors.[17]

EMERGENCE OF DYNAMIC MODELS OF NATIONAL POLICYMAKING

More contemporary models of the policymaking process have emerged in recent years to explain the expansion of the federal role since the 1960s. The constraint models just discussed have been at least supplemented, if not supplanted, by dynamic interpretations of the policymaking process. The older pluralistic models predicted only incremental changes to policy, due in large part to the dominance of each policy area by change-resistant iron triangles. However, these models failed to explain the rapid passage of previously unthinkable policy initiatives and reforms, such as tax reform, Medicare, and airline deregulation.

New models suggest a policy process far more open to major new policy initiatives. In one important work, Baumgartner and Jones depict a punctuated equilibrium model that describes how policy arenas that experience years of stability can suddenly come undone and be reformed when swept by a wave of enthusiasm for new ideas and interests.[18] John Kindgon describes agenda setting using the "garbage can" theory of organization to depict a process that is fluid and subject to rapid change.[19]

In an important study of the passage of the 1986 tax reform act, Beam, Conlan, and Wrightson posited a "new politics of reform" model as an alternative to explain the adoption of far-reaching, nonincremental policy change. In this view, ideas purveyed by influential experts and policy entrepreneurs find increasingly fertile ground in a more open, activist Congress that is anxious to take credit for legislation that appeals to broadly shared values championed by an all-pervasive media. Politicians compete not only for credit on these issues, but also to avoid blame for defeating such legislation.[20] The analysis by Derthick and Quirk of the politics of deregulation echoes this view by suggesting how emerging political forces now give political leaders a good chance of defeating narrow interests and overcoming particularism.[21]

Several important secular political developments underpin this new politics of reform. First, the party system has attenuated as a controlling influence on members' behavior. In contrast with Grodzins' view that our decentralized party system fosters decentralized government, more recent research in the field points to the dissolution of cohesive state and local parties. While Grodzins suggests that congressmen view themselves as ambassadors, representing their state and local governments to the nation, the weakening of party ties has led to a separation in the electoral interests of congressional actors and state and local officials.[22] Congressmen operate from their own political base, courting interest groups and other independent sources of support, not state and local party officials. In the era of split-ticket voting, candidates for office spanning all levels of government no longer have their electoral fortunes bound together by the tie of party. In fact, the relationship between congressmen and state or local elected officials of the same party often resembles a competitive or even antagonistic one between independent political entrepreneurs in search of money, visibility, and votes.[23] John Chubb argues that this trend toward electoral autonomy between federal and state office holders has removed a vital constraint on the growth of federal influence and has contributed to a congressional bias toward centralization.[24]

One consequence has been the transformation of members of Congress from loyal members of state and local party organizations to independent policy entrepreneurs searching for new issues to highlight their visibility to interest groups and the media. David Mayhew argues that members of Congress have become increasingly interested in position and credit-taking to maintain high profiles for reelection. Mandates are an ideal vehicle for this kind of activity because they permit the member to take credit for the policy's benefits without having to account for its costs.[25]

Congress has changed its institutional mores and rules to facilitate policy leadership by a broader base of entrepreneurs. By decentralizing policy initiative to subcommittees, new leadership opportunities were created across the board for even junior members of Congress. Changing institutional mores permitted even freshman members to assert strong leadership profiles in specific policy areas. Policy areas, once classified as iron triangles or policy monopolies controlled by long-standing rules and political relationships, came to be characterized as issue networks with more fluid, open, and fragmented political attachments.[26]

These trends toward congressional policy activism span party boundaries, obfuscating partisan differences on federal role questions that used to define the party system. Leaders of both parties increasingly have been found to engage in opportunistic competition to either champion federal leadership of compelling national causes or avoid being blamed for defeating such initiatives. One major study, for instance, concluded that the Nixon Administration presided over the greatest expansion of regulation over state and local governments in our history.[27] Mayhew found that more major regulatory statutes affecting both business and government were passed in the Nixon era than under any other postwar president through 1988.[28] Nixon's concern with courting a public that was clamoring for new environmental and consumer regulation clearly outweighed any residual support for business or federalism, prompting him to support and sign such path-breaking statutes as the 1970 Clean Air Act and the Occupational Safety and Health Act. Similarly, Ronald Reagan put cherished policy goals such as the conservative moral agenda and responding to seemingly irresistible public outcries for action such as legislation establishing a uniform twenty-one-year-old drinking age ahead of his commitment to reducing the federal role and enhancing the authority of states and localities.[29]

Within Congress, the differences between the parties on *Congressional Quarterly*'s Federal Role Index narrowed until *CQ* discontinued this index in 1969. Average Republican scores supporting a growing federal role increased from about 28 percent in the Senate in 1960 to about 55 percent in 1968.[30] These trends have prompted Theodore Lowi to write that the growth of the national state was "no longer a partisan matter" because both parties were equally willing to use federal power to achieve their own goals.[31]

Interest group analysis is also relevant in examining congressional consideration of mandates. The weakening of the parties has purportedly enhanced the influence of interest groups as political bases for many members of Congress. Many mandates are pushed by public interest groups concentrated in Washington, with little or no organizational bases in the states.[32] These groups are disposed by organizational mechanics to favor federal solutions. Many of these groups also have developed strong ties with key committee chairs and their staffs. The formation of politically assertive advocacy groups claiming to represent the diffuse interests of potential program beneficiaries has outpaced the formation of business groups since the 1960s, thanks in part to financing from foundations and federal grants and to a readiness of the media to embrace these claims.[33] Moreover, recent literature indicates that Olson's pessimistic assessment of the prospects for these kinds of broader interest organizations underestimated the intangible, noneconomic benefits that individuals derive from supporting such organizations.[34]

The growing concentration of media in Washington created a new resource for externality groups and entrepreneurs. Lacking the instrumental resources available to producer groups, and frequently without grassroots membership bases to tap, these groups use public opinion to gain leverage.[35] As Samuel Kernell documents, increasingly self-reliant and politically independent political leaders freed from traditional party moorings have also come to rely more on going public through the media to change the terms of the debate.[36] Studies of environmental and consumer politics note that the media often convert policy stories into morality plays, giving largely favorable coverage to the claims of groups that advocate the interests of regulatory beneficiaries.[37]

These forces facilitated the expansion of federal programs, but government itself also reinforced the expansion of the federal role in several ways. Once precedents were established for a federal presence in a policy area—often through financial assistance to states—it became far easier to enact subsequent expansions using regulation.[38] Bardach argues that further expansions become politically compelling as regulators plug gaps while uncovered groups press equity claims.[39] John Kingdon talks about how policies in one area become "contagious" and lead to adoption by imitation in other areas.[40] Moreover, programs create federal, state, and often local bureaucracies and clientele groups that subsequently become a source of program augmentation and expansion.

Though nationalizing forces have become a more compelling influence on national office holders, observers such as Timothy Conlan point to the eclipse of state and local government influence over national policy as well. Conlan argues that the Court's 1985 *Garcia* decision abandoned states and localities to the vagaries of the political process at the very time when their political resources had ebbed.[41]

Perhaps the most important political shift lies in the realm of the ideas undergirding policy—a factor gaining recognition as a key variable affecting policy outcomes.[42] As one analyst writes, ideas define conventional wisdom, define alternative policy options, and, most important, keep other options off the table.[43] In this regard, the record of mandating in recent years would suggest that the presumption against federal regulation of states and localities has been dropped as one of the unwritten rules of the game that guide the acceptable parameters of political debate. Timothy Conlan observes that, like most Americans, national political leaders pay homage to federalism but are generally unwilling to sacrifice more specific policy goals that call for federal action. He cites polling data indicating public support for political conservatism on general issues of federal power but also showing public support for a wide range of new federal policy interventions.[44] David Walker asserts that recent years have seen an erosion of distinctions between state and local concerns and federal issues, with an overloaded federal policy agenda as one of the outcomes.[45]

Students of the policymaking process have observed more generally that the character of policy debates has shifted from ideological
to pragmatic or instrumental grounds. James Q. Wilson, for example,
argues that debates over the propriety or wisdom of federal intervention are no longer characteristic of political conflict over new policies.[46]
The Advisory Commission on Intergovernmental Relations' studies
indicate that once policy precedents are set for federal involvement,
"familiarity undermines conceptions of propriety."[47] Similarly, Hugh
Heclo argues that once the thresholds legitimating federal activity are
crossed in a range of policy areas, policy conflict shifts its focus away
from basic ideological questions to instrumental concerns involving
program design and implementation.[48]

Some observers suggest that this political evolution has its roots
more in functional and economic trends than political ones. In this
argument, serious debates over the federal role become an academic
luxury in an increasingly national society whose economy and communications are ever more interdependent.[49] In this context, the operational
value of federalism no longer revolves around the independence of
the separate layers of government, but rather around the ways that
federal programs encourage joint implementation of national goals. In
this view, the federal role expands to meet the functional requisites of
a national community, sweeping aside ideological objections regardless
of the party in power.[50] No matter what the reasons, many argue that
key federalism values no longer set the principal parameters for a wide
range of domestic policy legislation, including the mandates studied
here.

In 1995, new Republican leadership was installed in Congress and
pledged to restore federalism values to a prominent place in the national debate. Proposals were advanced to block grant nearly 70 percent
of grant dollars to the states, and although only one major block grant
was passed for welfare, this new block grant devolved major responsibility to the states.[51] Passage of unfunded mandate reform became an
early downpayment on the federalism agenda of this congressional
leadership.

The Republican leadership also sought to change the policymaking
process in Congress, particularly in the House, to centralize policymaking and overcome the fragmented committee- and subcommittee-based
governance that had come to characterize Congress. New access to
congressional policy circles was provided for state elected officials,
particularly for Republican governors, which promised to restore some
of the broken links between national and state elected officials. Chapter
9 examines how sustainable these changes appear to be and what
impact they have had on Congressional consideration of mandates.

SHIFTING MODELS OF THE FEDERAL SYSTEM

The discussion just completed suggests that changes in national policy-making invariably prompt changes in our federal system as well. Models of our federal system have evolved to capture the shifting relationships between governments in our intergovernmental system. Specifically, the evolution of our system of federalism can be assessed by referring to three analytical models posited by Deil Wright: the coordinate authority model, in which states and federal government are essentially independent with their own sovereign powers; the over-lapping authority model, in which states and the federal government share concurrent powers; and the inclusive authority model, in which states have become surrogates of a dominant federal government.[52] Each of these models suggests different visions of policy outcomes for our federal system, based on contrasting views of the relationship between states and the federal government.

The first model—more commonly referred to as "dual federal-ism"—may have been appropriate to describe many domestic policy areas historically, but it is widely acknowledged to be irrelevant in describing contemporary intergovernmental relations in most areas. Indeed, some scholars like Grodzins and Elazar argue that dual federal-ism did not adequately capture the strong cooperative relationships between federal and state governments that developed even in the nineteenth century.[53]

Although not useful to characterize most contemporary intergov-ernmental relationships, the dual federalism model nonetheless re-mains the moral compass in the minds of many leaders as a normative guide for how our federal system should be restructured. President Reagan referred to the dual federalism model in his proposal to devolve authority for a broad range of education and infrastructure programs to the states. Other proponents of the sorting out of governmental functions between the federal government and the states assume that accountability and responsibility would be promoted by returning to a cleaner and clearer division of labor in our system.[54]

Most recently, as discussed in Chapter 1, the Supreme Court has underscored its allegiance to dual federalism in rulings restricting the federal government's ability to "commandeer" states in the service of national programs. In its 1997 ruling on *Printz v. United States* overturn-ing the Brady Handgun Violence Prevention Act, the Court held that "the Constitution established a system of 'dual sovereignty' " that limits the use of states as "instruments of Federal governance."[55]

Recognizing the growing influence of the federal government in this system, the other two models—the overlapping authority model and the inclusive authority model—compete in characterizing the kinds of federal tools used to project federal goals and the relative influence of the states over federal decisions. Wright argues that the overlapping authority model is most relevant in describing the contemporary intergovernmental system. Although the federal role has expanded significantly, states are viewed as having substantial independent political resources that are used to limit the scope and extent of federal influence and mandated actions. Cooperative bargaining characterizes the federal-state relationship, in which each level of government is mutually interdependent and brings independent political resources to the table.

Some adherents of this approach argue that the federal need for states as partners has conferred political resources on the states that have served to limit the scope of the federal role and introduce a decentralizing bias into federal program design and implementation. Richard Nathan, for instance, claims that successful federal grant programs must gain the support of a vertical coalition of state or local governments involved in service delivery, in addition to the traditional horizontal coalition of program beneficiaries and clientele. Programs with unreasonable design features and mandates could be vulnerable politically in the absence of state and local support or acquiescence.[56] Martha Derthick argues that states are given wide discretion in the administration of federal welfare policy and programs due to the need to maintain state cooperation and political support in congressional appropriation processes; she also suggests that state program officials, not federal bureaucrats, are the principal agents in enforcing federal mandates on state government.[57] As the federal government increasingly used states and localities to implement national programs, it acquired a vested interest in the welfare of its state and local partners.[58]

This cooperative, bargaining perspective was developed in the study of federal-state relations in grant programs. It proved particularly well suited to explain implementation patterns in many larger federal grant programs. Grants inherently rely on the voluntary cooperation of states for successful implementation, thereby generating cooperative behavior on the part of federal administrators and legislators. In these programs, states implicitly have leverage due to the threat that they can exit from the program, thereby defeating the program's goals of providing uniform or minimum levels of service throughout the nation. States and localities, however, may not enjoy this kind of leverage in the development of federal mandates, by which they are conscripted or compelled to serve the federal interest and cannot exercise the threat of exit from the program.

Advocates of the inclusive authority model point to the recent spate of mandate activity to argue that we have passed from an era of cooperative fiscal federalism, defined by our grant-in-aid system, to an era of coercive federalism.[59] Recent federalism writings depict the emergence of a more centralized federal system than the cooperative bargaining model that seemed to aptly define federal grants-in-aid. The more centralized models portray the federal government as playing an increasingly hierarchical role in directing the priorities and internal management of state and local governments. This literature, epitomized by David Walker's work and the voluminous studies published under his tutelage at the ACIR, suggests that mandating is becoming a modal federal response to interest group demands for national action, particularly in an era of severe federal budgetary crisis.[60]

In this view, traditional restraints on federal mandates have eroded as Congress has come to be more responsive to the claims of nationally oriented groups and less deferential to the prerogatives of their states or localities. Congress gives little consideration to the cost impacts of its actions when it enacts new mandate legislation. Chubb and Lewis Kayden, among others, have joined in this critique, arguing that Congress displays a bias toward centralization and an insensitivity to state autonomy claims, primarily due to the changes in political parties and congressional career patterns discussed earlier.[61]

It goes without saying that these three models are simplified for purposes of highlighting key differences in expectations and evaluations of our federal system. Functional theory, for instance, posits different federal-state relationships for different policy areas, based in part on the varying competencies and incentives of each level of government. Paul Peterson notes that redistributive policies such as income security have become more centralized with the federal government in recent years, whereas states and localities have assumed greater responsibility for distributive functions such as transportation and education.[62] Thus, differing models may be appropriate to characterize different policy areas.

IMPLICATIONS FOR THE POLITICS OF MANDATES

In broad terms, the three models correspond to essential choices Congress can make on the federal role in each major policy area or program. Martha Derthick has observed that in domestic affairs, Congress has three choices in dealing with the states, choices that parallel the models discussed here. It can choose to defer to states through inaction, permitting states to continue to occupy the policy area, as contemplated by the dual federalism model. Congress may instead choose interdependence, whereby collaborative arrangements are sought to involve the states cooperatively in pursuing national policy, a vision contemplated by the overlapping authority or cooperative model. Finally, Congress may decide to displace the states through preemptions or mandates to implement a uniform federal policy, as envisioned by the inclusive authority model.[63] For mandate decisions in particular, any one of these models may not fully explain congressional mandate decisions, and the empirical relevance of the various models may shift over time. The politics of mandates may very well differ both by policy area and by political era.

The dual federalism model, although recently of a more normative than empirical interest, would suggest that Congress would refrain from imposing mandates on states. The national government would legislate in its own sphere but leave the states in charge of their own exclusive areas of jurisdiction. Pure adherents of dual federalism may also denounce the federal reliance on grants and preemptions as intruding on formerly exclusive areas of state and local governance. Although clearly out of favor in recent times, dual federalism models appeared at least in the rhetoric of mandate reform advocates in the mid-1990s, and at least some reformers expected congressional mandate reform to bring about restraint on federal influence and a resurgence of state authority and autonomy.

The cooperative, bargaining approach would accept the inevitability or desirability of federal roles in domestic policy but would suggest that state and local governments retain significant leverage in how these roles are designed and implemented. This approach would suggest that Congress would rely more on grants and other forms of assistance to states and localities and would be wary of using the mandate tool. When mandates are adopted, the cooperative approach would suggest that they would be developed incrementally, only after cooperative financial assistance relationships had been tried and found wanting. Moreover, a Congress viewed as anxious about projecting federal authority may enact mandates only when a working majority of states have already adopted mandated programs on their own. Further, mandate programs would be designed to provide reasonable flexibility for state and local officials to implement national objectives and would seek, where possible, to delegate management responsibility for monitoring compliance to entities in the state and local community. Finally, efforts would be made to provide federal funding for at least part of the projected compliance costs expected to be incurred at the state and local level. Mandates, then, would be enacted and implemented as partnerships between the federal government and states and localities.

The more centralized inclusive authority model would suggest considerable mandating activity, with little regard for the costs or prerogatives of state and local governments. Congress would show little restraint in responding to new policy demands with mandating actions. The design of mandate programs would provide maximum feasible protection for program beneficiaries and clientele, with little federal funds provided to state and local governments. Mandates would frequently be adopted in a nonincremental fashion. It is argued that these trends would transcend party regimes, as both parties would become national policy activists who facilitate the centralization of policy decisions and outcomes.

These more theoretical themes form the backdrop for understanding the politics of mandates. The following chapters will unravel the political environment prompting the passage of mandates and explore the factors most responsible for congressional reliance on this tool of government. They will also address the impact of traditional sources expected to constrain centralization in our federal system, with an eye toward understanding whether the mandate reform of the mid-1990s presages a new era of federalism, one animated by the visions of dual federalism. Each of the models of policymaking and federalism discussed here may explain a portion of the evolving story of mandates that will unfold in the following pages.

NOTES TO CHAPTER 2

1. Charles Lindbloom, *The Policymaking Process* (Englewood Cliffs, N.J.: Prentice-Hall, 1968).

2. David Truman, *The Governmental Process* (New York: Alfred Knopf, 1951).

3. E. E. Schattschneider, *The Semi-Sovereign People* (New York: Holt, Rinehart and Winston, 1960), p. 35.

4. Mancur Olson, *The Logic of Collective Action* (New York: Schocken Books, 1965).

5. See Mancur Olson, *The Logic of Collective Action* (New York: Schocken Books, 1965); James Q. Wilson, *The Politics of Regulation* (New York: Basic Books, 1980).

6. Alexander Hamilton, James Madison, and John Jay, *The Federalist Papers*, No. 46 (New York: New American Library, 1961), pp. 294–300.

7. Morton Grodzins, *The American System* (Chicago: Rand McNally, 1966).

8. Edward C. Banfield and James Q. Wilson, *City Politics* (New York: Vintage Books, 1963), p. 2.

9. David Truman, "Federalism and the Party System," in *American Federalism in Perspective*, ed. Aaron Wildavsky (Boston: Little, Brown, 1967), pp. 81–108.

10. James Sundquist, *Dynamics of the Party System* (Washington, D.C.: Brookings Institution, 1973).

11. Samuel H. Beer, "Federalism, Nationalism, and Democracy in America," *American Political Science Review* 72, No. 1 (1978).

12. Herbert Wechsler, "The Political Safeguards of Federalism: The Role of the States in the Composition and Selection of the National Government," *Columbia Law Review*, 54 (April, 1954), pp. 543–560; Jesse H. Choper, *Judicial Review and the National Political Process* (Chicago: University of Chicago Press, 1980).

13. Commission on Intergovernmental Relations, *Report to the President for Transmittal to Congress* (Washington, D.C.: U.S. Government Printing Office, 1955), p. 66.

14. Quoted in Joseph Zimmerman, "Preemption in the Federal System," *Publius: The Journal of Federalism* 23, No. 4 (1993), p. 2.

15. Daniel Elazar, "Cooperative Federalism," in *Competition among State and Local Governments*, ed. Daphne Kenyon and John Kincaid (Washington, D.C.: Urban Institute Press, 1991), p. 75.

16. Advisory Commission on Intergovernmental Relations, *Regulatory Federalism: Policy, Process, Impact and Reform* (Washington, D.C.: ACIR, 1984), Chapter 3.

17. David Vogel, *Fluctuating Fortunes: The Political Power of Business in America* (New York: Basic Books, 1989).

18. Frank R. Baumgartner and Bryan D. Jones, *Agendas and Instability in American Politics* (Chicago: University of Chicago Press, 1993).

19. John Kingdon, *Agendas, Alternatives, and Public Policies*, 2nd edition (New York: HarperCollins, 1995).

20. David Beam, Timothy Conlan, and Margaret Wrightson, *Taxing Choices: The Politics of Tax Reform* (Washington, D.C.: Congressional Quarterly Press, 1990).

21. Martha Derthick and Paul Quirk, *The Politics of Deregulation* (Washington, D.C.: Brookings Institution, 1985). A more recent article explaining the emergence of this new politics of reform in the context of Mancur Olson's theories of policymaking is Gary Mucciaroni, "Unclogging the Arteries: The Defeat of Client Politics and the Logic of Collective Action," *Policy Studies Journal* 19, No. 3–4 (1991), pp. 474–494.

22. A good summary of this argument can be found in Robert Jay Digler, ed., *American Intergovernmental Relations Today: Perspectives and Controversies* (Englewood Cliffs, N.J.: Prentice-Hall, 1986). Also see Advisory Commission on Intergovernmental Relations, *Transformations in American Politics and Their Implications for Federalism*, A–106 (Washington, D.C.: U.S. Government Printing Office, 1985).

23. This point is made in Daniel Elazar, *American Federalism: A View from the States*, 3rd edition (New York: Harper and Row, 1984), p. 177.

24. John E. Chubb, "Federalism and the Bias for Centralization," in *The New Direction in American Politics*, ed. John E. Chubb and Paul E. Peterson (Washington, D.C.: Brookings Institution, 1985).

25. David Mayhew, *Congress: The Electoral Connection* (New Haven: Yale University Press, 1974).

26. See Hugh Heclo, "Issue Networks and the Executive Establishment," in *The New American Political System*, ed. Anthony King (Washington, D.C.: American Enterprise Institute, 1978).

27. Timothy Conlan, *New Federalism: Intergovernmental Reform from Nixon to Reagan* (Washington, D.C.: Brookings Institution, 1988), p. 84.

28. David Mayhew, *Divided We Govern: Party Control, Lawmaking, and Investigations, 1946–1990* (New Haven: Yale University Press, 1991), p. 83.

29. Timothy Conlan, "Federalism and Competing Values in the Reagan Administration," *Publius: The Journal of Federalism* 16 (Winter, 1986).

30. Advisory Commission on Intergovernmental Relations, *The Federal Role in the Federal System: The Dynamics of Growth*, A–78 (Washington, D.C.: ACIR, 1981), p. 124.

31. Theodore Lowi, "Europeanization of America: From United States to United State," in *Nationalizing Government*, ed. Theodore Lowi and Alan Stone (Beverly Hills: Sage, 1978), p. 18. This conclusion may be somewhat overdrawn, particularly considering findings of clear partisan conflict over new federal spending programs. See Demetrios Caralley and Yvette R. Schlussel, "Congress and Reagan's New Federalism," *Publius: The Journal of Federalism* 16 (Winter, 1986), pp. 49–79.

32. One analysis of eighty-three Washington public-interest lobby groups found that 67 percent of them had no local network of chapters. See Jeffrey M. Berry, *Lobbying for the People: The Political Behavior of Public Interest Groups* (Princeton: Princeton University Press, 1977).

33. For discussion of interest group growth patterns, see Jack Walker, "The Origins and Maintenance of Interest Groups in America," *American Political Science Review* 77 (June, 1983), pp. 390–406. Jeffrey Berry discusses how these public interest groups sustained themselves in the absence of grassroots organizations in *Lobbying for the People: The Political Behavior of Public Interest Groups*.

34. Russell Hardin, *Collective Action* (Baltimore: Johns Hopkins University Press, 1982).

35. Debra J. Salazar, "Conflict Expansion: Public Policy Typologies and Rational Choice" (paper presented at the 1988 Annual Meeting of the American Political Science Association, Washington, D.C., 1 September 1988).

36. Samuel Kernell, *Going Public: New Strategies of Presidential Leadership* (Washington, D.C.: Congressional Quarterly Press, 1986), p. 25.

37. See Mark Nadel, *The Politics of Consumer Protection*, (Indianapolis, Ind.: Bobbs-Merrill, 1971).

38. The ACIR calls this "breakthrough politics." See Advisory Commission on Intergovernmental Relations, *Federal Regulation of State and Local Governments*, A–126 (Washington, D.C.: ACIR, 1993), p. 54.

39. Eugene Bardach and Robert Kagan, *Going by the Book: The Problem of Regulatory Unreasonableness* (Philadelphia: Temple University Press, 1982), p. 19.

40. John Kingdon, *Agendas, Alternatives and Public Policies* (Boston: Little, Brown, 1984).

41. Timothy Conlan, "Politics and Governance: Conflicting Trends in the 1990's," *Annals* 509 (May, 1990), p. 129.

42. See Jane Mansbridge, ed., *Beyond Self-Interest* (Chicago: University of Chicago Press, 1990); Robert B. Reich, *The Power of Public Ideas* (Cambridge: Harvard University Press, 1990).

43. Mark Moore, "What Sort of Ideas Become Public Ideas?" in Robert Reich, *The Power of Public Ideas,* p. 72.

44. Timothy Conlan, "Federalism and Competing Values in the Reagan Administration," p. 45.

45. David Walker, *Toward a Functioning Federalism* (Cambridge, Mass.: Winthrop, 1981), p. 233.

46. James Q. Wilson, *Political Organizations* (New York: Basic Books, 1973), p. 341.

47. Advisory Commission on Intergovernmental Relations, *The Federal Role in the Federal System: The Dynamics of Growth.*

48. Hugh Heclo, "The Emerging Regime," in *Remaking American Politics,* ed. Richard A. Harris and Sidney M. Milkis (Boulder, Co.: Westview Press, 1989), p. 312.

49. Michael Reagan and John G. Sanzone, *The New Federalism* (New York: Oxford University Press, 1981), p. 168.

50. Advisory Commission on Intergovernmental Relations, *The Federal Role in the Federal System: Dynamics of Growth,* p. 222.

51. Paul L. Posner and Margaret T. Wrightson, "Block Grants: A Perennial, But Unstable, Tool of Government," *Publius: The Journal of Federalism* 26, No. 3 (1996), pp. 87–108.

52. Deil Wright, *Understanding Intergovernmental Relations,* 2nd edition (Monterey, Ca.: Brooks/Cole, 1982), p. 52.

53. Daniel Elazar, *The American Partnership* (Chicago: University of Chicago Press, 1962).

54. See Alice Rivlin, *Reviving the American Dream: The Economy, the States and the Federal Government* (Washington, D.C.: Brookings Institution, 1992).

55. Printz, Sheriff/Coroner, Ravalli County, *Montana v. United States,* 95–1478 (1997).

56. Richard Nathan, "State and Local Governments under Federal Grants," *Political Science Quarterly* 98, No. 1 (1983).

57. Martha Derthick, *The Influence of Federal Grants* (Cambridge: Harvard University Press, 1970). Another excellent presentation of the bargaining perspective is Helen Ingram, "Policy Implementation through Bargaining: The Case of Federal Grants-in-Aid," *Public Policy* 25, No. 4 (1977).

58. Samuel Beer, "Federalism, Nationalism, and Democracy in America," *American Political Science Review* 72 (1977).

59. John Kincaid, "From Cooperative to Coercive Federalism," *Annals* 509 (May, 1990), pp. 139–153.

60. See David Walker, *Toward a Functioning Federalism.*

61. John E. Chubb, "Federalism and the Bias for Centralization," in John E. Chubb and Paul E. Peterson, *New Directions in American Politics;* Lewis Kayden, "Politics, Money, and State Sovereignty: The Judicial Role," *Columbia Law Review,* 79 (1979).

62. Paul Peterson, *The Price of Federalism* (New York: Twentieth Century Fund, 1995), Chapter 2.

63. Martha Derthick, "The Enduring Features of American Federalism," *Brookings Review* (Summer, 1989), pp. 34–38.

3

Federal Mandates: Congressional Alignments

Congressional voting on mandates undoubtedly reflects a broad range of factors. The key issue to be addressed here is to understand the relative influence of federalism as a value in comparison with the influence of other policy goals on congressional decisionmaking. If voting on mandates is largely dependent on their contribution to more deeply held national policy goals, this could support the conclusion that federalism lacks institutional support in Congress as a value driving decisions. This chapter will examine congressional roll call votes on mandate issues from 1983 through 1990 to examine whether mandates themselves call forth distinct voting dimensions and alliances in Congress that center around federalism concerns or, alternatively, whether such decisions are a function of the underlying policy supported by the mandate. We will also seek to determine if support or opposition to mandates is systematically associated with the party affiliation, ideology, or region of members of Congress.

ROLL CALL VOTING ON FEDERALISM ISSUES

This chapter will examine trends in congressional support for mandates over four Congresses—the 98th through the 101st (1983–1990). Roll calls involving mandates over these eight years will be analyzed to ascertain: (1) what types of mandates called forth roll call votes over this period and (2) what factors disposed members to support or oppose federal mandates during this time. Although roll call analysis will help elucidate political trends, it will only do so for those issues or bills involving a vote sufficiently divided to qualify for roll call analysis.[1]

Roll call vote analysis is an important tool for describing patterns that underly congressional policy decisions. Once voting dimensions have been isolated, roll call analysis offers the potential for using linear regression to compare the relative impact of such independent variables as party, ideology, and constituency on voting patterns.[2]

Roll call studies of congressional decisions on federalism issues have been few and far between. Demetrios Caraley's work represents a continuing systematic study of congressional responses to federalism issues over time.[3] His work primarily focuses on congressional decisions on federal grant funding levels and on proposed shifts in control over those funds from the federal government to the states through block grants. His work shows consistently that party has been the principal variable predicting congressional positions on federal aid issues. For example, he found that House Democrats from every constituency were three to four times as likely to oppose Reagan's New Federalism legislation than were Republicans.[4] Region also helped explain critical swing voting blocks, as Southern Democrats could be counted on to join Republicans to support New Federalism. Eastern Republicans, normally more inclined to support federal aid than their party colleagues, deviated from this pattern in 1981–1982 to provide key votes permitting passage of many New Federalism initiatives.

Several other studies that attempt to analyze congressional voting on federalism have been identified. Rodney Hero found in his analysis of Senate votes from 1979–1982 that both party and ideology were strongly correlated with federalism voting, but that conservative ideology was a stronger predictor of profederalism voting than even party.[5] Other variables that capture the nature of senatorial constituencies (e.g., percentage that is urban, education levels, and intrastate party competition) were found to have little or no impact. Unlike Caraley, Hero did not focus on federal aid issues, but rather attempted to portray voting on federal-state authority issues. Although several mandate issues were included, his selection encompassed a broader set of policy issues implicating federalism as an issue, such as the creation of the Department of Education and a resolution supporting direct popular election of the president. In fact, the validity of his measure of federalism could be questioned since many of the issues captured by his votes more closely embodied a conservative ideological agenda than they did explicit policies supporting federalism. Thus, it would have been surprising if conservatism were not highly correlated with his index of "federalism."

The strong correlation between federalism voting and ideology or party is contradicted by another study of House and Senate federalism voting in the 101st Congress by Michael Malaby and David Webber.[6] Their roll call votes include both federal aid funding levels, as well as several federal mandates, and some broader federal-state authority issues such as the scope of a national education standards commission and campaign finance legislation. Unlike Hero, they collapse their votes into four separate, intercorrelated voting dimensions, which correspond to: (1) questions over funding or allocation of federal aid; (2) conjoint issues regulated jointly by federal government and the states; (3) explicit efforts to affirm federal regulatory authority in relation to state programs; and (4) federal preemption of state policies. Confirming Caraley's work, they found that only the federal aid funding dimension correlates highly with party and ideology, with liberals and Democrats more disposed to favor higher federal aid levels. However, they found weak or nonexistent correlation levels between these political variables and the other three dimensions of federalism voting.

Hero's relatively high correlations between political variables and his aggregate federalism voting index led him to conclude that federalism is in fact a unique and distinct congressional voting dimension. However, Malaby and Webber concluded the opposite, based on their differential findings once the federalism index was disaggregated into the four dimensions. They concluded that knowing the party or ideological affiliation of a member of Congress is a relatively poor predictor of the voting orientation of that member on such federalism issues as preemption and joint partnership programs.

This latter view would confirm the views of those who see federalism as more of an instrumental value whose support varies based on its contribution to more deeply held, fundamental policy goals. Timothy Conlan's work on the conflict between federalism and other conflicting objectives within the Reagan Administration adds credence to the notion of federalism as a subsidiary political dimension. Surveying a number of key policy areas, Conlan noted that Reagan's avowed federalism objectives usually were subsumed when they conflicted with more salient policy objectives such as mandating national conservative moral standards or preempting burdensome state regulations on its business constituency. Conlan concluded that Reagan resembled his more liberal predecessors in sacrificing federalism for other competing values.[7]

This view is confirmed by several other roll call analyses. In an analysis of federalism voting in the 96th Congress, Stephen Schecter concluded that liberals and conservatives in both houses chose their federalist stances based on the substance of the issue. On issues involving energy development and local funding of abortions, for instance, conservatives voted to curtail state and local authority.[8] A companion analysis of House votes revealed that other principles took precedence over federalism, as 86 percent of House Republicans showed no consistent pattern of federalism voting across relevant roll calls.[9]

Comparable results have been found in Senate voting by Margaret Wrightson. Analyzing Senate federalism votes in the 100th Congress, she was unable to find any significant correlation between an index of federalism support and any established political variables such as party or ideology. Even when disaggregated into three separate dimensions—budget, tax, and regulatory policy—no significant associations emerged. She concluded that support for federalism is more random than systematic, reflecting the relatively low importance placed on federalism values in the Senate. As she succinctly states, "Federalism values are insufficiently institutionalized to offer a stable basis for legislative choice."[10]

MANDATE ROLL CALLS: 98TH THROUGH 101ST CONGRESSES

Although the debate has been joined, these propositions have never been tested specifically on mandate voting. The federalism indexes are either based exclusively on federal funding votes or on a combined set of votes including a wide range of issues with real or possibly imagined federalism implications. Key questions that will be addressed in this section include: What types of mandates triggered divisive roll call votes in recent years, and how does the extent and nature of partisan conflict over mandates compare to that for federal aid issues and legislation in general? Which political variables have the greatest influence over mandate voting? To what extent do the political patterns vary by the nature and purpose of the mandate? Ultimately, do mandates constitute a distinct voting dimension, or is support dependent on more established programmatic or philosophical goals?

Selecting Roll Call Votes for Analysis

The mandates selected were based on theoretical and methodological criteria. Taking the universe of all roll calls for the 98th through 101st Congresses (1983 through 1990), all roll calls were identified where the vote specifically involved support or opposition to a federal mandate on state or local governments. Consistent with the definitions in Chapter 1, they were defined to include six different types of mandates:

- Direct orders
- Crosscutting requirements
- Crossover sanctions
- Partial preemptions
- Total preemptions
- Major grant conditions or requirements

The selection of roll calls screened out votes that clearly involved factors other than the mandate, such as most procedural votes to invoke cloture in the Senate or approve a rule in the House. To ensure measurement of support or opposition to state and local mandates specifically, only those votes where the mandate applied uniquely or in a different way to the state and local sector were included. Thus, for example, votes on the 1990 Americans with Disabilities Act were excluded since the regulatory issues applied equally to public and private sectors, but a vote was included that involved a proposal to give rural governments greater discretion in serving the transportation needs of the disabled. Only those votes where at least 20 percent of the members were opposed to one another were included, to assure a robust analysis of the reasons underlying congressional cleavages on mandate issues.[11]

The result was a universe of sixty-nine votes that met the criteria of mandate votes over these eight years, with thirty-one Senate votes and thirty-eight House votes. The mandates subject to eligible roll calls predominantly involved direct-order or crossover sanctions, followed closely by major grant conditions:

- Direct order: 18 votes
- Crossover sanctions: 18 votes[12]
- Grant conditions: 13 votes
- Total preemptions: 9 votes
- Partial preemptions: 8 votes
- Crosscutting requirements: 3 votes

Overall Congressional Voting Patterns

The position favoring the federal mandate prevailed in 55 percent of these votes, whereas the antimandate position won in 45 percent of the cases. Mandate votes in general were partisan—more so than general roll calls in Congress. Specifically, fifty-one of the sixty-nine votes, or 73 percent, featured a majority of Democrats voting against a majority of Republicans, with the remainder decided with majorities of both parties on the same side. The average of party votes to all roll calls, by contrast, was 52 and 45 percent party votes in the House and Senate respectively for the 98th through 100th Congresses.[13] Mandate votes also were more partisan than the early New Federalism votes analyzed by Caraley and Schlusse; in the 96th and 97th Congresses, 68 percent of the House New Federalism votes were partisan, whereas only 54 percent of Senate votes were partisan.[14]

One would expect Republicans and conservatives to vote against federal mandates. In general, they have been reluctant to expand the federal role, arguing that such actions would erode the values inherent in our federalist system. James Sundquist, in fact, argues that the extension of federal authority into new areas has been the principal line of cleavage dividing the two parties in recent times.[15]

Contrary to these expectations, Republicans had a higher overall mandate support score than Democrats during the period being considered. On average, 57 percent of the Republicans in both chambers across the eight years supported mandates, whereas only 52 percent of the Democrats and 51 percent of Southern Democrats did so. Moreover, the conservative coalition, that is, where a majority of Republicans and Southern Democrats joined together in opposition to the rest of the Democrats, emerged on only nine of the sixty-nine votes, or 13 percent of the votes. This is roughly comparable to the 12 percent of all roll calls characterized as conservative coalition votes by *Congressional Quarterly*.[16]

This result is clearly at odds with federal aid support patterns shown by Caraley and confirmed by this research. For comparison purposes, federal aid support scores were computed for the same four Congresses for twenty-six votes for which federal assistance levels to state and local government was the primary issue. As expected, Democrats uniformly had far higher scores than Republicans across the eight years studied. For these votes, 87 percent of the Democrats supported federal aid, compared to only 30 percent of the Republicans. Confirming research that showed the growing convergence of Southern Democrats with the mainstream of the party, 80 percent voted in support of federal aid.[17]

The mandate support results varied somewhat by chamber and by Congress, as shown in Table 3.1.

Table 3.1 shows significant differences in mandate support between the chambers and over time. Senate Republicans averaged 61 percent mandate support per roll call, five points higher than their House colleagues. Senate Democrats, on the other hand, averaged 41 percent support per vote, thirteen points lower than their House counterparts. Southern Democrats had the lowest promandate support scores in both chambers, with 38 percent in the Senate and 53 percent in the House. These trends vary somewhat over time. Senate Democrats actually had higher average mandate support scores than Senate Republicans in the 100th Congress, whereas House Democrats twice exceeded the mandate scores of their House Republican counterparts in the 99th and 101st Congresses.

This variability suggests that systematic explanations for House-Senate differences are not influential. For example, the differing nature of the House and Senate constituencies has been argued by Clausen

TABLE 3.1
Mandate Support Scores by Congress and Party*

	Republican	*Democrat*	*Southern Democrat*
98th Congress			
Senate	72%	47%	33%
House	63	41	39
99th Congress			
Senate	56	46	51
House	56	59	59
100th Congress			
Senate	46	54	49
House	53	50	46
101st Congress			
Senate	63	16	17
House	49	66	68

*Numbers in cells are percent of roll calls where a majority of each party supported mandates.

and Cheney to make a difference in voting patterns.[18] Yet, the chamber made little systematic difference in the overall mandate support score: Senate Democrats were lower than their House counterparts, whereas Senate Republicans were somewhat higher than House Republicans. The results could be accounted for by ideological differences between partisans in the respective chambers. Yet, the Senate and House Republicans both received essentially the same conservative support score, whereas Senate Republicans scored some fourteen points higher in support of mandates than did their House counterparts.[19]

A more likely explanation for the variance in party support between chambers lies in the types of issues triggering roll calls in each chamber. Specifically, in years where Senate Republicans had higher mandate support scores than their House Republican colleagues, a greater number of mandates generating Republican support, such as social policy and business preemption, were subject to roll call voting in the Senate than in the House.

Disaggregating Mandate Support by Policy Goals

A more productive approach to explain these patterns lies in the shifting composition of the mandate votes comprising the index.

For purposes of our analysis here, the contents of the legislation voted on was examined and grouped into six mutually exclusive categories. The categories were derived from the work of Conlan, as well as that of Lowi, suggesting that the preference for intergovernmental mandates varies based on the underlying policy or programmatic goals supported by the mandate. As noted above, Conlan argues that the Reagan Administration could be counted on to support federal mandates when they furthered the conservative social policy agenda of moral issues, preempted states from stronger regulation of the environment and other business issues, and restricted or placed conditions on welfare payments.[20] Lowi observes that Reagan's overriding goal was not to reduce regulatory burdens, but to "shift and extend government authority toward realms where government concerned itself with the morality of conduct."[21]

Consistent with these interpretations, the mandate index was disaggregated into six separate indexes. The six indexes were constructed around the hypotheses advanced by Conlan and Lowi that conservatives will generally support mandates regulating personal moral conduct or social behavior, preempting states from stronger regulation of business, or restricting welfare benefits. A separate category was added to capture the numerous votes on environmental mandates, which are hypothesized to capture Republican support due to Republicans' interest in preempting stronger state regulation. Democrats, on the other hand, are hypothesized to support mandates imposing additional service costs on state or local governments, as well as mandates restricting state authority to structure services or programs in areas other than the three Republicans are likely to support. Each vote was categorized into one of these six groupings and new indexes were computed.

The following is a description of each category, along with its frequency in the population of sixty-nine votes:

- *Social policy (19 votes):* mandates for state or local action to support national moral values or social policy objectives, including such conservative social agenda items as mandating school prayer as well as civil rights mandates.
- *Welfare mandates (7 votes):* mandates requiring state or local governments involved in administering welfare benefit programs to place certain controls or restrictions on program beneficiaries or administration.
- *Environmental (13 votes):* mandates regulating state or local participation as partners with the federal government in regulating compliance with national environmental standards, for instance,

permitting state standards to exceed federal standards in such areas as pesticides or oil spills.

- *Business (9 votes):* mandates restricting or preempting state regulation of the private sector, such as preempting state or local modular housing codes.
- *Authority (13 votes):* mandates with the principal impact of restricting state or local authority to implement services or policies in accord with local, as opposed to national, priorities (excluding environment, social policy, and business regulation covered by other indexes above), such as speed limits on interstate highways and voter registration procedures.
- *State or local costs (8 votes):* mandates with the primary impact of increasing budgetary or service costs faced by state or local government, such as requiring coverage of all new state and local employees under Medicare. (This excludes the environment, social policy, and business regulation areas covered by other indexes above.)

These six mandate indexes prove to have some value in further explaining the congressional response to mandates. Most intriguing is the variance captured in the partisan alignment on mandate issues. Table 3.2 illustrates the variance in party promandate scores across the six areas.

As predicted by Conlan and Lowi, Republican support for mandates was higher in the last three columns, that is, in business regulation, social policy, and welfare. Republicans, however, emerged as the strongest opponents of mandates on other authority issues. On cost

TABLE 3.2
Mandate Support by Area

	Authority	Costs	Environment	Business	Social Policy	Welfare
Republican	41	52	52	66	68	71
Democrat	58	54	49	47	44	30
Southern Democrat	49	51	54	43	43	43
Likeness*	55	58	66	38	38	52

*Index of Likeness measures the degree of conflict between the parties; the higher the index, the smaller the differences. The index is based on the average of all bills included in each area.[22]

issues, Republicans and Democrats were surprisingly similar. Republicans tended to oppose mandates imposing costs on state and local governments when only state and local costs were affected by the mandate, such as permitting smaller governments to be exempted from certain grant conditions or disability access requirements. However, when federal costs were at stake, Republicans more than Democrats tended to support mandates that shifted federal costs to the state and local sector, such as by increasing state and local matching rates or by denying entitlement status to a grant program that reimburses state and local costs involved in servicing illegal immigrants.

The Democrats, in contrast, supported federal mandates regulating general state and local authority but opposed mandates restricting welfare benefits or imposing national social agendas over the state and local sector. The low promandate score for Democrats on the social agenda is not due to some principled objection to this kind of federal activity, but to the fact that the preponderance of votes on this dimension—sixteen out of nineteen—involved attempts by conservatives to impose their moral or social agenda. The few votes involving national imposition of liberal social agendas, such as strengthening the application of civil rights requirements on grantees, generated strong Democratic support. Democrats tended to be somewhat more supportive of federal mandates imposing additional costs on the state and local sector than were Republicans, but they were also more supportive of federal funding and higher federal matching rates to help state and local governments cope with these kinds of mandates.

These results suggest that the underlying cleavages surrounding the programmatic or policy goal that gives rise to the mandate largely determine the political alignment on mandates. Sometimes this forces some very conservative members into awkward dilemmas. For example, Senator William Armstrong—a highly conservative Republican—found himself advocating an amendment to restrict states' authority to regulate hostile takeovers of corporations. Believing strongly in the need to curb the use of so-called poison pills by corporate managers seeking to forestall hostile takeovers, Armstrong authored a provision that banned poison pills unless approved by stockholders. When opponents argued that this would undermine the authority of states to regulate corporations, Armstrong claimed that he was a supporter of states' rights, but "that is not the case when you are talking about great national corporations."[23]

The first two columns in Table 3.2 show that when it does not conflict with more cherished priorities, federalism enjoys some residual support among Republicans. The dimensions of authority capture majority Republican support, such as permitting states to raise speed limits on interstate highways or deciding whether to adopt national standards over the voting registration process. Even in this category, however, mandates served for many as a stalking horse for other, more salient issues. For example, although Republicans used federalism arguments to oppose the so-called motor voter mandate requiring states to register voters when granting drivers' licenses, their opposition was at least in part motivated by concerns over the impact on the size of the electorate and potentially disproportionate mobilization of Democratic voters. And majority Republican support for speed limit increases was at least partly a function of the large numbers of Republican senators from the West with a constituency interest in higher speed limits.

The legislative success enjoyed by those opposing mandates similarly varies across these six areas. Though the promandate position prevailed in 55 percent of all votes, the passage of mandates varied from 78 percent for those restricting state regulation of business to 37 percent for those imposing social policy objectives on states and localities. The lower support for social policy mandates reflects the strong opposition to these kinds of mandates by Democrats, whose strong majorities in the House and close divisions in the Senate swing the entire Congress to the state and local side.

It can be argued that Republican voting patterns might be explained by the positions taken on these issues by the Reagan and Bush Administrations during this period. However, the administration took a position on only seventeen of the sixty-nine mandates during the eight-year period, and its positions tracked closely with those registered by congressional Republicans. Specifically, the Reagan and Bush Administrations supported the mandate in twelve of these seventeen bills, as shown in Table 3.3.

As expected, the administration supported mandates in social policy areas, involving such issues as state discretion over using Medicaid

TABLE 3.3
Administrations' Mandate Support by Area, 1983–1990

Type of mandate	Promandate	Antimandate
Authority	0	1
Costs	3	0
Environment	1	2
Social Policy	5	2
Business	1	0
Welfare	2	0
TOTALS	12	5

to fund abortion and schools' discretion over deciding whether to have prayer in public schools. Welfare mandates supported by the administration involved the imposition of workfare requirements. Administration positions on business and environmental mandates generally were driven by their support of the least stringent approach to regulation of the private sector. In cases where states were threatening more stringent regulation, the administration supported preemption of states' regulatory authority, whereas they opposed proposals to impose stricter federal regulations involving states. In the cost area, the administration's support for federal mandates reflected fiscal conservatism with regard to the federal budget; as with their congressional counterparts, the Republican administrations generally supported mandates shifting federal costs to the state and local sector and opposed additional funding to defray these costs.

Toward a Model of Mandate Voting

So far, the roll call voting data have been used to describe aggregate voting patterns. To confirm the analysis and to add other variables that could help further explain variance in mandate support, linear regression was used. In contrast to the above analysis, which was based on aggregate voting on bills, a mandate support score was computed for each member serving across the 99th through 101st Congresses for regression purposes. Only the most recent three Congresses were used to avoid dropping too many members from the analysis—as it was, approximately 20 percent of the members left the Congress over the six years studied and were consequently dropped from the study.[24]

This left fifty-three votes on mandates to be used as the universe from which the index of mandate support was developed for each surviving member. The dependent variable was operationalized both as the summative index of all mandate votes for each chamber over the six year period, as well as a similar summation for the disaggregated six dimensions discussed earlier: social policy, welfare, environment, business, authority, and costs.

The independent variables included party, ideology (a 100-point index calculated as the inverse of the score given each member by the American Conservative Union), region, the previous state or local office-holding experience of each member, and each member's federal grants-in-aid opposition score (a 100-point index based on roll call votes on major federal aid issues during the period). It was hypothesized that Republicanism, conservatism, southern or western region, and previous state and local experience would all lead to lower mandate support scores. Members opposed to federal aid were also expected to oppose mandates as well since both grants and mandates represent a stronger federal role in domestic policy.

The overall index did not prove to be too productive for either the House or the Senate, with a 0.21 R_2 value for the House and a modest 0.29 value for the Senate. As discussed earlier, this index includes a multitude of differing kinds of mandates, which tends to obscure key relationships. This further confirms the weaknesses of mandating itself as a separate voting dimension. Table 3.4 shows the relationships that proved significant for the House and Senate for the overall mandate support index.

The regression for all votes suggests that conservatives are more likely to vote for mandates than liberals, particularly in the House. The House equation indicates that the mandate support index falls by 1.3 points for every 10 percentage point increase in a member's liberalism index. The higher mandate scores are associated with declining values of liberalism. Democrats are also slightly less likely to support mandates in both chambers, although the results are not significant. Region is significantly associated with mandate voting in the House, with

TABLE 3.4
Regression of Overall Mandate Index on Independent Variables

	House	Senate
Intercept	0.6344**	0.5879**
	(0.0200)	(0.0395)
Party (Dem = 1)	–0.0106	–0.0555
	(0.0167)	(0.0299)
Liberalism (100 = liberal)	–0.0013**	–0.0007
	(0.0002)	(0.0005)
South	–0.0373**	–0.1048**
	(0.0145)	(0.0266)
Midwest	–0.0315**	–0.0308
	(0.0129)	(0.0231)
West	–0.0553**	–0.0470
	(0.0144)	(0.0249)
Prior state and local	–0.0063	–0.0054
experience (1 = none)	(0.0109)	(0.0177)
Federal aid opposition	–0.0134	–0.0498
(100 = no support)	(0.0180)	(0.0350)
R_2	0.2175**	0.2914**

* = variable significant below 0.05
** = variable significant below 0.01
(Numbers in parentheses are standard errors.)

members from the South, Midwest, and West all less likely to support mandates than Northeastern members.

Overall, the prior state and local office-holding experience of members had no statistically significant relationship to mandate voting, contrary to our expectations. Those opposed to federal aid did have somewhat lower mandate support scores also, but this relationship was not statistically significant.

As noted in the discussion of overall roll call results earlier, these counterintuitive results are likely due to the composition of the mix of roll calls used to score members. So, the roll calls were disaggregated into the six dimensions, and regressions were run for each of these dimensions for both House and Senate, as shown in Tables 3.5 and 3.6.

For the Senate, the disaggregated results are revealing and all except the cost dimension are better predictors of voting patterns than the aggregate model—explaining from 45 to 70 percent of the variation. Republican members tend to have high promandate scores for welfare, business, and social policy mandates. Party affiliation is most strongly associated with mandate voting on business preemption and welfare mandates in the Senate, with Republicans on average having 37 percent and 20 percent higher mandate support scores than Democrats on those dimensions, respectively. Republicans, in contrast, have lower mandate support scores on environmental votes, and their mandate support is also somewhat lower for authority and cost mandates, although the relationship is not statistically significant. These results, of course, parallel the earlier analysis of roll call by party.

Ideology is the only independent variable with statistical significance for five of the six mandate voting dimensions, but the direction of association varies by dimension. As shown in Table 3.5, liberalism has the greatest effect on reducing support for social policy mandates (7 percentage point drop in mandate support for every 10 percentage point increase in liberalism index) and for welfare mandates. Alternatively, liberalism tends to increase members' support for authority, the environment, and cost mandates. Recall that Hero had also found conservative ideology to be the single most important variable in predicting federalism voting, but his coefficients all pointed to a unidimensional positive impact on support for the federalism position. Here it is statistically significant, but the direction of association reverses depending on the underlying issue supported by the mandate. (Since party and ideology are highly correlated, with a Pearson coefficient of 0.77, the coefficients presented in Table 3.5 estimating the independent impact of each of these variables understates their combined impact on roll call voting.)

TABLE 3.5
Regression Results for Six Mandate Dimensions, Senate

	Welfare	Business	Authority	Cost	Environment	Social Policy
Intercept	0.8819**	0.5421**	0.3851**	0.2672**	0.2622**	1.0285**
	(0.1138)	(0.1935)	(0.0652)	(0.1150)	(0.0817)	(0.0883)
Party	-0.2005**	-0.3741**	0.0637	0.0245	0.1122*	-0.0323
(Democrat = 1)	(0.0813)	(0.0777)	(0.0466)	(0.0822)	(0.0584)	(0.0631)
Liberal	-0.0039**	0.0020	0.0016*	0.0030*	0.0033**	-0.0079**
(100 = liberal)	(0.0014)	(0.0013)	(0.0008)	(0.0014)	(0.0010)	(0.0011)
South	-0.0280	-0.1804**	-0.1432**	0.0167	-0.1656**	-0.0539
	(0.0737)	(0.0704)	(0.0422)	(0.0744)	(0.0529)	(0.0572)
Midwest	0.0077	-0.0299	-0.0556	-0.0614	-0.1063*	0.0294
	(0.0640)	(0.0611)	(0.0367)	(0.0647)	(0.0460)	(0.0497)
West	0.0630	-0.1338*	-0.0777*	-0.1623*	-0.1266*	-0.0539
	(0.0704)	(0.0910)	(0.0403)	(0.0711)	(0.0505)	(0.0546)
State and local experience	0.0111	-0.0581	0.0084	-0.0101	-0.0367	-0.0807*
(1 = none)	(0.0482)	(0.0460)	(0.0276)	(0.0487)	(0.0346)	(0.0374)
Federal aid opposition	-0.1212	0.2392**	-0.0011	0.1578	0.0930	-0.1196
(100 = no support)	(0.0953)	(0.0910)	(0.0546)	(0.0963)	(0.0685)	(0.0739)
R_2	0.4613**	0.5783**	0.4533	0.1539**	0.5317**	0.7005**

* = variable significant at 0.05 level
** = variable significant at 0.01 level
(Numbers in parentheses are standard errors.)

Region also has some independent impact on voting. Being from the South tends to lower mandate support scores for all but the cost dimension, with the greatest statistically significant impact on mandates pertaining to business, environmental, and authority dimensions. Southern senators, for instance, had, on average, 16 percent lower environmental mandate support scores when compared to Northeastern members. Midwestern senators had lower scores for four dimensions, but their regional background was statistically significant only for environmental mandates. Western senators had lower mandate support scores for all but the welfare dimension. Being from the West was most strongly associated with lower support for mandates with cost impacts, business preemptions, and environmental programs.

Over 60 percent of senators across the three Congresses had previous state and local office-holding experience, most as either state legislators or chief elected officials of states, cities, or counties. This kind of previous state and local experience was thought to dispose members to vote against mandates. However, state and local experience had very little independent effect on mandate voting, either in the overall index or for any dimension. The only statistically significant association was for social policy mandates, where prior state and local experience helped to reduce mandate support.

Opposition to federal aid was significantly associated with mandate voting for only business preemption, but contrary to expectations, those opposed to federal grants-in-aid tended to support these kinds of mandates. Other dimensions were not statistically significant and there was also no consistency in the direction of the relationship.

The House results for the various dimensions are less compelling for all but two dimensions—costs and social policy—and in fact result in a weaker R_2 than the overall House index for all but these two dimensions, as shown in Table 3.6.

House voting showed some different patterns from those of the Senate. Unlike the Senate, House Republicans were more supportive of mandates with cost impacts than Democrats on average and were slightly more supportive of environmental mandates. Also unlike the Senate, House Republicans were less supportive of welfare mandates than Democrats, although the relationship was not statistically significant. However, similar to their party colleagues in the Senate, House Republicans tended to be more opposed to authority mandates and more supportive of social policy mandates than Democrats.

Ideology had a statistically significant relationship to mandate voting for four of the dimensions. Like the Senate, House conservatives tended to be less supportive of mandates with authority and cost impacts than liberals; for every 10 percent reduction in the liberalism index, for instance, the support index for cost impact mandates dropped

TABLE 3.6
Regression Results for Six Mandate Dimensions, House

	Welfare	Business	Authority	Costs	Environment	Social Policy
Intercept	0.6273**	0.6404**	0.3836**	0.5634**	0.5156**	0.8799**
	(0.1163)	(0.0422)	(0.0413)	(0.0669)	(0.0461)	(0.0385)
Party	0.1652	−0.0440	0.1076**	−0.1374*	−0.0444	−0.1380*
(Democrat = 1)	(0.0970)	(0.0352)	(0.0344)	(0.0558)	(0.0380)	(0.0321)
Liberal	−0.0029	−0.0016**	0.0012*	0.0052**	−0.0005	−0.0070*
(100 = liberal)	(0.0016)	(0.0005)	(0.0005)	(0.0009)	(0.0006)	(0.0005)
South	−0.1706*	0.0032	−0.0192	−0.2074**	0.0581	−0.0365
	(0.0841)	(0.0305)	(0.0298)	(0.0484)	(0.0333)	(0.0278)
Midwest	−0.0909	−0.0298	0.0221	−0.2016**	0.0122	−0.0300
	(0.0751)	(0.0272)	(0.0266)	(0.0432)	(0.0297)	(0.0248)
West	−0.1351	−0.1146**	0.0351	−0.3994**	0.0384	−0.0761**
	(0.0836)	(0.0303)	(0.0297)	(0.0481)	(0.0331)	(0.0277)
State and local	−0.0485	0.0067	0.0292	−0.0585	0.0249	−0.0035
experience (1 = none)	(0.0631)	(0.0229)	(0.0224)	(0.0363)	(0.0250)	(0.0209)
Federal aid opposition	−0.0556	−0.0644	0.0382	−0.0823	0.0170	0.0432
(100 = no support)	(0.1049)	(0.0380)	(0.0372)	(0.0603)	(0.0415)	(0.0347)
R_2	0.0002**	0.1233**	0.1659**	0.3737**	0.0478**	0.7702**

* = variable significant at 0.05 level
** = variable significant at 0.01 level
(Numbers in parentheses are standard errors.)

by 5.3 points. Also like the Senate, the strongest linkage between ideology and voting was on the social policy mandates, with conservatives showing greater support for these types of mandates than liberals.

Regional variables also had an impact on House voting. Like the Senate, Southern congressmen tended to have lower support for welfare and authority mandates when compared to Northeastern colleagues. Unlike their regional counterparts in the Senate, House Southerners had significantly lower support mandates with cost impacts but slightly higher support for environmental and business preemptions. Midwestern congressmen were far more likely to oppose mandates with cost impacts than Northeasterners, and this was the only dimension where being from the Midwest made a statistically significant difference in voting.

Western congressmen had the greatest antipathy toward mandates with cost impacts, as members from this region had 40 percent lower support scores than Northeasterners. Being from the West made a statistically significant difference for only one other dimension, social policy, but the association was relatively weak. Being from the Western region had a greater impact on mandate voting in the Senate. Western senators were more likely to oppose cost, business preemption, environmental, and authority mandates, and these relationships were all statistically significant.

Like the Senate, the previous state and local office-holding experiences of congressmen had little relationship to mandate voting. The associations were weak for all dimensions, and none were statistically significant. Relationships with federal aid opposition were not statistically significant either.

The disparity in the specific votes comprising the indexes in the House and Senate help explain differences in the strength and direction of the model between the two chambers. For example, for the environmental dimension, Senate Democrats and liberals were more likely to support these kinds of mandates, whereas their House counterparts were slightly less likely to vote for environmental mandates than House Republicans. When compared to the Senate environmental mandate votes, the House votes consisted disproportionately of mandates to preempt state regulation of oil spills and pesticide residues—mandates favored by Republican conservatives who were anxious about the burden of varying and strong state regulatory policies on their business constituencies for the environment. In the welfare area, the weak relationship between party and ideology in the House undoubtedly is largely due to the fact that the House welfare index consisted of only one welfare mandate roll call during the six-year period, compared to six in the Senate.

IMPLICATIONS

The strong programmatic and policy thrust behind much of the mandate voting suggests that federalism is largely a secondary value, overshadowed and often overwhelmed by other, more primary goals. Roll call voting is largely prompted by the underlying policy issue involved, not by the principle of federalism at stake. When conflicted, members of Congress will tend to vote based on their policy preferences rather than on their views on the use of mandates as a generic tool of government action.

This pattern suggests that successful battles against federal mandates by state and local government interest groups must engage other allies who have a policy-oriented reason to oppose the mandate. Whether it be enlisting environmentalists to protect state authority to exceed federal environmental standards or public-employee unions to fight against an extension of Medicare that would impose costs equally on state and local employers and employees, coalitions are the path to success in a system that appears to have such weak support for federalism values.

Although roll calls lend a view of congressional behavior on those mandate issues prompting floor divisions, they by no means synoptically determine, let alone explain, the political patterns giving rise to the significant mandates passed by Congress during this period. First, it is possible that many mandates do not prompt divisive floor roll calls. Second, regardless of how conflict is resolved, roll call analysis does not help explain important parts of the political puzzle that enable mandates to reach agenda status and move to floor consideration in the first place, including the impetus for legislation, the responses of different committees, and interest group behavior patterns.

The next chapter analyzes specific conflict surrounding the consideration of the twelve most significant mandates of the 99th Congress to help us better understand the variables most responsible for mandate outcomes.

NOTES TO CHAPTER 3

1. For purposes of this analysis, only votes with more than a 20 percent voting split among the members in either direction were used. Votes with sufficient variance are needed to statistically analyze independent variables affecting voting behavior. See Jerrold Schneider, *Ideological Coalitions in Congress* (Westport, Conn.: Greenwood Press, 1979).

2. Of course, such an analysis is only part of the story explaining congressional behavior on mandates—many mandates are approved without divisive

roll calls and the crucial stage of agenda setting, that is, determining which issues are presented and how they are presented for voting, is obviously left out. Further, such analysis is fraught with methodological pitfalls, including the assumption of the equal significance of each vote and the complex and often multiple dimensions involved in many roll call votes. See Lee F. Anderson, et al., *Legislative Roll-Call Analysis* (Evanston, Ill.: Northwestern University Press, 1966).

3. See Demetrios Caraley, "Congressional Politics and Urban Aid," *Political Science Quarterly* 91 (1976), pp. 19–43; "Do Congressional Liberals Really Need to Tremble? A Quick Look at Some Hard Data," *Political Science Quarterly* 96 (Spring, 1981), pp. 27–30; and (with Yvette R. Schlusse), "Congress and Reagan's New Federalism," *Publius: The Journal of Federalism* 16 (Winter, 1986), pp. 49–79.

4. Demetrios Caraley (with Yvette R. Schlusse), "Congress and Reagan's New Federalism", p. 56.

5. Rodney Hero, "The U.S. Senate and Federalism Policy: An Examination of Selected Roll Call Votes in the 96th and 97th Congress," in *Congress and Public Policy: A Source Book of Document and Readings*, 2nd edition, ed. David C. Kozak and John D. Macartney (Chicago: Dorsey Press, 1987), pp. 322–328.

6. Michael R. Malaby and David J. Webber, "Federalism in the 101st Congress," *Publius: The Journal of Federalism* 21 (Summer, 1991), pp. 77–92.

7. Timothy Conlan, "Federalism and Competing Values in the Reagan Administration," *Publius: The Journal of Federalism* 16 (Winter, 1986), p. 45.

8. Stephen Schecter, "Federalism in the 96th Congress," *Publius: The Journal of Federalism* 11, Nos. 3–4 (1981), p. 157.

9. Martin O. Sabo, John E. Haynes, and Louis Dvorak, "U.S. House Votes in the 96th Congress on Issues with Major Implications for Federalism," *Publius: The Journal of Federalism* 11, No. 3–4 (1981), p. 166.

10. Margaret Wrightson, "Support for Federalism in the U.S. Senate: Analysis of Key Votes in the 100th Congress," unpublished paper, 1991.

11. To target the analysis on only those votes involving a mandate alone, I excluded votes on broader legislation that encompassed several other issues in addition to mandates, for example, some of the votes on reconciliation bills. Further excluded were votes involving mandates applying to a single locality, state, or region, in the interests of focusing exclusively on national mandates affecting all or most states and/or communities. Finally, certain redundant votes were excluded when roll calls were reconsidered, taking the most recent vote as determinative.

12. Crossover sanctions are closely related to grant conditions, with the primary distinction involving the relevance of the condition to the purposes of the grant program to be withheld in the event of mandate noncompliance. In some cases, subjective judgments had to be made on categorization; for example, five votes that conditioned receipt of AIDS funds on major state policy changes regarding marriage licensure or patient disclosure were viewed as crossover sanctions. By contrast, for example, votes that changed cost-sharing rules or sanctions for erroneous eligibility determinations were viewed as grant conditions.

13. David W. Rohde, "Electoral Forces, Political Agendas, and Partisanship in the House and Senate," in *The Postreform Congress*, ed. Roger H. Davidson (New York: St. Martin's Press, 1992), p. 34.

14. Demetrios Caraley (with Yvette R. Schlusse), "Congress and Reagan's New Federalism."

15. James L. Sundquist, *The Dynamics of the Party System*, (Washington, D.C.: Brookings Institution, 1973).

16. "Conservative Coalition History," *Congressional Quarterly Almanac, 1990* (Washington, D.C.: Congressional Quarterly, 1991), p. 42.

17. David H. Rohde, "Electoral Forces, Political Agendas, and Partisanship in the House and Senate."

18. Aage Clausen and Richard Cheney, "A Comparative Analysis of Senate-House Voting on Economic and Welfare Policy: 1953–1964," *American Political Science Review* 64 (March, 1970), pp. 138–52.

19. "Ratings Find Ideological Edges Softened," *Congressional Quarterly Almanac, 1990* (Washington, D.C.: Congressional Quarterly, 1991), p. 22-B.

20. Timothy Conlan, "Federalism and Competing Values in the Reagan Administration."

21. Theodore Lowi, "Ronald Reagan—Revolutionary?" in *The Reagan Presidency and the Governing of America*, ed. Lester M. Salamon and Michael S. Lund (Washington, D.C.: Urban Institute Press, 1985), p. 38.

22. Lee F. Anderson, et al., *Legislative Roll-Call Analysis*.

23. "Anti-Takeover Bill Pulled from Senate Floor," *Congressional Quarterly Almanac, 1988* (Washington, D.C.: Congressional Quarterly, 1989), p. 251.

24. The potential bias induced by dropping members would have been a concern if the data were used to describe the universe of voting over this period. However, the primary purpose of the regression modeling here is to test the existence and strength of relationships between mandate voting and various independent variables.

4

The Rush toward Consensus

The most significant and costly mandates passed over the 1983–1990 period for the most part did not prompt divisive roll call votes, and thus are not included in the analysis in Chapter 3. In fact, mandates with the greatest cost impacts on state and local governments were most often passed unanimously in both committee and floor voting in both houses. Although conflict was assuredly present, it was resolved early in the congressional process, and most mandates became politically unassailable as they moved through formal committee and floor consideration.

The surprising consensus for important mandates can best be explained by examining the behavior of intergovernmental "constrainers"—state and local governments and conservative congressional Republicans who could be expected to mobilize in alliances to oppose these programs. Because mandate advocates succeeded in defining the issue in ways that appealed to widely supported public values, state and local groups were reluctant to frontally and openly oppose proposals. Instead they successfully pressed for concessions in the form of federal funding and modest regulatory easements early in the bill drafting process. Republicans in some cases emerged as leaders in championing mandate proposals. In other cases, the more conservative Republicans became "reluctant mandators," pressing for concessions to ameliorate the most egregious impacts but unwilling to risk political careers by opposing mandate passage. These concessions showed that Congress exercised surprising restraint when mandating, but this restraint actually facilitated consensual passage of the mandates themselves.

INVENTORY OF SIGNIFICANT MANDATES, 1983–1990

The assessment of the politics leading to the passage of the most significant mandates is predicated on identifying those mandates during the 1983–1990 period, the same period covered by the roll call analysis in Chapter 3. For purposes of this analysis, an inventory was developed based on ACIR's 1993 report that catalogued the most important new

TABLE 4.1
Features of Major Mandate Legislation, 98th–101st Congresses

Mandate Type	Number	Costs (state & local savings)[a]	Roll Calls (by type)[b]
Direct Order	14	$16 billion	6 (43%)
Crossover Sanction	6	($0.2 billion)	2 (33%)
Crosscutting	2		1 (50%)
Partial Preempt	3	1.9 billion	1 (33%)
Total Preempt	1		1 (100%)
Grant Condition	5	7.8 billion	2 (40%)
TOTALS	31	27.2 billion	13 (42%)

[a] Total costs for the column includes $2.5 billion in state and local savings for two mandates—Immigration Reform and Child Support Enforcement. Cost estimates are five-year numbers and are for fifteen of the thirty-one mandates. Of the fifteen mandates, CBO data was used for twelve and federal agency data was used for the remaining three, where CBO was either not able to do a full cost estimate or where federal agency data were more complete and current.
[b] Numbers of divisive roll calls prompting at least a 20 percent division on the floor.

mandates defined as direct orders, crosscutting requirements, partial preemptions, and crossover sanctions. This listing was supplemented by additional major grant conditions and total preemptions tracked in the Congressional Budget Office's (CBO's) database of state and local cost estimates.[1]

The thirty-one major mandates passed in the 98th through 101th Congresses are listed in the Appendix, along with five-year cost estimates for fifteen of these mandates, based largely on CBO numbers for the bills as they emerged from committee.[2] Table 4.1 summarizes the data across the eight years on the thirty-one most significant mandates passed.

For the thirty-one major mandate laws passed during the eight-year period, over $27 billion in net costs were estimated to be imposed on the state and local sector over a five-year period. This includes two mandates—Immigration Reform and Child Support Enforcement—where additional mandated responsibilities were accompanied by sufficient federal funding or cost avoidance to provide savings to the state and local sector, according to CBO.[3]

SIGNIFICANT MANDATES PASSED WITH BROAD SUPPORT

The data in Table 4.1 also show that only thirteen of the thirty-one most significant mandates were subject to a divisive roll call vote engaging more than 20 percent division on the floor of either chamber. If one conceives of at least two opportunities per bill for floor contests to emerge as the bill moves through both chambers, then in only fourteen of a minimum of sixty-two potential opportunities did this occur—or 23 percent of the minimum possible occasions for floor conflict.

A 23 percent overt floor conflict level appears low. It is particularly low when compared with aggregate figures over the eight-year period, showing that a majority of each party opposed each other on an average of 45 percent of roll calls in the Senate and 55 percent in the House.[4] For the 98th Congress, by our broader definition of floor conflict (more than 20 percent disagreement among members voting), 71 percent of the roll calls in the Senate and 66 percent of House votes were divided. Even when adding in the 408 bills passed in the House under suspension of the rules, typically by voice vote, still over 46 percent of all House votes in total were divided. This included many pieces of legislation passed by suspension of the rules that do not carry the stakes or potential for controversy of the significant mandates reviewed here.

How does the level of floor conflict for these mandates stack up against the more significant legislation passed during the same eight-year period? Using David Mayhew's list of important enactments by Congress in the postwar period, thirty-six public laws passed the threshold for significant legislation by his standards during the eight-year period from 1983 to 1990.[5] With only a handful of exceptions, each one of these laws was subject to a divided roll call vote in each chamber during consideration. Thus, by any measure, we can conclude that the significant mandates passed during the eight-year period were subject to far less floor conflict than other legislation.

The level of floor conflict, however, varies considerably across the mandate issues covered by these statutes, as shown in Table 4.2. The most highly symbolic issues in the social policy dimension prompted the greatest floor conflict, as conflict emerged in three of the eight

TABLE 4.2
Floor Conflict over Significant Mandates

	Social Policy	Costs	Authority	Welfare	Environ-ment	Business
Roll Call Conflict	3	5	2	1	2	1
Number of Conflict Opportunity	8	28	10	4	10	2

opportunities. The issues supported by these mandates were among the most controversial and highly partisan of the day and included civil rights, religion in the schools, and euthanasia.

One would expect that the mandates with the greatest cost impacts would occasion the sharpest floor conflict, as state and local governments and their congressional supporters would mobilize to expand the scope of conflict to overturn mandate legislation on the floor that they could not contain at the committee level. But this was not the case. Specifically, of the forty opportunities to vote on the legislation imposing costs, a roll call vote was taken in only eight, or 20 percent of the time. Legislation whose primary impact was not costs but state or local authority sparked roll calls in 25 percent of the cases. Bills without floor conflict included major new environmental legislation such as the 1986 Safe Drinking Water amendments, estimated to cost over $10 billion, and the Asbestos Hazard Reduction legislation, with a $500 million cost.

Explaining this extraordinary consensus requires more than data on roll calls. Rather, in-depth research on the legislative histories, interest group alignments, and policy dynamics of major mandates is necessary to understand both how the issues attained agenda status and how the key variables influenced subsequent outcomes. Legislators certainly struggle to resolve conflicts over these mandates, but apparently they resolve differences before the bill reaches committee or floor voting stages.

A qualitative exploration of the histories of a group of mandate bills will help us explore how conflict arises and is resolved and, most important, what variables can predict state and local success and failure. Needing a smaller sample for deeper analysis, we decided to focus on significant mandate activity in the 99th Congress.

MANDATES IN THE 99TH CONGRESS

The 99th Congress offers a good test bed for some of the questions and hypotheses about mandate activity. Nine significant mandates from the listing in the Appendix were passed during this period—more than in any of the other three Congresses. Five of the mandates imposed an estimated $15.3 billion in five-year costs. Further, two significant mandate relief and funding actions were passed during this term as well—the Fair Labor Standards Amendments and the Immigration Reform Act, with accompanying appropriation. Thus, those for and against mandates were active, and each was successful in several cases.

To understand the forces at work in promoting passage and floor consensus, we reviewed twelve mandate statutes, consisting of the nine mandates listed in the Appendix and three additional actions, to provide a more robust set of mandates with which to test independent variables.[6]

Overall, the 99th Congress was a highly divisive and partisan term. *Congressional Quarterly* noted that it was the most partisan Congress in three decades.[7] Over 55 percent of the roll call votes were partisan votes, and the party unity scores were the highest ever recorded by *Congressional Quarterly*.[8] Over 85 percent of Democrats voted with their party on a majority of these votes—a thirty-year high, brought about largely by the growing convergence of Southern Democrats with their party's mainstream.[9]

The 1986 congressional elections held promise for Democrats to retake control of the Senate that was lost to the Republicans in 1980, a prospect that no doubt had something to do with the increasing partisanship and posturing in this Congress. One article noted that increasing tensions between the Reagan White House and Congress provided "a formula for legislative stalemate."[10] This conflictual environment made the consensual passage of major mandates in the 99th Congress appear even more surprising.

IMPETUS FOR THE MANDATES OF THE 99TH CONGRESS

The group of twelve mandates offers a convenient test to ascertain the applicability of many of the themes discussed in Chapter 2 purporting to explain the impetus for mandates. Many of the factors promoting rapid policy change and adoption were active in the creation of these mandates.

In the 1980s, the president was viewed as setting the federalism agenda for the nation, and President Reagan certainly took leadership in promoting broadscale devolution of federal program responsibilities to the states through block grants and program turnbacks, as well as through his deregulation initiatives discussed in Chapter 1.[11] However, Congress was most often the initiator of the mandate actions passed in the 99th Congress, just as it was of the regulatory policies of the 1970s.[12] Specifically, Congress initiated eight of the twelve mandates, with the Reagan Administration and some part of Congress bearing joint responsibility for the other four mandates. Three of the four mandates initially sponsored by the administration had the primary objective of shifting federal costs to the state and local sector, whereas all of the congressionally initiated mandates had a policy rather than fiscal thrust.

As noted in Chapter 2, much congressional policy activism is promoted by congressional policy entrepreneurs whose emergence is the product of a number of institutional changes. Members of Congress enhance their electoral profiles by championing grant programs and mandates that promote media attention within their constituencies.[13] Nearly all of the mandates concerned obtained momentum thanks to the efforts of a congressional policy entrepreneur, most often the chair of the committee responsible for the legislation. In five of the cases, Republican members were the primary entrepreneurs pushing the mandate—three environmental mandates and two handicapped education mandates.

Congress was prompted to act in five of the cases due to perceived policy crises precipitated by either the courts or the administration. In three cases, Supreme Court rulings challenged the policy status quo by extending a mandate. In two cases, the Court extended mandates: *Garcia v. San Antonio Metropolitan Transit Authority*, which resulted in the extension of Fair Labor Standards requirements to state and local employees, and *Wyoming v. EEOC*, which outlawed mandatory retirement for public safety officers. In the other case, the Court overturned a mandate: *Smith v. Robinson*, which absolved schools of the responsibility to pay attorneys' fees for parents prevailing in court suits.[14] Congress reacted to both the *Garcia* and *Wyoming* decisions by modifying the mandate to reduce state and local costs and increase flexibility, permitting state and local governments to award compensatory time off for overtime and by permitting mandatory retirement for public safety officers. In the other case, Congress reinstated requirements for school districts to pay attorneys' fees and expanded the mandate to include payments for parents prevailing in administrative proceedings. Two environmental mandates were enacted in response to perceptions of administration foot-dragging in promulgating safe drinking water regulations and in requiring schools to abate asbestos hazards.

The "logic of regulatory expansion" fueled the growth of mandates in many cases.[15] Though ACIR found that 90 percent of the mandates of the 1970s broke new ground by applying regulation to a policy for the first time, they discovered that the intergovernmental regulatory statutes passed in the 1980s were largely modifications of those earlier regulatory policies.[16] It is a reflection on the maturation of regulatory federalism that while the programmatic antecedents to the regulations of the 1970s were earlier grant programs, the programmatic antecedents to the regulations of the 1980s were earlier regulatory programs.

Specifically, ten of the twelve mandates in the 99th Congress involved expansions of earlier regulatory policies, either from the private to the state and local sector or from one type of service or beneficiary to another. Having broken through the political barriers to establish the regulatory policy in the first place, its extension to new areas proved to be a far less difficult political task. Regulators seek to plug gaps and loopholes, whereas uncovered groups press equity claims to extend benefits. Bardach and Kagan referred to this self-generated expansion of regulatory programs as the "logic of regulatory expansion."[17]

Bardach and Kagan further argue that the increasing articulation of interest groups speaking on behalf of regulatory beneficiaries, including the growth of public interest groups that represent broader publics affected by regulation, adds political momentum to these claims.[18] Significant growth has taken place in what Robert Salisbury calls "externality groups"—organizations that represent broader interests and values, such as environmental protection and handicapped children.[19] Adroit use of the media by these groups helps to expand the scope of conflict and place issues on the federal agenda in ways that appeal to broad public values.

For the twelve mandates under review here, externality groups emerged as leading members of broader coalitions. Handicapped or child-welfare advocacy groups took the lead for four of the mandates, whereas environmental groups were leaders for another three bills. Coalitions most often included narrower groups with specific economic interests at stake as well. For instance, the safe drinking water amendments were enacted with environmental group leadership, but the group representing larger water systems joined in supporting expanded federal mandates partly due to their belief that federal requirements might prompt smaller water systems to relinquish their independent status.

The Ironic Role of the States

State policies helped paved the way for many of these mandates. Popular conceptions hold that federal regulation often emerges due to the failure of states and localities to adequately address a policy problem. Although the relationship between federal policy initiation and state action has received little academic attention, state regulatory activism, ironically, paved the way for federal regulatory policy in a number of cases.

Richard Nathan argues that states' emergence as policy innovators is to be expected when the national government is dominated by conservatives, as it was in the 1980s. States were endowed with greater fiscal and policy management capacities, thanks to reforms initiated in the 1960s in revenue systems, redistricting, and state legislative and administrative organization. With a conservative administration and a Republican-controlled Senate in Washington, states became the focal point for policy advocates frustrated at the national level. State initiatives undertaken during these conservative national periods subsequently become the basis for a ratcheting up of national policy action, in Nathan's view.[20]

The twelve mandates reviewed here were classified based on whether the federal policy was enacted before most states had similar regulations or when a majority of states had similar regulations.[21] Limited data on the prior state programs permit assessments of this dimension for only seven mandate bills. The federal action generally followed similar actions in most states for all seven mandates. For example, forty-two states offered at least some schooling to handicapped children of preschool age; thirty-five states had mandatory retirement ages for public safety officers; thirty-one states had some program to inspect and abate asbestos in schools as early as 1981; and 75 percent of state and local employees were already covered under Medicare by virtue of their participation in Social Security.

Of course, the high relative frequency of state programs most likely masks significant variations in quality among state programs, and federal mandates often seek to upgrade quality to some national minimum standard.[22] For example, although forty-two states offered some kind of preschool for handicapped children, many of these programs by no means covered the range of children called for in the 1986 handicapped education amendments.

Nevertheless, the prevalence of state programs remains intriguing and suggests that state regulatory programs may, in fact, be an important if overlooked factor prompting federal regulatory initiatives. This could occur in one of several different ways:

- *Stimulating interest.* State programs often first identify the scope of problems and suggest the benefits of public policy actions in terms readily understood by a national media and policy activists. For example, horror stories about asbestos in public schools emerged from states like New Jersey, whose inspection and abatement programs had uncovered the problem.
- *Demonstrating feasibility.* States' programs offer vital precedents for federal programs, often establishing the legitimacy of public action to address a problem. The implementation of mandates in states serves as "laboratories" to test the feasibility of programmatic strategies. National program advocates seize upon successful state programs as models to design federal programs, as well as for evidence on the workability of regulatory strategies. For example, when state and local governments challenged the proposed age discrimination amendment that banned mandatory retirement for all employees including public safety officers, mandate advocates were able to point to thirteen states with

comparable prohibitions, as well as to cities where such bans had not impeded effective performance. States' adoption of mandate policies gives advocates of federal mandates even more support in arguing against budgetary concerns of state and local officials; for example, Senate proponents of Medicare coverage for all existing state and local employees argued that incremental costs would actually be quite low since 75 percent of state and local employees were already covered.

- *Eliminating variability.* Significant variation in policies across states often tempts advocates and worries national businesses, and both seize on federal mandates to achieve some level of uniformity across all states. James Sundquist articulates most clearly this now conventional model explaining the etiology of the federal role. He suggests that activists first propose federal aid to entice states and communities to adopt nationally desired programs, but when the problem finally becomes recognized as a national one, more coercive means are used to ensure a uniform national response.[23] Proposals for mandated education for preschool handicapped children, for instance, were inspired by advocates who felt that it was inequitable for such children to benefit from education in some states and not others. The asbestos industry attempted with little success to gain adoption of a uniform national standard for school asbestos programs that would have prohibited removal of asbestos by local school districts.

Policy Concerns Drive Mandates

Numerous analysts suggest that the federal budget deficit tempted federal policy activists to resort more to mandates than to spending programs to achieve national goals. As Wallace Oates observes, from a federal perspective, state and local costs are "free."[24] In fact, ACIR found a growing tendency for more recent administrations to propose nonspending as opposed to spending initiatives to address national issues.[25]

It is possible, albeit impossible to prove, that in better fiscal times Congress might have chosen to implement these twelve programs using grants to state and local governments instead of regulatory coercion. Nonetheless, circumstantial evidence suggests that the federal deficit may not have been the primary consideration in the choice of the mandate tool. Of the twelve mandates reviewed, for instance, nearly all were preceded by another regulatory program, and it is difficult to imagine that Congress, even in the best of times, would have filled the gaps left by a prior regulatory program with a grant program. Bardach and Kagan argue that regulatory programs usually become more, not less, extensive and comprehensive, thanks to the logic of regulatory expansion discussed earlier.[26]

For instance, the 1986 safe drinking water mandates were enacted to strengthen the rules and fill the gaps left by the safe drinking water mandate of the 1970s, and it is difficult to conceive that Congress would have chosen a voluntaristic grant to address the perceived environmental deficiencies of the prior regulatory program. Mandate advocates, in fact, often reach for coercive tools because grants and other voluntaristic instruments are perceived to be ineffective in achieving a uniform level of services with desired quality throughout the country. The primary rationale for mandates in the view of advocates, then, was programmatic, not fiscal, although the absence of large federal costs may have facilitated congressional adoption.

Indeed, only two of the twelve mandates examined—water resources cost sharing and Medicare premiums for state and local workers—had the primary intention of producing federal budgetary savings by passing costs on to state and local governments and their employees. Moreover, as the following section will discuss, mandates often prompted higher federal spending to gain support of state and local governments for their passage. Federal funding was a state and local concession that mandate advocates could wholeheartedly support since it promoted greater levels of service and compliance throughout the nation.

CONSENSUS EXPLAINED: DISARMING THE CONSTRAINERS

As was pointed out earlier, mandates were passed with a minimum of overt conflict on the floor in comparison with other legislation. This was also the case with committee voting—eleven of the twelve bills were approved unanimously by the respective committees, with supplemental views expressing member concerns filed for only five of the bills. Consensus was so strong on five of the twelve bills that a conference between the two chambers was not needed.

How did mandates pass with such broad acclamation? The search for explanations must focus on the behavior of the actors who, by virtue of ideology and interests, would be expected to oppose mandates. Republicans, using their leadership platforms in the Senate and the White House, are expected to act as a force of restraint on most of these mandates. Ten of the twelve mandates fall into the cost and authority categories, which earlier roll call analysis showed to elicit

Republican opposition. Democrats, on the other hand, are expected to be likely to favor most of these mandates, as suggested by the roll call analysis.

The intensity and cohesiveness of state and local government interest groups is also likely to have a major impact on mandate outcomes. State and local governments, as the bearers of concentrated costs, would be expected to have the greatest interest in defending their prerogatives and fiscal pocketbooks against federal mandates. Another major variable affecting mandate outcomes is the nature and importance of coalitions allied with or opposed to state and local governments. Although the behavior of interest groups on mandates will be more fully discussed in Chapter 5, the following section will discuss how state and local views and party leaders in Congress affected congressional behavior.

Mandate Legislation Defined and Designed to Disarm Opponents

A number of variables may influence the extent to which these natural mandate opponents became engaged in political conflict over mandate legislation. The success of mandate advocates in appealing to symbolic and widely shared values was critical to disarming conservatives and fostering consensus. Conservative Republicans as well as state and local interest groups did not want to publicly oppose bills promoting such causes as safe drinking water or handicapped education. And advocacy groups have become very skilled at using the media to keep public attention on such causes and on any political actor brave enough to wander from the consensus supporting such goals.[27]

However, the political acclamation given to these mandates was also founded on substantial concessions won by state and local governments and their congressional allies during consideration of the legislation. Although state and local groups did not typically venture to oppose most of the mandates outright, they nonetheless won key modifications to seven of the twelve bills prior to committee voting and, further, gained a surprisingly generous level of new federal funds for some of these mandates. These major modifications included the following:

- Fair Labor Standards—to permit state and local governments to award compensatory time off in lieu of pay for overtime work
- Immigration Reform—to provide $1 billion on an entitlement basis to cover state costs for each of four years, modified from

House and administration proposals requiring subsequent appropriation action to fund the program

- Age Discrimination—to exempt state and local public safety officers from a House committee–proposed ban on mandatory retirement
- Handicapped Education—to convert a Senate-proposed mandate requiring service to all preschool disabled children to a voluntary grant program with less severe sanctions
- Medicare—to modify a Senate-proposed mandate extending coverage to all state and local employees to a final bill requiring coverage only for newly hired employees
- Commercial Motor Vehicles—to modify an original bill establishing a federally administered commercial driver's licensing program to provide for administration by states whose laws conformed to federal standards
- Rehabilitation Services—to modify the proposed increased state match to kick in only when federal funds exceed levels authorized for fiscal year 1988

Interestingly, mandates were considered but replaced with voluntary assistance programs in several areas in which most states had not developed programs—groundwater regulation, where only seventeen states had programs, and early intervention programs for disabled infants, where only seven states had comprehensive programs. In the case of early intervention, Senator Weicker's staff conceded that limited state involvement suggested that more experimentation was needed by more states before prescriptive national standards could be applied, so a voluntary grant program was established to entice more states into the field.[28]

Moreover, some federal funds accompanied the mandate in nine of the ten cases in which additional state and local costs were imposed. In several cases, the federal money was relatively minor, such as for the preschool education mandate, where the federal funds were expected to cover a minor share of the total costs.[29] Funding for asbestos in schools also was relatively low at $50 million per year. Funding for other mandates was considerably more significant: $1 billion per year for four years was provided in a new federal entitlement program to reimburse states for costs of serving illegal immigrants, and the federal government is obligated to fund an average of 55 percent of the costs for the new Medicaid mandates.

In some cases, funding came some years after the initial passage of the mandate, reflecting the delayed recognition by states and localities of their burden. For example, ten years after the passage of the

Safe Drinking Water Amendments in 1986, the Clinton Administration obtained congressional approval for a new drinking water fund to defray the costs of local compliance, albeit through federal upfront funding of loans that must be paid back.

The provision of increased federal funding for most mandates is surprising, particularly for a Congress that also enacted the Gramm-Rudman-Hollings deficit reduction legislation and eliminated general revenue sharing. Given the strength of the budget deficit as a political issue, it suggests unexpected political strength for program advocates and perhaps for state and local governments as well. It also gives credence to those fiscal conservatives' fears that the passage of mandates ultimately generates additional claims on the federal budget.

Both the funding additions and the concessions reducing the mandate burden reflect some degree of apparent congressional consideration of state and local concerns on mandate issues, a restraint that belies common views of a Congress with a voracious and virtually untamed appetite for unfunded mandates. This finding, however, comports with views of Congress as an institution averse to conflict. A Congress disposed toward consensus will seek, wherever possible, to couple mandates with funding to maximize support from both mandate advocates and state and local government mandate implementors. Thus, members can both vote for the benefits of a mandate and save their constituents from its cost effects.

Coalitions that support mandates also find it advantageous to seek federal funding to accompany new regulations. Program advocates seek program expansion and higher spending at both levels of government and are thus disposed to combine funding and mandates. Funding alone risks uneven participation by states, whereas mandates alone risk insufficient programs by poorer or less enthusiastic states. Mandate advocates have a vital interest in enhancing the fiscal wherewithal of state and local governments, the implementors of mandates, to provide sufficient resources to make the program work. Funding is particularly important for jurisdictions with low fiscal capacity because, as the Urban Institute notes, mandates have a regressive impact in imposing a greater fiscal burden on those governments with the least ability to pay.[30] Some mandates, such as the safe drinking water requirements, also impose a disproportionate burden on smaller jurisdictions due to scale diseconomies; substantial investments made to comply are financed by a small base of taxpayers or users.[31]

Perhaps most critically, such concessions help gain the acquiescence and even support of state and local interest groups for passage of the mandate itself, as will be discussed further in Chapter 5. It should be acknowledged that these modifications and funding provisions did not vitiate the mandates themselves, but they largely softened their state and local impacts. Thus, it could be argued that these concessions actually facilitated consensual passage of these mandates.

Although effective in winning these modifications at the committee level, state and local interest groups then became bound to accept the overall legislation reported out of committee. As will be discussed in Chapter 5, they generally did not choose to overturn committee decisions on the floor, instead permitting unanimous passage of such costly mandates as safe drinking water and asbestos in schools.

Parties' Role in Mandate Advocacy and Restraint

Neither party emerged as a consistent supporter or opponent of mandates. As with the roll call votes, mandate support was predicated on the particular policy objectives and constituency groups involved. Moreover, even when disposed to oppose mandates, members—particularly Republicans—did not state their position outright, fearful of opposing programs appealing to such broad symbolic values as clean air or handicapped education. Rather, these members became "reluctant mandators," pressing for concessions and modifications to ease the impact on states and localities, while supporting the mandate itself.

Table 4.3 illustrates that both parties earned roughly equivalent mandate support scores.

The passage of these twelve bills began and ended with substantial bipartisan agreement in the Senate, but not in the House. Across all twelve bills, the parties began with bipartisan agreement on eight of the twelve bills in the Senate, but only on three of the twelve in the House.

TABLE 4.3
Mandate Support by Party, 99th Congress[a]

Position	Senate Dem.	Senate Rep.	House Dem.	House Rep.
Support	6	7	4	5
Modify/Support	1	0	1	1
Oppose	2	3	1	3
Modify/Oppose	3	2	4	3

[a] = Absent roll calls on most of the bills, party positions were measured based on the initial positions taken by members of each party involved in leadership roles on each bill in each chamber. There was a possible universe of twelve bills in each of the two houses, except for the House Democrats, where internal divisions among the leadership on the age discrimination and handicapped protection mandates prevented characterization of party position.

For those cases where the parties disagreed, the nature of the disagreements may partly explain the apparently successful resolution of conflict for these bills; only two of the cases disagreed on involved one party supporting the mandate, with the other opposed. The remaining cases found one party supporting the mandate with the other party serving as either "reluctant mandators," pressing for modifications to ease the state and local impact or as "reluctant relievers," pressing for modifications to advance federal objectives for mandate relief statutes.

With regard to the Republicans, Chapter 3 showed that the Republicans' historic aversion to the expansion of the federal role for spending programs did not manifest itself in consistent opposition to proposed mandates. An analysis of Republican positions on the twelve bills in the 99th Congress indicates that there were several reasons for their apparent support for mandates.

First, the mandate, or in one case, the mandate relief bill, had attained such a popular compelling status that public opposition even by conservatives became hazardous; Republicans concerned about the state and local impacts of environmental or handicapped mandates did not feel that they could oppose such measures, due to the strong public support and fear of arousing inattentive publics.[32] Accordingly, they gave vent to their policy conservatism through nonpublic bargaining for concessions to reduce the mandate's impact, while supporting the mandate in recorded committee or floor votes.

For example, Republican Congressman Norman Lent bargained with Congressman Florio to modify the asbestos in schools mandate to provide schools with more flexibility, but he did not publicly oppose the mandate for its "demagoguery potential."[33] Congressman Steven Bartlett, the ranking Republican on the committee reporting on the preschool handicapped mandate, sought changes in the preschool handicapped mandate to reduce its burden but remarked that conservatives had to be careful to pursue only those alternatives that could be justified as ways to better serve the beneficiaries.[34] Later chapters on asbestos and preschool handicapped mandates show that the conservatives' options and effectiveness dwindled once mandate legislation achieved agenda status and required public position taking.

Second, in some cases, Republicans assumed roles as mandate advocates and leaders. Support by Senate Republicans for seven of the twelve mandates was particularly surprising. Indeed, Senate Republicans emerged as their party's leaders on these mandates, largely by virtue of their chairmanship of the relevant committees with jurisdiction. Republican committee or subcommittee chairs who led their party on four of the seven mandates supported were moderate to liberal members with relatively high Americans for Democratic Action support scores: Robert Stafford, Chairman of Senate Environment and Public Works, with an ADA score of 60; Lowell Weicker, Chairman of the Handicapped Subcommittee of Senate Human Resources, with an ADA score of 80; and Robert Packwood, Chairman of Senate Finance Committee, with an ADA score of 60.

Stafford and Weicker, for example, were both federal policy activists who realized that the impending 1986 congressional elections might cost the Republicans control of the Senate.[35] The 99th Congress could be their last chance to claim credit for bringing favored issues to the congressional agenda. Further, the 99th Congress saw Republican congressional deference to the Reagan presidency wane, as members realized that the president's policy positions on such issues as environmental and social issues could make them unelectable. So, members already disposed to disagree with the conservative policy agenda felt greater license to distance themselves from White House control.[36]

Weicker used his position as Chairman of the Handicapped Subcommittee to aggressively push two important mandates advancing handicapped education: the handicapped protection bill, expanding parents' rights to claim attorneys fees for administrative proceedings, and the handicapped education amendments, extending earlier federal special education mandates to preschool children. In both cases, Weicker authored tough bills that provided for the strongest federal role and the greatest state and local burden of any of the alternatives considered.

Stafford's embrace of the asbestos in schools mandate reflected his desire to leave a policy legacy on environmental issues before the Democrats resumed the committee chairmanship. As will be discussed further in Chapter 6, the asbestos bill was presented as a "done deal" by a broad coalition of Stafford's interest group allies from the environmental movement, the education community, and the public-employee labor unions. Given the support and momentum generated for the bill by Congressman Florio in the House, it would have been difficult for any chair of the Senate's environment committee to keep it off the committee's agenda without losing significant support from these key groups. Indeed, Stafford advocated even stricter federal controls than those in Florio's bill, including the extension of federal asbestos abatement standards from just schools to all private buildings. Both Stafford and Weicker illustrate how institutional expectations for leadership can generate policy activism; as Derthick and Quirk note, institutional leaders have a bias toward policy action because of their own and others' expectations that they should make a difference.[37]

House Republicans' mandate positions were somewhat more in keeping with expectations. Although supporting five of the twelve mandates, three of those five had a primary goal of shifting federal costs to states and localities, thus reflecting fiscal conservatism. House Republicans further reflected their fiscal conservatism in seeking to curtail the federal reimbursement payment for state immigration costs[38] and to oppose new Medicaid mandates, due to concerns for their impact on the federal deficit.[39] House Republicans used their position to modify three other mandates passed by Senate Republicans to reduce their state and local cost impact.

Unlike their Senate counterparts, only one of the mandates supported by House Republicans involved a member acting as a policy advocate or entrepreneur. Congressman Edward Madigan of Illinois used his position as ranking minority member of the relevant House subcommittee to develop and champion the safe drinking water mandate bill to neutralize environmentalists outraged at his opposition to federal controls over acid rain.[40]

Significantly, Republicans in both houses had no better record than Democrats in opposing or modifying mandates to protect state and local prerogatives. Republicans and Democrats in both houses each sought to reduce mandate burdens on five of the twelve bills, but in most cases they chose different bills to defend state and local prerogatives. Republicans in the House opposed mandates or pressed for modifications in environmental, health, and fair labor standards.

Democrats, as expected, supported these kinds of mandates. However, Democrats also confounded expectations by opposing or modifying mandates to reduce their impact in five of the bills in both houses. Democrats tended to oppose mandates when perceived to harm key party constituencies. For two mandates, the opposition of public-employee unions was instrumental in turning Democrats against the Medicare mandate, which burdened public employees, and against banning mandatory retirement for public safety officers. In both cases, an alliance of two major Democratic constituencies—labor and larger cities—turned Democrats against these mandates. For example, Congressman Austin Murphy, chairman of the subcommittee responsible for Fair Labor Standards and Age Discrimination, though not beholden to local governments, overturned the ban on mandatory retirement, reflecting the opposition of public-employee unions to this mandate.[41]

Four of the five mandates opposed by Democrats would have shifted federal costs to the state and local sector, and Democratic opposition appeared to reflect their overall aversion to conservative efforts to trim federal domestic discretionary spending at least as much as their support for greater state and local discretion or burden reduction. Freed from the Republicans' burden of supporting these fiscal conservative mandates, opposition to these mandates permitted Democrats to give free rein to congressional localism by positioning themselves as the party favoring continued or expanded federal expenditure benefits to local districts.

For example, Democrats from the four states uniquely burdened by costs associated with Immigration Reform defined the party position to support a $4 billion entitlement grant to fully fund states' estimated costs, a position opposed by Republicans encumbered by fiscal conservatism and an administration opposed to new domestic social spending. Senior Democrats on the House Committee on Education and Labor could press to effectively nullify the increased rehabilitation matching requirement, due to its impact on their fiscally distressed Midwest states.

IMPLICATIONS

A qualitative analysis of the passage of significant mandates of the 99th Congress confirms the results of the roll call analysis: Federalism is a secondary value, overshadowed and often overwhelmed by other, more primary policy goals. The impetus for mandates is a fundamental feature of our political system, as entrepreneurs from both parties are disposed to act on the claims brought by a wide range of increasingly organized groups representing potential mandate beneficiaries.

Once mandates were on the agenda, actors traditionally expected to oppose them were neutralized. Thanks partly to the broad symbolic appeal of many mandates, Republican conservatives often became "reluctant mandators," resigned to rear-guard actions, such as modifying mandates to alleviate their most egregious effects. That broad symbolic appeal, as well as the state and local concessions often granted, go a long way toward explaining the surprising consensus surrounding the passage of these significant regulatory programs.

But what of the presence or absence of state and local government opposition? We turn to this question in the next chapter.

NOTES TO CHAPTER 4

1. Advisory Commission on Intergovernmental Relations, *Federal Regulation of State and Local Governments: The Mixed Record of the 1980's*, A–126 (Washington, D.C.: ACIR, 1993). For discussion of CBO's database and responsibilities under the State and Local Government Cost Estimate Act of 1981, see Theresa Gullo, "Estimating the Impact of Federal Legislation on State and Local Governments," in *Coping with Mandates: What Are the Alternatives?* ed. Michael Fix and Daphne A. Kenyon (Washington, D.C.: Urban Institute, 1990), pp. 41–48.

2. For the remaining sixteen mandates, CBO estimated there were no additional direct state and local costs for some, such as the Age Discrimination Amendments; they were not required to prepare estimates for some, like the Drug-Free Workplace Act of 1988, which was a floor amendment; or they were not able to prepare full estimates in the short time provided by congressional committees.

3. The inventory excludes several other statutes enacted during the period that ACIR found provided states and localities with at least partial regulatory relief, including the Fair Labor Standards Amendments of 1986, which blunted the impact of the *Garcia* decision by permitting states and localities to give compensatory time off instead of overtime pay; the Local Government Anti-Trust Act of 1984, which reversed a Supreme Court ruling holding local governments liable for damages in antitrust suits; and the 1987 statute permitting states to raise speed limits to 65 miles per hour on rural interstates.

4. "Proportion of Partisan Roll Calls," *Congressional Quarterly Almanac, 1990* (Washington, D.C.: Congressional Quarterly, 1991), p. 33.

5. David R. Mayhew, *Divided We Govern: Party Control, Lawmaking, and Investigations, 1946–1990* (New Haven: Yale University Press, 1991).

6. The three added included one mandate relief statute—the Fair Labor Standards Amendments. Two other mandates were added that did not make the threshold for the most significant mandates during the eight-year period but were the next most significant for this Congress after the first nine already included in the Appendix—the Medicaid mandates passed during this term and the Rehabilitation Services grant program's increased state matching share, with estimated state costs exceeding CBO's major mandate cost threshold.

7. "Partisanship Hit New High in 99th Congress," *Congressional Quarterly Almanac* (Washington, D.C.: Congressional Quarterly, 1987).

8. *Ibid.*, p. 29-C.

9. Norman J. Ornstein, *et. al., Vital Statistics on Congress* (Washington, D.C.: American Enterprise Institute, 1988), p. 209.

10. Richard E. Cohen and Dick Kirschten, "An Era of Deadlock," *National Journal,* 18 January 1986, p. 126.

11. John Kincaid, "The State of American Federalism—1986," *Publius: The Journal of Federalism* 17 (Summer, 1987), pp. 1–33.

12. Advisory Commission on Intergovernmental Relations, *Regulatory Federalism: Policy, Process, Impact and Reform* (Washington, D.C.: ACIR, 1984), p. 65.

13. David Mayhew, *Congress: The Electoral Connection* (New Haven: Yale University Press, 1974).

14. *Garcia v. San Antonio Metropolitan Transit Authority*, 105 Sup. Ct. 1005 (1985); *EEOC v. Wyoming*, 460 U.S. 286 (1983); *Smith v. Robinson*, 468 U.S. 992 (1984).

15. Eugene Bardach, "Social Regulation," in *Beyond Privatization: The Tools of Government Action*, ed. Lester M. Salamon (Washington, D.C.: Urban Institute Press, 1989), p. 201.

16. Advisory Commission on Intergovernmental Relations, *A Decade of Change: The Mixed Record of the 1980's* (Washington, D.C.: U.S. Government Printing Office, 1993).

17. Eugene Bardach and Robert Kagan, *Going by the Book: The Problem of Regulatory Unreasonableness* (Philadelphia: Temple University Press, 1982), p. 19.

18. Jeffrey M. Berry, *Lobbying for the People: The Political Behavior of Public Interest Groups* (Princeton: Princeton University Press, 1977).

19. Robert Salisbury, "The Paradox of Interest Groups in Washington—More Groups, Less Clout," in *The New American Political System*, 2nd edition, ed. Anthony King (Washington, D.C.: AEI Press, 1990), p. 210.

20. Richard Nathan, "Federalism—the Great 'Composition,' " in *The New American Political System*, 2nd edition, ed. Anthony King (Washington, D.C.: AEI Press, 1990).

21. William Lammers, "Health Policy Regulations and the States: Sources and Implications of Variations in the Speed and Scope of Federal Action" (paper prepared for delivery at the 1991 Annual Meeting of the American Political Science Association in Washington on 1 September 1991).

22. *Ibid.* Lammers' study found that new federal regulations were largely more stringent than regulations prevailing in most states.

23. See James L. Sundquist with David W. Davis, *Making Federalism Work* (Washington, D.C.: Brookings Institution, 1969), p. 11.

24. Wallace Oates, *Fiscal Federalism* (New York: Harcourt, Brace, and Jovanovich, 1972).

25. Advisory Commission on Intergovernmental Relations, *Regulatory Federalism: Policy, Process, Impact and Reform*, p. 68.

26. Eugene Bardach and Robert Kagan, *Going by the Book: The Problem of Regulatory Unreasonableness*.

27. See Thomas J. Anton, *American Federalism and Public Policy* (New York: Random House, 1989), p. 189, for a discussion of symbolic politics surrounding intergovernmental regulation.

28. Interview with Loni Florian, staff to Senate Subcommittee on the Handicapped.

29. Interview with Joel Hamilton, Office of Special Education, U.S. Department of Education.

30. Michael Fix and Daphne A. Kenyon, *Coping with Mandates: What Are the Alternatives?* p. 19.

31. Arnold M. Kuzmack, "The Safe Drinking Water Act: A Case Study," in *Ibid.*, pp. 69–77.

32. R. Douglas Arnold, *The Logic of Congressional Action* (New Haven: Yale University Press, 1990).

33. Interview with Teresa Gorman, staff to Congressman Lent.

34. Interview with Congressman Steven Bartlett, May, 1989.

35. This section on Stafford and Weicker was drawn from interviews with their committee staffs.

36. "Hill Support for President Drops to a Ten-Year Low," *Congressional Quarterly Almanac, 1986* (Washington, D.C.: Congressional Quarterly, 1987), p. 21-C.

37. Martha Derthick and Paul J. Quirk, *The Politics of Deregulation* (Washington, D.C.: Brookings Institution, 1987).

38. Positions to modify a mandate to increase the state and local costs or promote a stronger federal role were scored in Table 4.3 as modify/support.

The House Republican position on immigration reimbursement was scored in this fashion.

39. The federal government is obligated to pay an average of 55 percent of all eligible state Medicaid expenditures.

40. Interview with Michael Mason, legislative staff assistant to Congressman Madigan.

41. Interview with James Riley, staff with the Subcommittee on Labor Standards, House Education and Labor Committee.

5

State and Local Government Interest Group Behavior

A key variable affecting congressional adoption of mandate concessions is the balance of interest group pressures brought to bear on the legislation. Justice Blackmun's majority decision in the *Garcia* case recognized this by noting that state and local governments must rely on their own political resources and prowess, not the Constitution, to protect their prerogatives and costs from federal encroachment. This is true to a point, and state and local governments have shown that they have considerable influence when they choose to apply their political resources.

However, it fails to account for the frequent ambivalence shown by state and local governments toward new mandates, an ambivalence that hampers their ability to marshall the requisite internal political consensus and intensity to wage an effective campaign against mandate legislation. Their ability to overcome this ambivalence and their success in obtaining powerful allies willing to join their fight against new mandates proved to be the two most important variables affecting state and local success in gaining major mandate concessions. But states and localities were often unable to marshal sufficient intensity, unity, or allies in the fight against mandates, which helps to explain the consensual passage of mandates during the 1980's and early 1990's.

STATE AND LOCAL GOVERNMENT OPPOSITION

The literature on interest groups suggests that state and local governments would be expected to intensely oppose the imposition of mandates. As Jeffrey Berry reports, the most common reason cited for organizing business interest groups is opposition to impending or actual federal regulation.[1] David Vogel notes that the expanded advocacy of business interests in the late 1970s was due to the costs imposed by environmental protection, occupational safety and health, and other regulatory programs enacted earlier that decade.[2] More broadly, traditional interest group theory suggests that formal groups arise due to disturbances in their socioeconomic environment; in fact, the rate of interest group formation could serve as an index of the stability of a society.[3] If interest groups did not already exist, in this view, the recent outpouring of mandates would guarantee the formation of state and local lobbies.

The literature also suggests that interest groups with a narrow focus and pursuing their own economic self-interest are likely to be more successful in maintaining themselves and in pressing their claims than groups representing broader or "purposive" interests.[4] With regard to mandates, state and local governments have a concentrated, narrowly economic-based interest, whereas mandate advocates seek to reflect the broader and more diffuse interests of those who might benefit from mandated programs. Mancur Olson would predict that state and local governments would have an easier time sustaining opposition to mandates than mandate advocates since they do not suffer from the free-rider problem that plagues advocates of a "public interest."[5] Similarly, James Q. Wilson argues that mandate advocates face a struggle to represent the more diffuse beneficiaries of regulatory programs, and their success requires the effective leadership of policy entrepreneurs who can mobilize latent publics and define the issue as promoting widely shared values.[6]

Notwithstanding their theoretical advantages, studies of state and local government interest groups conclude that their influence on significant legislation is limited.[7] First, the necessity of organizing as an interest group marked an implicit recognition of the waning informal influence state and local officials had in national politics through the party system. Only thirty years ago, Banfield and Wilson wrote of the strong connection between local and national politicians through the party system.[8] Grodzins concluded that the decentralized nature of our parties worked to disperse power away from Washington.[9] Under this regime, members of Congress owed their nominations to state and local party leaders and could be depended on to protect the institutional and fiscal integrity of states and localities.

As noted in Chapter 2, dramatic changes have occurred that have severed these informal ties between national and local leaders. Governors and mayors lost pivotal positions in the nomination process for presidential and congressional offices, as party organizations and labels lost their grip on the election process and the electorate in general. One manifestation of the growing independence is a decline in the portion of congressional leaders having held previous local elected office from 55 percent in 1903 to 18 percent in 1983.[10] Another indicator is the decline in gubernatorial elections held in presidential election years from thirty-three in 1944 to ten in 1980[11] and the rise in split-party control of the Senate and governorship within the same state from 18 percent on average prior to 1960 to nearly 47 percent since 1960.[12] Far from allies, the relationship between congressional members and their state and local elected counterparts resembles a competitive or even antagonistic one between independent political entrepreneurs in search of money, visibility, and votes.[13]

Donald Haider wrote that it is no coincidence that the establishment of such groups as the National Governors' Association and the National Association of Counties as major Washington lobbying organizations can be traced to the early 1960s—roughly the same period when state and local influence over nominations waned. As their political influence within their parties decreased, their collective identity as an interest group increased.[14]

David Vogel discusses a similar transformation in his study of American business. Before the 1960s, business achieved its influence not through political organization, but through the broad acceptance of business prerogatives in the political culture. Subsequently, it had to become better organized and represented as an interest group once public support for business values declined.[15]

The membership of state and local interest groups is both their greatest strength and their greatest weakness.[16] As elected officials, state and local leaders have considerable legitimacy to members of Congress and greater access to congressional offices than many other groups. Their influence arises in large part from their direct electoral relationship with members' constituencies, a relationship that can be used to either help or hurt the member. Successful state or local politicians are, at the very least, a force that members of Congress must respect and acknowledge. Moreover, their role as implementors of most federal policies also gives them some leverage in developing legislation. Richard Nathan called states and localities the "vertical coalition" that supports a program's implementation, as contrasted with horizontal coalitions of program beneficiaries. As implementors, they can often threaten exit or noncompliance to gain leverage in changing the terms and conditions for their participation.[17]

However, precisely because their members are elected officials, state and local interest groups find it difficult to achieve the kind of internal cohesion needed to effectively formulate and communicate group positions on the important intergovernmental issues of the day. As with most interest groups, internal consensus is a prerequisite to the groups' articulation and advocacy of positions. Berry argues that consensus is more difficult with state or local organizations since the members are reluctant to delegate the formulation of positions to staff.[18]

With members from both parties, it is often difficult to obtain consensus from political officials on important issues. Haider calls the nation's governors fifty prima donnas, each with his or her own national policy ax to grind.[19]

Further, positions on issues often differ among different groups of state and local officials, as well as within each group, as elected officials such as governors often have different interests and positions than state program officials for such areas as highways or welfare. The term "picket fence federalism" was coined to describe how like-minded program specialists within federal and state governments form alliances across governments in implementing federal programs, often against their nominal elected superiors.[20] As with any interest group, the failure to achieve consensus diminishes their effectiveness—either they take no position and therefore gain no influence, or their disunity is exploited by opponents.[21]

State and local government interest groups face another liability: They are uniquely geographic groups seeking influence in a policymaking process that is organized along functional lines.[22] The major committees in Congress, for example, are all based on programs or functions such as transportation, health, or agriculture. And the interest groups that form the core of subsystems or issue networks are also functionally based. States and localities come to the table pressing a different set of concerns. To be effective, they must usually form alliances with functionally based interest groups, whether they be groups representing disabled citizens, environmentalists, or teachers. Reviewing a series of case studies used in his analysis, Haider says states and localities succeeded only when they allied with others in a coalition.[23]

Perhaps as a result of these limitations, both Haider and Camissa conclude that state and local groups avoid controversial issues and have difficulty supporting new policies or opposing them due to imponderables that affect implementation. Their greatest success typically centers around narrow issues and in gaining concessions on implementation questions.[24]

STATE AND LOCAL GROUPS' MIXED VIEWS ON MANDATES

Although states and localities might be expected to be vigilant opponents of mandates, the record was actually quite mixed, as state and local interest group positions varied considerably across the twelve mandates reviewed in the 99th Congress. Organizations that represented elected officials and top management officials reporting directly to elected officers (e.g., school superintendents and state budget officers) initially supported the mandate in four of these twelve cases, while registering opposition for seven bills.[25] However, once committees modified the proposed mandates to provide federal funds and address some of the state and local concerns, as reported in Chapter 4, state and local government groups generally dropped their opposition to the passage of the mandate itself. In only three of the twelve bills—Medicare coverage of state and local employees, age discrimination, and Medicaid—did the groups seek to overturn committee decisions on the floor.

The positions and intensity of these interest groups were strongly associated with the congressional outcomes. Of the seven bills that the groups opposed, Congress adopted major concessions urged by these groups in six of them. Conversely, all four of the mandates favored by the groups were passed without significant modification, including such expensive mandates as the safe drinking water amendments.

An analysis of all National Governors' Association (NGA) positions taken during the 99th Congress affirms that the organization supported mandates or preemption in a surprising number of cases.[26] Of thirty-five positions taken on mandate or preemption issues, the association opposed these federal actions in sixteen cases, as expected. However, the NGA supported federal preemption or mandates in seven cases, several of which were contingent on federal funding availability, including drinking water, asbestos in public buildings, and air pollution standards for solid waste disposal plants. In the remaining twelve cases, the governors supported preemption or mandates but with the condition that states be permitted to exceed the federal standard or be given flexibility in implementing the regulation. These cases included support for national preemption of state energy efficiency standards for appliances, national minimum benefit standards for public assistance with work requirements, and stronger federal clean air and clean water standards.

As suggested by Haider and Camissa, state and local groups were not always united in their positions. In several cases, groups representing state agencies advocated mandates that were opposed by their generalist bosses. State program bureaucrats perceived mandates to be a useful club to use in budgetary battles within the state. Thus, for example, whereas organizations representing school boards and school superintendents mounted a vigorous grassroots campaign to modify Senator Weicker's handicapped education bill, the state association of special education administrators actually helped Weicker draft the bill. State rehabilitation administrators pronounced themselves to be "enthused" about the increased state matching requirement in the initial rehabilitation services bill. It is no wonder that the senior lobbyist for the National Governors' Association remarked that he spends much of his time fighting organizations of state bureaucrats.[27]

SOURCES OF STATE AND LOCAL AMBIVALENCE

On first glance, the support given to certain significant mandates by state and local elected officials appears puzzling. Although often gaining modifications, these groups would nevertheless support the final mandate in both houses. Some might suggest that group leaders have somehow failed to do their jobs of protecting their state and local members from the effects of this increasingly dominant federal policy tool. But there are more fundamental factors at work, relating to the nature of these groups' members and to unique issues posed by mandates as a tool of government action.

Compelling Political Appeal

First, as with congressional officials, the goals supported by mandates sometimes overshadow federalism issues and cost concerns, thereby crosspressuring state and local officials. State and local officials are politicians who are prone to be captured by the same causes and interest groups sweeping through Washington. The broad public appeal of many goals supported by mandates makes public officials at all levels reluctant to oppose such measures outright. And public officials are often reluctant to take public positions that oppose politically sensitive beneficiaries.

Accordingly, state and local organizations resort more often to seeking modifications rather than try to defeat such mandates.[28] Public water officials, for example, could not publicly oppose the safe drinking water mandate, whereas the organization representing private for-profit water suppliers did take a public position against the bill, due to the cost impacts of some of its key provisions. Similarly, the chief Washington lobbyist for the National Governors' Association laments how difficult it has been to get a governor to publicly oppose Medicaid mandates for pregnant women and children.[29]

Moreover, the appeal of such mandates can compel entrepreneurial politicians within the state and local community to support the mandate. For example, Governor Anaya of New Mexico lobbied the National Governors' Association to support the pending asbestos in schools mandate. Joining forces with lobbyists from the labor and environmental groups supporting the mandate, the governor succeeded in overcoming the objections of fellow governors concerned about potential costs to gain full NGA support at the organization's annual conference.

Furthermore, as was noted in Chapter 4, mandates themselves often have intergovernmental origins. When many states and localities have already adopted comparable programs prior to the federal mandate, it is more difficult to arouse intense and unified state and local opposition to it. In fact, if a mandate stimulated new federal money to help with compliance, such a program could be welcomed by state and local officials as a source of fiscal aid for ongoing programs.

Mandates Protect Leaders from Internal and External Competition

State and local officials can use the political cover provided by mandates to implement their own internal political agendas. In an increasingly litigious and politically organized system, unbridled discretion can pose dilemmas for state and local leaders. External constraints can provide political comfort and deflect opposition to federal, not state and local, officials.

For example, various state and local groups perceived some political utility in the new federal safe drinking water mandate. The National Governors Association supported stronger federal standards, taking the Environmental Protection Agency (EPA) to task for failing to promulgate sufficient national standards, and associations representing public water systems and large metropolitan water districts also supported strong national standards. National standards would provide politically useful cover for these officials to guard against public overreaction to frequently harmless local contamination incidents.[30] Further, larger water systems viewed federal standards as a way to promote consolidation of smaller, less efficient water authorities. Smaller systems would face higher per capita costs to comply than would larger systems with a larger customer base and more advanced water supply technologies.[31] Advocating federal regulations by business to gain competitive advantage is alleged to be widespread in the private sector but less commonly observed in restructuring public-sector service delivery.[32]

A federal mandate helps state officials achieve policy goals by presenting controversial positions as federal decrees. For example, Southern governors sought federal Medicaid mandates during the 99th Congress to help them gain support from reluctant state legislatures in reforming a benefit structure perceived to be excessively restrictive and out of step with the rest of the nation.[33] Though the legislation mandated benefits to low-income pregnant women and children, it also enabled these states to provide Medicaid for these groups without also providing them with welfare coverage under the Aid to Families with Dependent Children program (AFDC).

Further, state and local officials often find federal mandates help them to overcome the pressures of intergovernmental competition on service levels or regulatory standards. Policy analysts have long noted that states are vulnerable to adopting "lowest common denominator" policies in order to compete successfully with other states.[34] States may, accordingly, be driven to weaken environmental regulations or public welfare benefits below a level that state officials themselves feel is advisable.

Susan Rose-Ackerman argues that progressive states with stronger environmental regulations or public welfare would have an interest in putting a floor under intergovernmental competition by pressing for national mandates. Otherwise, they might lose their tax bases to states with lower service levels.[35] She suggests that thanks to intergovernmental competition, a federal system may result in adoptions of nationally mandated policies by political officials or voters who might not favor such policies in a unitary system.

A study of the federal adoption of state policy innovations indeed found that states pressed for nationalization of innovations particularly for redistributive social programs, for which states are mandated to serve the underclass.[36] As Peterson, Rabe, and Wong observe, these programs are especially difficult for states to sustain, due to their potential harm to each state's competition for business; higher benefits for low-income programs may cause an influx of the poor and an exodus of middle- and upper-income taxpayers.[37] Federal adoption or standardization helps states contain the competition problem without losing program benefits for their citizens.

Thus, mandates or preemptions can save states or localities from their worst competitive instincts by putting a floor under state policy competition. James Martin, senior lobbyist for the National Governors' Association, notes that for this reason, NGA has increasingly come to favor federal preemption of states in such areas as product liability, appliance energy standards, and air pollution. The governors, for instance, did not oppose national driver's license standards for trucks in the Commercial Motor Vehicle Safety Act of 1986 (PL 99-570). The act was passed in recognition of the limited ability of states to engage in concerted action on their own to uniformly regulate commercial drivers and vehicles. Although thirty-one states had joined in a voluntary regulatory program using common standards and reciprocal agreements, other states did not require special licenses, tests, or screenings for truck drivers. This permitted drivers with histories of driving problems to register in states with weak requirements, undermining the thirty-one states' attempts to promote safer highways within their borders.

FEATURES OF MANDATES THAT LIMIT
STATE AND LOCAL INFLUENCE

In addition to their own ambivalence, mandates as a policy tool put states and local governments at a particular disadvantage, especially when compared with federal grant programs. Unlike grants, mandates make it more difficult for state and local groups to form alliances with program beneficiary groups. And the benefits of mandates are immediately visible, whereas the costs are often vague and recognized only when agency regulations are later issued.

Alliances with Other Groups

As noted earlier, Haider's research suggests that state and local groups succeed when they find programmatically or functionally based allies. Lobbying for federal grant funds permits state and local government groups to more easily form alliances with other functionally or pro-grammatically oriented interest groups representing program benefi-ciaries. For example, when state and local governments join in close alliances with advocacy groups for the handicapped to gain more funds to implement federal handicapped education mandates, both the state and local treasuries and program clientele benefit.

Mandates, in contrast, are more divisive because they promise benefits to program clientele while imposing costs on governments. Thus, they often pit state and local groups against program beneficiaries and deprive state and local groups of the alliances so vital to their success. Given the importance of such alliances, state and local govern-ments are likely to be more successful in lobbying on federal funds since program beneficiaries are more likely to share their interests in continuing or increasing the flow of federal funds. Beneficiary groups could also become allies in fighting for federal funding to help state and local governments implement mandates more effectively. Beneficiaries, however, are not likely to help states and localities reduce mandated costs.

The ability of state and local groups to gain allies proved to be critical to the outcome of the mandate legislation studied. Recall that the roll call analysis, as well as the evaluation of mandates in the 99th Congress, showed that programmatic and policy goals overshadowed federalism as factors influencing mandate outcomes. Accordingly, state and local governments' success depended on enlisting interest group allies who could help redefine mandate issues in programmatic or policy terms. Of the twelve mandates examined for the 99th Congress, state and local governments engaged the support of other interest group allies on five occasions, and they attained their goals of significantly modifying the mandate in four of these five cases.

Public-employee labor unions were the principal allies with state and local governments in four of these five cases, and their support proved to be instrumental in winning over key Democrats in both houses. State and local governments and their unions often found common interests in Washington on funding issues, as both frequently joined forces to lobby for continued federal funding through revenue sharing and other programs.[38] Labor and management were able to find common ground on these four mandates as well. Fair labor standards overtime provisions and mandatory retirement bans threatened to overturn hard-fought contractual benefits enjoyed by public employees, such as compensatory time off and early retirement for public safety officers. The extension of Medicare would have required employees and employers to pay an equal share for a benefit already received by many public employees, with spouses covered under Social Security. Finally, the school boards and superintendents were joined in their fight against preschool handicapped education mandates by the American Federation of Teachers, who were concerned that salary gains promised by education reform could be wiped out by a new and expensive federal mandate.

Conversely, state and local governments did not fare as well when interest group coalitions were aligned against them. Of the eight bills against which other interest groups worked to oppose the state and local mandate position, state and local governments prevailed in only three cases, and these involved bills for which state and local governments were able to build alliances of their own with other interest groups. In the cases in which mandates were passed without modification, the alliance of interest groups was often broad-based.

For example, the asbestos in schools mandate was supported by a broad coalition of environmental groups, public-employee labor groups, teachers' organizations, and other components of the education community such as the national association of PTAs; further, the asbestos industry itself favored national standards to preempt large-scale asbestos removal and to undercut schools' lawsuits against the industry to recover asbestos removal costs. The Medicaid mandate was supported by another broad coalition that consisted of child health organizations such as the Children's Defense Fund, business groups concerned about the burden borne by employer-financed health insurance policies in financing care for the uninsured, and the health insurance industry, seeking to shift these costs from their policyholders to the states.[39]

Timing of Benefits and Costs

Though the benefits of mandates are compelling, their costs are often vague and dependent on agency regulations published several years after passage of the mandate legislation. Thomas Anton writes that maintaining regulatory policy coalitions calls for mandate legislation to be cast in largely symbolic terms to emphasize the benefits. Because specifying implementation and cost impacts threatens to unhinge coalitions and arouse state and local lobbyists, these kinds of "details" are left for subsequent elaboration by the federal agency.[40] The CBO often finds it difficult to estimate costs for major proposed mandate legislation, due in no small part to these implementation uncertainties.[41]

The delay in mandate implementation triggers a delayed reaction by state and local officials to the cost issues. Characteristically, state and local groups will either acquiesce to or support the initial passage of a mandate, only to experience a groundswell reaction from its grassroots members once the federal agency begins implementing the regulations. State and local officials often wonder how they could have let such onerous legislation "sneak by," leading to pressure on Congress to modify the original mandate.

This pattern occurred with several mandates originally passed in the 99th Congress, including the asbestos in schools mandate, which passed with state and local support, only to be modified two years later when local schools realized the costs prompted by the EPA's regulations. Similarly, the safe drinking water mandate, which was passed in 1986 with state and local support, ran into trouble when later EPA regulations made the costs clear to communities. Pressure welled up for Congress to pass an amendment sponsored by Senator Domenici in 1992 to suspend and ease the regulations, and it was defeated by only ten votes. One water commissioner in a rural county wrote to Domenici in 1992 that "this letter should have been written in 1986 . . . but (the mandate) is just now being felt by us and our customers."[42] Subsequently, significant deregulation was enacted in 1996, as discussed in Chapter 9.

Interestingly, the most intense state and local grassroots opposition to the initial passage of a mandate in the 99th Congress occurred with the Fair Labor Standards provisions imposed by the *Garcia* decision. A major factor prompting the intensity and eventual state and local success in modifying the mandate was that the costs were immediate and even retroactive, causing a crisis atmosphere as states and localities were forced to modify budgets and labor agreements to accommodate the ruling.

The uneven nature of the state and local response to mandates stands in stark contrast to their interest groups' responses to federal grant funding or tax subsidy issues. For these issues, state and local governments have mounted vigorous efforts to retain or increase federal funds for critical state and local programs. In the 99th Congress alone, they mounted major grassroots efforts to retain general revenue sharing, which they lost, and to defeat the Reagan Administration's proposed elimination of state and local tax deductibility, which they won. State interest groups sponsored a federal grant information and tracking service ten years before they began such a similar effort on mandates.

State and local interest group staffs have commented that it is easier to arouse their memberships on federal funding issues.[43] Federal grants provide benefits to state and local officials of all political persuasions, and their loss poses an immediate threat to fiscal balance or service delivery. As attested to by the near universal participation of states and localities in federal aid programs, state and local officials rarely turn down a federal grant, irrespective of local priorities, since these funds provide a partial return to the state of federal taxes paid by its residents.[44]

The Washington Political Environment

State and local interest groups' positions on mandates are, as those of most interest groups, moderated by their need to adapt to norms and values prevailing in Washington policy arenas or issue networks. Their Washington lobbyists can ill afford to stray too far from the consensus or risk disenfranchisement from the bargaining table on this and other issues. As a result, for instance, the National Governors' Association recognized that seeking complete exemption from Fair Labor Standards Act requirements following the *Garcia* decision would place them outside the governing consensus on the issue, so the association instead pressed for legislation modifying the mandate's burden.[45] Private interest groups are also affected by such moderating influences.[46]

IMPLICATIONS

Congressional staff involved in developing mandate legislation often expressed surprise by the absence of significant state and local opposition to major mandates. They compared state and local governments to a "wild card," which was feared more for its potential influence than its actual assertion of power. State and local officials are feared due to their daily connection with local voters and their credibility that ensues from this.[47] Staff members indicated that even when the groups are not active, congressional mandate champions fear rousing state and local officials and their allies and will sometimes modify mandate legislation to anticipate the worst reactions and dampen the potential for retrospective political blame from these officials. The power reputation of state and local officials, then, sometimes outpaces their inclination to use their political resources on mandate issues.

Nevertheless, the experience of the 99th Congress shows that state and local interest groups could successfully change mandate legislation if they were able to rouse sufficiently intense opposition. But, thanks to their ambivalence on mandates, these programs often disarmed these groups and prevented such opposition. This consequence comes from the nature of mandates as a policy tool, as well as from the nature of state and local officials as political leaders reluctant to appear to be on the wrong side of issues with broad public appeal. Mandates also help government officials seeking leverage over competitors both within their jurisdictions and in other states.

What factors dispose state and local governments to marshall the intensity and alliances needed to defend themselves against mandates? Since this has a great bearing on congressional mandate decisions, more in-depth understanding of the role of such factors as the nature of the policy area, visibility of costs and benefits, and prior histories of state and federal programs will help us ultimately determine the reasons for differing mandate decisions.

To understand these factors better, the next two chapters will analyze the politics underlying the passage of two mandates with very different outcomes, those of asbestos in schools, for which a costly mandate was passed with little modification, and handicapped preschool education, for which an expensive mandate was converted into a voluntary assistance program. Both mandates principally affected the schools, but the interest groups representing the schools and other affected state and local officials had dramatically different postures on them, with acquiescence and support for the asbestos in schools mandate and intense grassroots opposition to the handicapped preschool education mandate. The two case studies should thus help further illuminate the variables that influence mandate outcomes in Congress.

NOTES TO CHAPTER 5

1. Jeffrey M. Berry, *The Interest Group Society* (Boston: Harper Collins, 1989), p. 35.

2. David Vogel, *Fluctuating Fortunes* (New York: Basic Books, 1989).

3. David Truman, *The Governmental Process* (New York: Alfred Knopf, 1951), p. 57.

4. Jane J. Mansbridge, "A Deliberative Theory of Interest Representation," in *The Politics of Interests*, ed. Mark P. Petracca (Boulder, Co.: Westview Press, 1992), p. 47.

5. See Mancur Olson, *The Logic of Collective Action* (New York: Schocken Books, 1968).

6. James Q. Wilson, *The Politics of Regulation* (New York: Basic Books, 1980), p. 370.

7. Major works include Suzanne Farkas, *The Urban Lobby: The U.S. Conference of Mayors in a Policy Subsystem* (New York: Columbia University Press, 1969); Donald Haider, *When Governments Come to Washington* (New York: Free Press, 1974); Anne Camissa, "Intergovernmental Lobbying: State and Local Governments as Interest Groups" (unpublished dissertation, Graduate School of Georgetown University, Washington, D.C., 1992).

8. Edward Banfield and James Q. Wilson, *City Politics* (New York: Vintage Books, 1963), p. 2.

9. Morton Grodzins, *The American System*, ed. Daniel J. Elazar (Chicago: Rand McNally, 1966).

10. Advisory Commission on Intergovernmental Relations, *The Transformation of American Politics*, A–106 (Washington, D.C.: U.S. Government Printing Office, 1986), p. 76.

11. Aaron Wildavsky and Nelson Polsby, *Presidential Elections*, 6th edition (New York: Charles Scribner's Sons, 1984).

12. Joe Soss and David T. Canon, "Partisan Divisions and Voting Decisions: U.S. Senators, Governors, and the Rise of a Divided Federal Government" (paper presented at the Annual Meeting of the American Political Science Association, Washington, D.C., 2–5 September 1993).

13. Daniel Elazar, *American Federalism: A View from the States*, 3rd edition (New York: Harper and Row, 1984), p. 177.

14. Donald Haider, *When Governments Come to Washington*, p. 111.

15. David Vogel, *Fluctuating Fortunes*.

16. Anne Camissa, "Intergovernmental Lobbying," p. 28.

17. Richard Nathan, "State and Local Governments under Federal Grants," *Political Science Quarterly* 98, No. 1 (1983).

18. Jeffrey Berry, *The Interest Group Society*, p. 69.

19. Donald Haider, *When Governments Come to Washington*, p. 24.

20. Term was coined by Terry Sanford, *Storm over the States* (New York: McGraw-Hill, 1967).

21. In their analysis of the politics of deregulation, Paul Quirk and Martha Derthick report that divisions within the airline industry on the benefits of deregulation were exploited by proponents of deregulation. See Paul Quirk and Martha Derthick, *The Politics of Deregulation* (Washington, D.C.: Brookings Institution, 1985).

22. Donald Haider, *When Governments Come to Washington*, p. 223.

23. *Ibid.*, p. 222.

24. See *Ibid.* and Anne Camissa, "Intergovernmental Lobbying."

25. The state and local elected and top management officials took no public positions on the rehabilitation services matching requirement, but governors' offices in several fiscally distressed Midwestern states successfully persuaded key Midwestern House Education and Labor Committee members to lead a successful effort to significantly modify the requirement.

26. National Governors' Association, *Policy Positions, 1985–86* (Washington, D.C.: National Governors' Association), 1986.

27. Remarks by James Martin at an ACIR critics' session convened to kick off the ACIR study "A Decade of Change," Washington, D.C., 26 March 1991.

28. Interview with Martha Fabricus, Washington staff for the National Conference of State Legislatures.

29. Interview with Jim Martin, National Governors' Association.

30. Interview with Jack Sullivan, director of the Washington office of the American Association of Water Authorities.

31. EPA officials estimate the compliance costs for initial standards to average $50 per family for larger systems and $300 per family for smaller systems. See Arnold M. Kuzmack, "The Safe Drinking Water Act: A Case Study," in *Coping with Mandates: What Are the Alternatives?* ed. Michael Fix and Daphne A. Kenyon (Washington, D.C.: Urban Institute Press, 1990), p. 73.

32. Robert E. McCormick alleges that "there is hardly a regulatory program anywhere that does not benefit some industry . . . most often at the expense of rivals or consumers." See his study, "The Economics of Regulation," in *Regulation and the Reagan Era: Politics, Bureaucracy and the Public Interest*, ed. Roger E. Meiners and Bruce Yandle (New York: Holmes and Meier, 1989), p. 28.

33. Interview with Marina Weiss, staff with the Senate Finance Committee. Ms. Weiss indicated that the persistent pleas from Southern governors for these mandates were the catalyst behind the committee's endorsement. Republicans on the committee also endorsed the mandates, partly because they came from states already providing the mandated services.

34. See Daphne Kenyon and John Kincaid, eds., *Competition among States and Local Governments* (Washington, D.C.: Urban Institute Press, 1990). Also see Paul Peterson, *Making Federalism Work* (Washington, D.C.: Brookings Institution, 1990). Peterson argues that states are particularly prone to underprovide services of a redistributive nature that can threaten the exodus of their tax bases to competing jurisdictions.

35. Susan Rose-Ackerman, "Does Federalism Matter? Choice in a Federal Republic," *Journal of Political Economy* 49, No. 1 (1981), pp. 152–163. Although the economic competition argument is compelling to state lawmakers, recent studies suggest progressive environmental and education policies may give some states an advantage in competing for business and higher income taxpayers. See David Beam, "Reinventing Federalism: State-Local Government Roles

in the New Economic Order" (paper delivered at the Annual Meeting of the American Political Science Association, Washington, D.C., 2 September 1989).

36. Keith Boeckelman, "The Influence of States on Federal Policy Adoptions," *Policy Studies Journal* 20, No. 3 (1992), pp. 365–375.

37. Paul Peterson, Barry Rabe, and Kenneth Wong, *When Federalism Works* (Washington, D.C.: Brookings Institution, 1986).

38. Interview with Roger Dahl, labor-management relations specialist, U.S. Conference of Mayors.

39. Robert Pear, "Deficit or No Deficit, Unlikely Allies Bring about Expansion in Medicaid," *New York Times*, 4 November 1990, p. A–24.

40. Thomas Anton, *American Federalism and Public Policy* (New York: Random House, 1989), p. 189.

41. Advisory Commission on Intergovernmental Relations, *Federal Regulation of State and Local Governments*, A–126 (Washington, D.C.: ACIR, July, 1993), p. 63.

42. Letter from Eden Water Company in Eden, Az., *Congressional Record*, 9 September 1992, p. S13045.

43. Interviews with James Martin, National Governors' Association; Cynthia Pols, National League of Cities.

44. Nearly all state agency officials contacted by GAO in a study of state legislative oversight of federal grants reported that their legislatures accepted all available federal funds. See Comptroller General of the United States, *Federal Assistance System Should Be Changed to Permit Greater Involvement by State Legislatures*, GGD–81–3 (Washington, D.C.: U.S. General Accounting Office, 15 December 1980), p. 47.

45. National Governors' Association, *Policy Positions, 1985–86* (Washington, D.C.: National Governors' Association, 1986), p. 35.

46. Lewis Anthony Dexter, *How Organizations Are Represented in Washington* (New York: Bobbs-Merrill, 1969), p. 103.

47. Interview with James Riley, staff with House Education and Labor Committee.

6

Asbestos and the Politics of Consensus

In 1986 Congress passed a major new regulatory program requiring the nation's 37,000 local school districts to clean up asbestos in their school buildings. This legislation—the Asbestos Hazard Emergency Response Act of 1986 (AHERA)—had projected costs for local schools ranging from just over $1 billion to over $3 billion, making this legislation among the more expensive intergovernmental mandates to be enacted in the 1980s. Asbestos manufacturers also were concerned that legislation could support schools and parents seeking to recover their asbestos removal and related medical costs in liability suits. On the other side, advocacy groups warned about the dangers of asbestos exposure both to children and to the teachers and maintenance workers in school buildings. Finally, the issue invited conflict between a Republican administration opposed to this legislation specifically and to greater federal regulation in general, and Democratic congressional policy entrepreneurs whose careers could be enhanced by its passage.

Given this political constellation, it would be expected that congressional consideration of this issue would be marked by intense intergroup and partisan conflicts.[1] Yet, the bill passed each step in the legislative process unanimously and was signed unceremoniously by a conservative president at the urging of conservative members and the asbestos industry. More remarkably, this was accomplished during a purported nadir of federal regulatory activism, presided over by an ideologically conservative president and a Republican-controlled Senate.

The story of this consensus illustrates how the political process can be skillfully manipulated to achieve regulation by acclamation. More broadly, it shows how the constraints on federal activism and regulatory intrusiveness can be overcome when the issue is defined in a compelling manner to appeal to widely held consensual values. Under these circumstances, even those who must bear the costs—

specifically, local school districts—become politically crosspressured and immobilized.

THE POLITICAL EXTRAPOLATION OF SCIENCE

The concerns about asbestos in schools that culminated in the passage of the 1986 Asbestos Emergency Response Act had their scientific roots in numerous studies of the risk of exposure of workers in asbestos manufacturing plants and other industrial settings. Beginning in the 1930s, epidemiological studies showed a strong link between the exposure of asbestos workers and lung diseases such as asbestosis and lung cancer, as well as a rare cancer of the chest and abdominal lining known as mesothelioma.[2] These findings led the World Health Organization's International Agency for Research on Cancer to list asbestos as one of thirteen chemicals known to cause cancer in humans.[3]

With the enactment of the Occupational Safety and Health Act of 1970 (OSHA), the federal government gained jurisdiction over the entire range of workplace hazards, and a regulation specifying exposure limits for asbestos became its first health standard.[4] Some workers contracting asbestos-related diseases took to the courts and filed product liability suits against the asbestos manufacturers, prompting three major corporations to file Chapter 11 bankruptcy petitions.[5]

However, scientists had not directly recorded the long-term effects of low-level exposure to occupants of buildings where asbestos was used for insulation, ceilings, or other structural purposes. Lacking studies of the effects of low-level intermittent asbestos exposure to building occupants, extrapolations were made by scientists and environmental organizations based on the worker exposure data. Accordingly, the data were more open to various interpretations, and a 1984 study by the National Academy of Sciences concluded that significant uncertainties existed, due to the near absence of information on health effects for the general population.[6]

Consequently, to fully understand how the issue came to the federal agenda, we must look beyond science to the political manipulation and interpretation of research. Absent scientific consensus, political actors sought to gain congressional and public acceptance of their own interpretations of the research. As John Kingdon notes, research and indicators can play a major role in placing issues on the public policy agenda, but they need a "little push" to gain attention in a favorable manner.[7]

The asbestos industry touted research by two British researchers—Dahl and Peto—that indicated that asbestos in structures posed minimal hazards to occupants. They calculated a 1 in 100,000 chance of cancer from such hazards. Advocates of federal action on asbestos in schools took heart from other research and researchers. Dr. Irving Selikoff, perhaps the nation's leading asbestos researcher, concluded that even one day's exposure to asbestos fibers in the air can increase the risk of lung cancer, and one week can double the risk.[8] One study showed that people working with asbestos for as little as five weeks had higher than normal rates of cancer.[9] This notion that even limited exposure to asbestos could be harmful became a critical intellectual premise for those groups arguing for federal control of asbestos in schools. It also helped foster a crisis atmosphere once asbestos was discovered in schools, a discovery that prompted parents and teachers to call for its immediate removal. As the Environmental Defense Fund stated, "Only no exposure can guarantee no cancer."[10]

Reporting in 1979 on the first bill establishing a grant program to assist local schools in abating asbestos hazards, the House Education and Labor Committee concluded that "for want of definitive proof to the contrary," the overwhelming scientific opinion was that there is no safe level of asbestos and all unnecessary exposure levels should be avoided.[11] As will be discussed at the end of this chapter, more recent studies following the passage of AHERA cast new doubts on the dangers faced by building occupants.

THE SCHOOLS: TARGET FOR REGULATORY EXPANSION

Eugene Bardach and Robert Kagan conclude that a good deal of the growth in federal regulations can be explained by "the logic of regulatory expansion."[12] Thus, in our case, having already extended federal controls over asbestos in the workplace in the early 1970s, extending federal regulations to asbestos in other settings was not only politically easier, but also logically compelling.

Why were schools selected as the first target outside the workplace? Why didn't Congress seek to regulate exposure in all publicly accessible buildings? In other policy arenas, Congress had chosen to regulate the private sector first, exempting state and local employers, at least for a time. For example, under the OSHA program, all private employers are covered, but state and local employers are exempt in the twenty-seven states where the federal labor department enforces the standards without using state government. Federal pension regulations and insurance apply to private employers under the Employee Retirement and Income Security Act (ERISA), but public employers are not covered.

Politically, schools are an inviting target for advocates. The population at risk is a specific, targeted group with highly organized and influential interest group representation. Children are represented by the Parent-Teacher Association (PTA); teachers, by several important unions, including the National Education Association (NEA); and maintenance workers, by the Service Employees International Union (SEIU), among other unions. Although the school boards and superintendents who must pay for asbestos abatement are also well represented, their leverage is at least equally matched by that of these other beneficiary groups. Further, school board concerns about costs are likely to be offset somewhat by their political responsiveness to parents' and teachers' worries about asbestos exposure; these crosspressures might be expected to dilute their opposition to federal standards.

In contrast, regulating exposure in all publicly accessible buildings is fraught with more political danger. First, the beneficiaries are diffuse, disorganized, and not well represented by any membership group.[13] Although public interest environmental lobbies do attempt to articulate these concerns, they are more effective when allied with strong membership groups, such as those representing children and school workers. Second, unlike school boards, those thousands of building owners are less likely to be beholden to the population benefiting from regulations and therefore more likely to intensely lobby against the program. Although initially proposing in 1986 to regulate all public buildings in addition to the schools, Senator Stafford, principal sponsor and floor manager of AHERA in the Senate, backed off, due to expected opposition from the hotel and restaurant industries, among others.[14]

Further, advocates of a federal policy response for schools were able to make a number of substantive arguments that sounded compelling to policymakers. The use of asbestos materials in schools expanded after World War II, and alarming stories reported that the asbestos had become "friable" (i.e., most vulnerable to release dangerous fibers into the ambient air). One study in New Jersey, funded by the U.S. National Institute of Environmental Health Sciences, revealed that thirty-three schools had damaged or deteriorating asbestos surfaces, releasing air concentrations of fibers exceeding the then current OSHA workplace standard.[15] Another study in Massachusetts indicated that twenty-seven schools in that state had asbestos dangers hazardous enough to warrant immediate action.

EARLY FEDERAL POLICY ACTION FOLLOWS THE INCREMENTAL MODEL

The first federal policy responses came in the late 1970s with the EPA's technical assistance program, closely followed by the enactment of a financial assistance program for asbestos inspection and cleanup in schools in the early 1980s. In both cases, the initial federal responses avoided the mandate approach, preferring instead to assist states and localities that were already moving to address the problem. The etiology of the federal response was consistent with the incremental model suggested by James Sundquist: Initial impetus is provided by the progressive actions of some states and localities, followed by federal help to aid them in dealing with what is still perceived as a local problem, and capped by transformation of the issue into a national problem accompanied by a more regulatory response.[16]

By the late 1970s, the concerns about asbestos had become widely known, and several states moved to address the problem in the schools. New York State, for instance, enacted legislation in 1979 requiring local schools to inspect for asbestos and to remove the substance where warranted.[17] The GAO visited eleven states with active asbestos programs of varying scope and coverage and found that nearly all states had begun their programs in 1977, nearly two years prior to the EPA's first technical assistance program.[18] A 1979 EPA survey found that thirty-one states already had programs to address asbestos in their schools.[19]

Ironically, these progressive state and local actions served to highlight the extent of the problem and prompted some advocates to seek federal action to extend these programs to those other inactive states and localities. Advocates pointed to the lack of uniformity in state and local program coverage and quality.[20] For example, over 33,000 schools remained uninspected, and the GAO found that many states made local asbestos inspections optional. Criteria for action varied as well— Florida required all friable asbestos to be removed, whereas Houston decided to take no abatement action, pending issuance of EPA standards.[21]

The first policy initiative at the national level was led by a public interest environmental group—the Environmental Defense Fund (EDF)—and it was directed at the federal agency, the EPA, not at Congress. The EDF, like many public interest groups, had no grassroots membership structure.[22] Rather, it specialized in using the courts to force federal agencies to regulate under their statutes. The group initially asked the EPA to regulate asbestos in schools by: (1) requiring schools to inspect for asbestos; (2) forcing schools to develop and implement abatement plans; and (3) requiring the EPA to regulate exposure in all public buildings. Interestingly, the EDF petition asked that the asbestos industry collectively be required to fund the costs of abatement. The governor's office of New Jersey filed a similar petition in late 1978.

The EDF was able to take advantage of a law enacted just two years earlier—the Toxic Substances Control Act of 1976 (TSCA)—which gave the EPA broad authority to control chemical substances, filling the gaps left by other legislation. Section 21 of TSCA permits suits to be brought against the EPA by private parties and entitles the group to a de novo proceeding in court without having to satisfy more traditional and stringent tests for judicial review of agency action (e.g., proving that the agency acted arbitrarily or capriciously).[23]

Perhaps in partial response to the petition, the EPA announced a technical assistance program (TAP) in March 1979 to help states and local schools carry out inspections and abatements.[24] Under threat of a subsequent EDF suit, the EPA then agreed to initiate a two-stage rulemaking effort. The first rule required local schools to inspect their facilities and notify parents and workers, and it became final in 1982.[25] The second rule, forcing local schools to abate asbestos that posed potential health hazards, was dropped in April 1981 as part of the Reagan Administration's deregulation thrust. EPA officials argued that the inspections would provide local schools with the needed impetus to address the problems on their own. Nevertheless, the first inspection rule ultimately set the stage for the eventual congressional passage of the 1986 act that mandated inspection and abatement regulations on local schools.

While these groups petitioned the EPA, other actors brought the issue to Congress in 1979, leading to congressional passage of the first piece of legislation addressing the problem—the Asbestos School Hazard Detection and Control Act of 1980. Similar to the EPA's initial efforts, the first congressional response came in the form of a voluntary financial and technical assistance program, rather than as a regulatory mandate.

The 1980 law was a product of some of the same forces that would be present in the 1986 act, namely a coalition of policy advocates in and out of Congress; prior governmental actions (in this case, progressive state actions and EPA actions) that sparked federal interest in extending these programs to all states; the definition of the issue as a compelling public health cause that thwarted open public opposition to legislation; and the consequent collapse of constraints on federal role expansion.

A key congressional policy entrepreneur and several pivotal interest groups put the issue on the congressional agenda. Congressman George Miller, a member of the 1974 Watergate class, epitomized the congressional policy entrepreneur.[26] An activist on a host of issues, his interest in asbestos stemmed initially from both his Northern California constituency, where workers were exposed in a Manville asbestos factory, and his chairmanship of a subcommittee with jurisdiction over the workmen's compensation program facing asbestos-related claims. Although the bill was clearly initiated and drafted by Miller, it was actively championed by an interest group coalition that included environmental public interest groups, notably the Environmental Defense Fund, that had been active in seeking EPA regulation, and groups that represented parents and children in the schools, most notably the PTA. Those facing the concentrated costs—the school boards and the school superintendents—were initially supportive of a federal financial assistance program, but they tempered their advocacy with trepidation about the potential for a new federal mandate.

The bill's sponsors emphasized the absence of mandates on local school districts. Congressman George Miller, seeking to placate some Republicans, pointed out that not only was there no mandate, but that "if the school district wants to ignore the program, we do not intervene."[27] In fact, Congressman Miller recognized that it was too early in the genesis of the issue to propose a nationwide mandate. Too little was known about the extent and nature of the hazard, and schools were just beginning to address the problem on their own. Congressman Miller was not "shy about mandating," but he thought that a mandate could convert what promised to be a consensual process into a conflictual one that would call on the congressman to devote considerable time and scarce political resources to the bill.[28]

The Education and Labor Committee, which reported the bill, was disposed to adopt an assistance approach, as opposed to a regulatory approach, consistent with its role as supporter of federal aid to schools. Had the bill gone to the House committee responsible for environmental regulation, a different set of tools, perhaps featuring regulation, might very well have been selected.

In commenting on the reasons for government growth, Aaron Wildavsky once observed that "government is its own cause."[29] In a similar vein, the congressional interest in the asbestos in schools issue came partly from the various federal, state, and local efforts already taken to address the problem. The progressive actions of some states and local schools helped sow the seeds of federal interest, whereas the failure of many other states and localities to follow suit voluntarily led many to believe that a federal role was necessary. The EPA's proposed rule mandating local inspections also lent some urgency to providing funding to quickly meet this forthcoming requirement.

E. E. Schattschneider observed that political conflict is largely a struggle over the displacement of conflict and that the outcome of politics depends on which of numerous potential conflicts gains the dominant position.[30] In this case, advocates of federal action defined the issue as a public health question that made outright public opposition to the goals of the program politically untenable, a strategy that promoted ultimate bipartisan consensus in Congress. The costs faced by local schools for inspection and abatement did not gain the status of a competing issue for the 1980 act because the act retained a largely assistance approach rather than a regulatory one.

Defining the issue in compelling public health terms neutralized conservatives who normally could be expected to oppose new federal programs. In fact, the record from the early 1980 deliberations suggests that, far from partisan deadlock, the parties competed for public approbation on the issue. In other arenas, such as passage of the Tax Reform Act of 1986, such partisan competition has been shown to transform a cause from "the unmovable to the seemingly unstoppable."[31] Indeed, Republicans felt obliged to offer an alternative way of providing federal aid to local districts for asbestos by giving states and localities the option of using up their existing federal education grant funds on asbestos inspection and abatement. As Republican Congressman Goodling argued, "Everyone wants to do the same thing. We want to help children. I think it is just a matter of how can we get the dollars the quickest."[32] Such was the power of the public health formulation of the issue.

Although no funds were ever appropriated to implement this program, pressure built to enact a similar program several years later. The implementation of the 1982 EPA inspection rule increased costs faced by schools. The advocacy coalition found a Republican ally in Senator James Abdnor of South Dakota, who had become concerned with asbestos removal costs for Native American schools in his state. Using his positions on the Senate Appropriations HUD-Independent Agencies Subcommittee, which was responsible for the EPA's budget, and the Senate Environment and Public Works Committee, the EPA's authorizing committee, Senator Abdnor developed an assistance program for schools to be administered by the EPA. The provision received about three minutes of debate and then bipartisan unanimous support. The House accepted the entire Senate bill, including the new Asbestos Schools Hazard Abatement Act of 1984 (ASHAA). The program thus never received a hearing. Most important, Abdnor was successful in obtaining $50 million in funding.

REGULATION BEGETS REGULATION

While Congress was moving to enact the new assistance program, schools were proceeding to implement the EPA's new regulation mandating local school inspections. EPA officials were profoundly correct in their prediction that the inspection rule alone would unleash a torrent of local pressure from parents and employee groups that would, if nothing else, prompt an overreaction.[33]

In the absence of EPA standards regulating abatement, parents and employee groups appeared to be more vigilant overseers than the EPA. When notified of the presence of asbestos, parents and employee groups pressured school boards to completely remove the material, a response that sometimes released more fibers than if nothing were done. For instance, the GAO found that although asbestos in the Philadelphia schools was not considered hazardous by the district's asbestos coordinator, it was nonetheless all removed or encapsulated due to public pressure.[34] The EPA regulation requiring asbestos to be removed from buildings prior to demolition also encouraged removal since it would have to be done eventually anyway. As one reporter observed, "Asbestos can withstand heat far better than local school boards can."[35]

The EPA's decision to forego issuance of abatement standards—ostensibly designed to promote more local flexibility and discretion—was prompting concerns over inappropriate response actions. The GAO concluded that the absence of regulatory abatement standards would cause schools either to overreact and waste money or to underreact and expose school occupants to hazardous asbestos.[36] One survey of the EPA's regional staff found that 75 percent believed local abatement actions to be improper or inappropriate.[37] Consequently, schools and the asbestos industry welcomed additional federal standards as political relief and protection from seemingly extreme demands from parents for total removal of asbestos discovered during inspections. The 1982 regulations thus started the nation on the road to passage of the AHERA legislation in 1986.

MANY ROADS LEAD TO WASHINGTON

Faced with this situation, an odd coalition found it in their interest to call for definitive EPA standards governing the abatement of asbestos found in schools. The coalition included most of the advocacy groups discussed earlier who were pressing for financial assistance before Congress, including the National Education Association and the PTA. Although the National Association of School Boards did not join in this effort, the American Association of School Administrators (AASA), who represented school superintendents, did call for federal standards. When asked in a 1985 symposium what he wanted for Christmas that year, the Washington lobbyist for the AASA said he wanted the EPA to issue standards governing the local abatement of asbestos to help them fend off local pressures from parents for extreme and costly solutions to the problem. In subsequent testimony on AHERA before the Senate Environment and Public Works Committee in 1986, the AASA called for federal or state governments to certify local compliance with abatement rules to aid in the "abatement of hysteria" generated by the EPA 1982 rule.[38]

Another seemingly odd partner in this nascent coalition was the asbestos industry itself and its umbrella group, the Safe Buildings Alliance. This industry was besieged by a spate of product liability lawsuits from families of their employees who had contracted diseases shown to be strongly linked to long-term asbestos exposure.[39] The industry was also sued by school districts faced with the costs of removing asbestos. By 1989, the industry had lost most of the twenty-one asbestos property damage trials involving suits brought by building owners, mostly school districts.[40]

The industry feared that, absent strong federal guidance, schools would choose to remove all asbestos and release fibers into the air that would have remained dormant, thereby animating additional lawsuits from concerned parents. In contrast, federal standards might rationalize the state and local response, particularly if the EPA limited circumstances warranting removal. Others saw less noble motives at work. In many states, plaintiffs have from one to six years to pursue cases against manufacturers.[41] Congressional staff and school attorneys speculated that the industry was actually attempting to slow down the local removal of asbestos to take advantage of the statute of limitations. Delay in removal beyond this period would thus free the industry from liability.

National businesses now often seek federal preemption of state and local regulation in the interests of uniformity and business efficiency. Traditionally, business opposed new federal regulatory programs because state and local governments were presumed to be friendlier territory. Grant McConnell expressed the conventional view that politics in smaller communities gives great advantages to private interests; federalism is, accordingly, an instrument of conservatism and particularism.[42] Faced with what some have suggested is a resurgence of state government, many national corporate leaders have come to favor federal solutions preempting state authority. Preemption not only constrains the most progressive states but, more important, institutes a single regulatory standard that better reflects the operating realities of large national industries.[43]

The Service Employees International Union served as the catalyst for the coalition pressing for strong EPA abatement standards. The SEIU is the fourth largest union in the AFL-CIO, with nearly 850,000 members, including over 200,000 janitors who are vulnerable to asbestos exposure in boiler rooms and basements of office buildings and public schools. The issue was politically appealing to the union to convince Congress and its own members that it could influence policy affecting so many of its members. The issue also allowed the union to challenge the Reagan Administration when labor was still recovering from the president's 1981 firing of the air traffic controllers on an "easy" issue with wide appeal.[44]

A federal regulatory strategy was preferable to pursuing asbestos cleanup at the bargaining table, where costs might be deducted from monetary compensation and potentially place union employers at an economic disadvantage. A federal regulatory solution, on the other hand, would apply standards across the board to union and nonunion employers alike. Moreover, it placed the SEIU in the position of champion for all workers, even those not members of the union, thereby strengthening the union's membership drive.[45]

The union filed a formal rulemaking petition with the EPA under the authority of Section 21 of the Toxic Substances Control Act discussed earlier. The petition asked the EPA to: (1) establish standards for determining when asbestos in schools is hazardous and requires appropriate abatement action; (2) develop rules for the performance of abatement activities, including protection for the workers involved; and (3) extend the inspection and abatement rules to all public and commercial buildings.

The Section 21 citizens' petition section of TSCA looked to be a win-win situation for the union: Either the EPA would agree to initiate rulemaking, or the union could begin a de novo proceeding in a district court that would review the agency's failure to regulate, using more lenient judicial review standards than are traditionally applied by courts in reviewing agency actions.[46] Expecting no change in the EPA's position, the SEIU's counsel indicated that the primary objective of their suit was not to get the EPA to regulate, but to develop through these court discovery proceedings a "smoking gun" to generate political support and raise the issue on the congressional agenda. In this sense, the court case was to be a tool to expand the scope of conflict to a broader congressional and interest group audience.

Though the EPA refused to proceed with the rule, the court discovery process brought to light internal EPA documents that revealed considerable internal dissension by the EPA's professional staff with the formal position of the agency and suggested the possibility that the Office of Management and Budget (OMB) was really behind the agency's decision to avoid regulating. The disclosure of internal dissension and possible OMB involvement undercut the EPA's position and rallied further congressional and media interest in the issue. Although the court supported the union after AHERA was passed in 1986, the decision was anticlimactic and real impact was the disclosure.

A NEW CONGRESSIONAL CHAMPION EMERGES

As occurred with the 1980 passage of the first assistance legislation, a developing interest group coalition joined a congressional policy entrepreneur to place the regulatory issue on the congressional agenda. Congressman James Florio, like Congressman George Miller, was a member of the Watergate class of 1974. Like Miller, he was an aggressive policy entrepreneur, forging new ground, especially on the environment and consumer issues, and by 1984 he had become known as the father of the 1980 Superfund legislation. Florio was chairman of a subcommittee with potential jurisdiction over the asbestos in schools issue. The Subcommittee on Commerce, Transportation, and Tourism of the House Interstate and Commerce Committee had given him a platform to write the Superfund legislation and to pursue other environmental issues.

Although a national policy champion of mandates, Florio was almost atavistic in the closeness of his ties to the local county party organization. His strong ties enabled his former chief of staff to become county administrator, prompting some to charge that Florio had become the boss of Camden County.[47] Such ties made him more oriented toward home than were many Washington actors. He spent only three nights a week in Washington and lived in a one-room efficiency apartment several blocks from his Capitol Hill office.[48]

Although his close ties to county government made him an advocate for more federal aid for cities, he also advocated various environmental mandates with cost implications for his local governmental colleagues. As the population base of the City of Camden fled to the suburbs, he appealed to the new suburbanites through such cross-partisan issues as day care, transportation, and the environment. With his ear close to his constituency, the way he defined his constituency sometimes found him in conflict with the local government he allegedly controlled.[49] For example, his home city of Camden reported spending $900,000 to remove asbestos, an amount which the school president said should have been used for educational programs in that hard-pressed city.[50]

Florio had one attribute not shared by most of his House colleagues—his ambition for the governorship. Though 24 members of the 103-member Watergate class of 1974 ran for the Senate, Florio was one of only three who ran for governorships.[51] His continued pursuit of the governorship became the spur for his sponsorship of asbestos in schools legislation. Asbestos in schools had become a major issue in New Jersey, and Governor Kean had launched a program to oversee asbestos cleanup, with a hidden agenda of upstaging Florio on the issue.[52] In 1984 the state's *Public Advocate* reported that 200 schools might not open due to problems experienced with asbestos removal.[53] Governor Kean was vulnerable and could be held responsible for not guiding the schools. Florio saw an opportunity to gain political mileage within the state on the issue by using his subcommittee position to investigate.[54]

In today's politics, strong ties between a national political official and the local party organization no longer provide a solid bulwark against policy centralization. Though members of Congress may have considered themselves ambassadors to the nation when they owed their nominations to state and local party leaders, the advent of open primaries and the media's assuming the gatekeeper function of parties prompted congressional candidates seeking higher state office to pursue new alliances and find new supporters beyond officialdom. Much like members use federal public works projects or grant dollars to cement or expand local alliances, Florio sought to embarrass his own state's governor on a federal regulatory issue.

As his staff noted, this was the "New Jersey explanation" for the development of new legislation in 1986. The "Washington answer" involved the existence of an established interest group coalition that had already worked together to gain funding for federal assistance and greater EPA regulations. Once the EPA denied the SEIU regulatory petition in November 1984, this coalition began to press for a legislative solution. The coalition advocating legislation became more formalized and was coordinated by the National Education Association and the Service Employees International Union. Although the school boards and school administrators had dropped out, the number of organizations supporting legislation grew to sixteen and encompassed other unions, environmental advocacy groups, and children's groups.

The push for regulation was abetted by the reaction to the administration's deregulation philosophy epitomized in the EPA by the team brought in by Administrator Ann Gorsuch. By 1983, opinion surveys revealed stronger public support for federal environmental controls than in the Carter years.[55] These trends in public support found expression in the 99th Congress and were reflected in bipartisan congressional passage of legislation enacting stronger mandates in the drinking water and hazardous waste areas, as well as in funding increases for sewage treatment, overriding a presidential veto.[56]

THE POLITICS OF UNANIMITY

Some legislation aims to define partisan differences and sharpen lines of political cleavage to favor the bill's sponsors and are introduced not with serious hope of passage, but rather to embarrass other groups or policy actors. However, consensus, not conflict, characterized the development of the asbestos in schools legislation. First, the nature of the supporting coalition generated widespread bipartisan political support, and the issue was defined to tap deeply held public values that compelled political support and consensus. Florio summarized the appeal when he argued that the costs should not dissuade the people from providing its "most valuable asset, school children, with a safe environment for learning."[57] Even if they wanted to derail the legislation, the schools' lobby and the asbestos industry could not dissuade congressional conservatives from ultimately supporting the legislation because they failed to provide a politically defensible argument that could publicly justify opposition. In the presence of such a compelling public issue, their only real hope was to keep the issue off the congressional agenda.

Despite the compelling nature of the issue, Florio sought to accommodate the concerns of all actors, including potential opponents from the asbestos industry and school boards. Such efforts would not only broaden support but reduce the intensity of potential opponents. Although the bill would probably have been approved overwhelmingly on a roll call vote, Florio was worried that some potential opponents could derail it at several key points.

First, because the bill was not introduced until the second session, time became a factor and opponents could preclude a vote on the floor, particularly in the Senate, where one member's hold can prevent a bill from coming to a vote. The quickest way to get a bill passed on the floor of the House is to place it on the consent calendar. Requiring the approval of the Rules Committee and the concurrence of three members selected from each party, this procedure is reserved for those bills garnering unanimous support. The objection of one member can return it to the regular process. The Senate has a similar process through unanimous consent rules. These procedures place a premium on consensus building and can give inordinate leverage to a single member, who can by one objection force the bill to go through the regular process.

Second, the chairman of the full Energy and Commerce Committee—Congressman Dingell—could keep a bill from going to the floor. Dingell and Florio had been in conflict before and were locked in battle on the 1986 Superfund reauthorization bill.[58] Dingell tended to be more cautious according to Florio's staff.[59] So, Florio wanted to gain his support by demonstrating overwhelming political support for the measure. As Florio's staff said, Mr. Dingell was known to only cosponsor bills that become law.[60] Further, Florio had invested considerable political energy and resources on the Superfund fight and could ill afford another contentious battle at the same time.

Third, Florio's staff noted that President Reagan might be expected to veto the legislation, particularly in view of the administration's tenacious resistance to additional regulation by the EPA. They were particularly worried that an aggrieved asbestos industry could find a direct channel to the president through Peter Grace, a Reagan confidant and president of an asbestos manufacturing firm. Although the president had "nondecisional" power, he was largely on the sidelines in the congressional process, as advocates perceived that the White House would not be helpful in developing a bill.

Finally, moving legislation quickly helps contain the scope of conflict. Having succeeded in expanding the scope of conflict and placing the issue on the congressional agenda, advocates then sought to reduce the opportunities for schools or the asbestos industry to generate congressional opposition. Moving the bill quickly under cover of consensus would also reduce the risk of arousing the broad constituency of private-building owners, restaurateurs, and hostelries, all of whom might be concerned that this bill would set a precedent for regulating asbestos in their buildings.

In seeking consensus, Florio was averse to risk. The potential power and intensity of opposing groups was consistently overestimated. Some potential opponents later said that the issue was so compelling that they could not have openly opposed a stronger bill. In hindsight, they believe Florio could have pushed through a stronger bill. But reputation, not reality, governed the strategy and the eventual substance of the bill.

Nearly all groups involved were given an opportunity to comment, and efforts were made to accommodate many of their concerns, including those of the asbestos manufacturers and the schools. Florio's staff worked on twenty drafts for six months before formally introducing a bill. In subcommittee, the bill was approved unanimously in a markup that consumed all of fourteen minutes. However, the bill was once again revised to accommodate concerns raised by schools and the asbestos industry and then reintroduced with a different bill number. Ten more drafts of the bill were prepared before the second bill was formally introduced for full committee consideration. The full committee also approved it unanimously by voice vote.

The bill Florio introduced required the EPA to establish federal standards mandating: (1) proper inspection procedures, including the use of personnel accredited through the states or EPA training programs; (2) appropriate response actions by schools to abate the hazards found in inspections; and (3) operations and maintenance programs by schools to regulate and periodically inspect the friable asbestos not removed.[61]

In developing these standards, the bill required the EPA to use the "protection of human health and the environment" criteria under the Resource Conservation and Recovery Act (RCRA), instead of the less stringent "unreasonable risk" standard applied under the Toxic Substances Control Act, the standard the EPA had used in promulgating its 1982 inspection rule. This was a major concession to the advocates of stronger federal regulatory action because the RCRA criteria did not require costs or degree of risk to be weighed in the response.

Further, the bill required local responses when friable asbestos was either visibly damaged or located in a heavily used area that posed a "reasonable likelihood" of prospective damage or deterioration to the asbestos material. For example, the committee report noted that a school gym with undamaged asbestos ceiling tiles could nevertheless release fibers when hit by a basketball. Adopting this standard was a rebuff to the asbestos industry, who had argued for using the results of air-monitoring tests as the trigger point for response actions. They had maintained that the actual presence of airborne fibers, not some subjective assessment of damage potential, would provide a more solid basis for local action and would avoid the needless removal of asbestos materials that did not pose a threat to occupants. Florio's subcommittee, however, was persuaded by the opposition of the EPA's professional staff, who argued that local abatement actions should protect against not only current hazards, but also the potential for episodic release of fibers that would not be captured by air-monitoring equipment.

The bill also set forth a timetable for schools to develop management plans describing response actions to be taken. School districts were to begin implementing the plans within 900 days from the date the bill was enacted. Due to the variability of local actions, no date was provided for completion, although they were urged to complete actions in a "timely fashion."

To prod a reluctant administration, the bill provided for an alternative set of criteria and local implementation timetables should the EPA fail to promulgate the mandated regulations within the bill's time frames. Borne from the congressional mistrust of the Reagan Administration's regulatory intentions and from the EPA's regulatory resistance on the asbestos issue, this unusual provision articulated specific criteria for fiber concentration following the completion of an abatement action. The bill also provided for citizens to sue the EPA to compel timely issuance of regulations.

Significantly, the bill did not go beyond regulating asbestos in schools. Although the SEIU suit against the EPA had petitioned the agency to rule on exposure to occupants of all publicly accessible buildings, Florio's bill only required the EPA to study this issue and report back within a year.

Gaining Conservative Support

As noted earlier, the bill went through many iterations to gain the support of key members and groups. The changes included provisions to ameliorate the impact on the schools, including lengthening the timetable for schools' submission of implementation plans; substituting gubernatorial review of local plans for a previous provision calling for gubernatorial approval; and a deletion of a requirement to complete the abatement action one year from the approval of local plans.

The changes also accommodated several concerns of the asbestos industry. First, a provision was added that permitted local schools to use "the least burdensome methods" that would adequately protect against asbestos hazards. Although schools could conceivably benefit from it, this provision was added at the behest of the industry to discourage local schools from removing asbestos. A provision was also added that stipulated that AHERA could not be used as evidence in court to bolster claims by plaintiffs in suits against manufacturers. This so-called neutrality provision was sought by the industry in its battle with local schools that were suing to recover inspection and abatement costs from manufacturers. Significantly, attorneys who were prosecuting the major school cases were not contacted until after the bill passed the House. As will be discussed later in this chapter, this provision became a major issue in House-Senate negotiations over the final bill.

A principal objective of these changes was to obtain the support of the ranking minority member—Norman Lent, Republican from New York—as a way to secure bipartisan consensus throughout the remainder of the legislative process. Florio's staff believed that Lent's support would impress Chairman Dingell and convince him to permit a full committee vote on the bill. Equally important, bipartisan support might ward off a veto from an avowedly deregulatory administration.

In Florio's 1985 oversight hearings, Lent expressed skepticism about the scientific basis for the problem and cited a British study that suggested that building asbestos exposure was not particularly hazardous. He also expressed his wariness about the prospect of another federal mandate and drew a parallel with the problems schools were facing in implementing the handicapped education mandate without substantial federal reimbursement.[62] However, once Florio brought the bill before the subcommittee, Lent worried that opposition could hurt him in his district due to the "demagoguery potential" of the issue on the House floor.[63] Lent had opposed expanding funding for the Superfund in the 1986 reauthorization and was looking to favor environmentalism in some way. He had also heard from the PTA and the NEA on the issue but had not heard any intense opposition from the schools. In addition, Florio's staff had worked with the PTA to apply local pressure on Lent from his home district on Long Island.

His staff explained that Lent, as a Republican, was inclined to be more concerned about the costs of new initiatives than a Democrat would be. However, on the asbestos issue, the costs seemingly could not be avoided, as local schools had to comply with the 1982 EPA rule and the subsequent abatement actions without federal guidance. Ultimately, it was hoped that AHERA would provide support for school boards to use against the more extreme and radical demands of parents. Lent negotiated with Florio to further assure that the legislation would be sensitive to the burdens faced by local schools.

The changes made to accommodate schools and the industry, as well as the funding authorized, became an important part of the advocates' strategy to hold the schools and their congressional supporters at bay. With these concessions, Florio could appeal to conservative supporters such as Congressman Lent and, later in the Senate, Senator James Abdnor. Essentially, these changes permitted Florio and others both to pose as the advocates of the mandate and to take credit for saving their constituents from its effects.

The consultation paid dividends in political support. The version reported out of the committee had obtained 104 cosponsors, including 18 Republicans. The voting at subcommittee, full committee, and on the House floor was unanimous. Although the bill was clearly Democratic in origin, Republicans knew enough to bargain for some changes in its drafting and then stay out of the way. Predictably, the House passed the bill unanimously on a voice vote.

THE AMBIVALENT POSITION OF THE SCHOOLS

Both lead staffers for the House and Senate committees on the bill believe a broad coalition of state and local elected officials opposed to the legislation could have significantly altered the legislation or perhaps killed it.[64] However, because the regulated community itself was ambivalent and crosspressured on the need for regulation, they largely stood by and watched the legislative juggernaut gain momentum. David Truman recognized long ago how crosspressures can weaken both the solidarity and intensity of interest groups. Given their penchant for unanimity, these organizations have trouble dealing with the consequent internal conflicts and, most often, decide either not to decide or to withdraw from active lobbying for the majority position.[65]

The school boards, superintendents, and asbestos industry had decidedly mixed feelings about stronger federal regulatory standards governing asbestos abatement. As noted before, the results of the inspections mandated by the 1982 EPA regulations alarmed parents and school employees and often prompted schools to remove asbestos at great cost. Federal standards that specified what levels of exposure warranted specific responses such as removal could help provide political support to the voices of restraint at the local level and perhaps limit removals that posed legal hazards of their own to the asbestos industry. The regulated community thus wanted direction, not discretion. As Florio's staff noted, unlike the EPA's regulations, AHERA would tell schools when they were done.[66]

Moreover, lobbyists for both the school boards and the school superintendents said they could not have aroused the vast bulk of their grassroots membership on the issue even if they had wanted to. The costs associated with complying with new regulations were at least three years away and awaited EPA regulations before they would be known with sufficient specificity to prompt member concerns. These lobbyists further reported that threats of potential cuts in grant money being received were more pressing concerns among their memberships than the prospective impact of a new regulatory program whose costs may not be felt for at least three years in the future.[67] And the Florio bill did increase authorization ceilings for the grant and loan program first funded in 1984. Elected school officials were also crosspressured as local politicians who could ill afford to alienate the very same advocacy groups at the local level concerned about asbestos in schools.

The electoral appeal of the issue actually prompted state and local political leaders to press for national regulation. Governor Toney Anaya of New Mexico approached the SEIU to look for an opportunity to assert national leadership on the issue. The governor and the union lobbied the National Governors' Association and gained their support for AHERA. Although several governors proposed to modify the proposal to avoid advocating a mandate, Anaya succeeded in gaining NGA support for his position and testified in favor of the bill.[68]

The NGA's position was useful to the bill's advocates as a powerful symbol of the widespread political support and consensus behind the bill. The National Association of Counties also supported the need for Florio's legislation. Consequently, the schools were not only isolated from their traditional allies in the education community, they were also cut loose from potential supporters among the general-purpose state and local government interest groups.

The schools also had trouble gaining allies among other education interest groups whom they normally joined on federal funding issues. The AASA had appealed to the American Federation of Teachers and the NEA to consider the cost implications of additional regulation for teachers' salaries, but its appeal fell on deaf ears.[69]

Once the issue had been placed on the agenda, the regulated groups moderated their positions to gain leverage at the bargaining table; outright opposition might have deprived them of any influence at all over the bill. The regulated groups had to fend off their more radical members to avoid appearing to be too negative and strident—a posture that might alienate or embarrass Florio and his staff. Washington lobbyists for both the school boards and the asbestos industry said they were concerned when several of their corporate or state association members took overly negative positions on the bill in direct communications with members.[70] Indeed, the Wyoming Association of School Boards opposed the legislation and sought to enlist Senator Simpson—the Republican Whip and key member of the Senate Committee on Environment and Public Works—in the effort to derail the bill.[71]

A REPUBLICAN SENATE ENACTS A STRONGER BILL

Florio and the asbestos coalition succeeded in getting the Senate involved in early 1986, prior to the formal introduction of his bill. The Senate Environment and Public Works Committee was chaired by Senator Robert Stafford, a Republican from Vermont. Stafford was known as a supporter of environmental issues and greater federal aid to education, in spite of the positions of his administration. The full committee was in favor of strong environmental regulation in general. Most important, from the standpoint of Florio and the advocates, Stafford was a Republican, and his support would buy further insurance against a presidential veto.

When Florio's staff approached Stafford's committee staff, however, Stafford's staff initially rebuffed the Florio proposal because their legislative plate was already full. However, the PTA appealed this decision and obtained Stafford's approval to place the issue on the committee's 1986 agenda, using the strong ties they had built with the senator on federal education issues. Stafford was swayed by the presentation of the issue as virtually a "done deal" with widespread political support.

The school boards and superintendents were again ambivalent in the Senate. They supported the need for national standards for abatement but suggested a number of changes to provide more funding, ease compliance deadlines, and recognize the efforts of schools already seeking to abate their asbestos hazard. In fact, the school superintendents asked for a federal certification of compliance with the federal standards to protect against subsequent lawsuits.[72] Their positions, coupled with the support from the National Association of Counties (NAACO) and NGA, enabled the Senate staff to indicate in markup that all school groups favored more prescriptive national standards.[73]

The schools were not used to dealing with the environmental committees, and this unfamiliarity was reflected in their positions. Senate staff indicated that some school lobbyists asked for voluntary guidelines that would give schools seeking protection from concerned parents something to fall back on without mandating a new set of federal requirements. The Senate committee staff said that this reflected the naivete and inexperience of the schools in working with the Environment and Public Works Committee. He said that they should have known that the committee favors regulatory solutions to national environmental problems and would quickly dismiss a voluntary compliance approach.[74]

The schools were also isolated from conservative Republican senators, who might have been their natural allies in fighting new federal regulation. The school boards thought at one point that Senator Alan Simpson of Wyoming, the Senate Minority Whip and one of that chamber's more conservative members, would put a hold on the bill, which could have derailed the consensual strategy discussed earlier. Yet, even though he often was a lone conservative voice opposing environmental bills in the Senate Environment and Public Works Committee, Simpson did not wish to be the lone dissenter on this compelling issue, joking that he had learned "never to kick a fresh turd on a hot day."

The Subcommittee and full Committee on Environment and Public Works unanimously approved the legislation. Although the schools raised the sensitivity of some Republican members to the potential cost burdens, the cost issue was dealt with in several ways by the Senate staff managing the bill. First, they argued that much of the costs in the EPA's $1 billion estimate would have been incurred in the absence of the AHERA legislation by schools abating asbestos on their own, so only a small portion of these costs were truly incremental in nature. Second, they suggested that the new legislation would in fact moderate the costs of the EPA's 1982 regulations because the bill would give local schools more moderate options to contain asbestos exposure, short of removal. Third, they argued that the health costs of asbestos-related diseases should be considered alongside the purported costs of compliance. Fourth, some advocacy groups felt that alleviating asbestos exposure in schools was a benefit worth the price.[75]

Ironically, the cost issue almost proved to be the bill's undoing in the Senate. The House legislation had included the provision establishing federal neutrality in court suits that were being brought against the asbestos manufacturers by local schools. Without that provision, AHERA could give leverage to the schools in recovering their abatement costs from manufacturers in court because their actions could be portrayed as a response to a federal mandate enacted to protect children from a dangerous material. The neutrality provision foreclosed this strategy, thereby depriving schools of a potentially lucrative source of reimbursement for mandate implementation. Predictably, the schools wished to remove the neutrality clause in the Senate, whereas the asbestos industry hoped to retain it.

The asbestos industry lost in the Senate. The bill reported out of the full committee told courts not to construe the legislation as precluding them from awarding costs and damages associated with the removal of asbestos. The Senate bill also did not contain the House language that called on schools to use the "least burdensome" methods to abate asbestos hazards. On 10 September 1896, the Senate passed the committee's version unanimously without objection. The bill was praised by leaders on both sides of the aisle.

HOUSE-SENATE NEGOTIATIONS

The Senate had been prepared to adopt any changes made by the House to their bill prior to passage to avoid the need for a conference. However, concerns over the impact of the House bill on ongoing school suits converted a consensual process into a conflictual one. It also introduced the product liability issue as a line of conflict that would compete with the other issues for prominence. Further, it also threatened to make opposition to the House bill on cost grounds respectable, if not compelling. With the end of the congressional term approaching, failure to reach agreement quickly could kill the bill and require advocates to start over with a new Congress.

Senate staffers and advocates mounted a public campaign to mobilize support for the Senate bill, centered around the court suit provision. One *New York Times* report suggested that Florio was collaborating with the asbestos industry on the legislation—a story that capitalized on the negative public image of the industry and threatened to undermine the environmental image Florio had been trying to cultivate through this legislation. Senate staff attempted to mobilize the school boards, particularly to pressure the House members to abandon their neutrality and least burdensome methods provisions. The school boards association supported the Senate bill to the hilt, recognizing that the Senate's intransigence on neutrality could kill the bill in a publicly defensible manner. At last, they had found a publicly defensible way to defeat the bill without leaving their fingerprints.

The Senate staff threatened to let the bill die rather than accept the House liability provisions. Yet, it would not die, because too many other interests needed a bill to be passed. Florio had staked a good deal of his reputation on the bill, and he needed a victory after setbacks on the reauthorization of Superfund. Florio's staff was flexible on the neutrality provision and had informed the asbestos industry that the provision may not survive a conference.[76] The advocacy coalition wanted a regulatory bill, and they urged Florio's staff to agree to the Senate position to avoid jeopardizing the bill. The industry needed a bill to help head off court suits prompted by the ongoing asbestos abatement but was reluctant to accept a bill that could be used in court to hurt their cause. They were particularly worried that courts could interpret the conference committee removal of neutrality and least burdensome provisions as reflecting congressional support for the schools' case.

The final agreement gave both sides something. On neutrality, the final bill kept the Senate language that declared that the legislation should not preclude courts from awarding costs and damages associated with asbestos abatement, including removal. However, the industry felt mollified by a separate provision that stated congressional intent to avoid supporting either side in the court suits. The final bill retained the House provision that called on the EPA to specify the "least burdensome" methods that could be used by schools in responding to asbestos hazards. Although this appeared to be a concession to the industry, floor colloquy by both Florio in the House and Stafford in the Senate clarified that schools could go beyond these least burdensome approaches and remove asbestos.[77]

Both houses adopted the same version of the legislation unanimously. A presidential veto was only a theoretical possibility. The supporting coalition behind the bill was too broad, and too many Senate and House Republicans had become committed to the bill to permit a veto. Further, letters were sent to the president endorsing the bill not only from the asbestos in schools coalition, but also from the asbestos industry that ultimately viewed passage of the final bill as better than no bill at all.

A LEGISLATIVE POSTSCRIPT ON COSTS

The harmony surrounding the passage of the act soon disintegrated during its implementation, as schools recognized the costs and burdens of the mandates being placed upon them. As the EPA geared up to implement its regulations, the bill's timetables for submission of local plans for inspection and abatement drew nearer and caught a number of districts short.

Schools in rural areas lacked qualified inspectors and available contractors to survey schools and help prepare the required abatement plans that were to be submitted to the Governor in October 1988, just eleven months after the EPA promulgated the regulations specifying the requirements. These plans had to go into effect in July 1989. Members were also hearing that the shortage of trained inspectors was dramatically inflating costs to local schools; one Texas congressman reported that a small district containing five buildings that required inspection received a bid from a contractor for $125,000.[78] Senator Melcher of Montana noted that schools in his state had to send their personnel over 1,000 miles to Salt Lake City or Denver for overbooked training courses.[79] The Democratic Chairman of the Hazardous Wastes and Toxic Substances Subcommittee, Max Baucus from Montana, shared these concerns.

Unlike the struggle over the 1986 legislation, the National School Boards Association could mobilize their grassroots state associations to seek relief from these pressing near-term problems. Schools now were facing definitive EPA regulations fortifying a deadline established in statute, and the EPA did not have the power to grant local flexibility.[80] As the costs of the law became more pressing and immediate, the earlier ambivalence of the schools disappeared.

Like the original enactment of the mandate, providing relief proved to be a bipartisan affair. Seven separate bills were introduced that called for extensions of the planning and implementation deadlines by from six months to eighteen months—four authored by Democrats, three by Republicans.[81] Constituency strongly affected members on this issue, as both Democrats and Republicans from largely rural states competed for the leadership to gain extensions.

Recognizing the growing pressure and the potential that a bill might reach the floor without their input, Florio and the advocacy coalition negotiated a bipartisan settlement with the schools to contain both the relief offered and the scope of conflict. Schools were given a seven-month delay until May 1989 for submission of the management plans, and extensions had to be reviewed by the states and explained to local parent and teacher organizations. The bill did not, however, delay the July 1989 starting date for implementation. True to the political history of this issue, the extension bill passed all committees and the floor in both the House and Senate on a unanimous voice vote.

In retrospect, the schools did not actually achieve any major reform or reduction of the regulatory burden, just an implementation delay. The strength of the public argument and the advocacy coalition prevented any stronger challenges to the fundamental mandate underlying the act. One member—Congressman Bereuter, a Republican and former state legislator from Nebraska—dissented from the prevailing consensus and introduced a bill to reimburse schools for inspection or management plan costs exceeding 2 percent of the school's annual budget. Yet, this bill attained no significant support.

The schools' failure to win more basic changes is even more remarkable in light of recent research casting fresh doubts on the underlying dangers faced by building occupants from asbestos. Recent studies do not support the advocates' initial premise that any exposure, regardless of how minimal, is alarming. A 1989 symposium at Harvard's Energy and Environmental Policy Center concluded that "fiber phobia" among the general public was all out of proportion to the actual public health risk from building exposures. The report further concluded that ten excess deaths could be expected for each one million schoolchildren exposed to low levels of asbestos—a risk estimated to be nearly 400 times less than other indoor air pollution threats, including radon exposure and passive exposure to cigarette smoke.[82] A 1989 article that appeared in the *New England Journal of Medicine* points to studies showing no excess cases of cancer from low exposure levels, which prompted the authors to conclude that the idea that there are no safe exposure levels is an "unproven hypothesis."[83] These more authoritative studies were not available to inform the debate leading to the AHERA legislation.

IMPLICATIONS

The unanimous adoption of an expensive mandate is surprising in a conservative era during which Republicans controlled the presidency and the Senate. The issue gained agenda status thanks to forces responsible for the rapid expansion of the federal role in other areas of domestic policy: the presence of strategically placed congressional entrepreneurs whose own political ambitions became identified with stronger federal action and the forceful advocacy by public-interest groups and unions representing the beneficiaries of the program. This infrastructure championing the interests of diffuse beneficiaries of regulatory programs was clearly not reversed in the Reagan era. Asbestos in schools proved to be the right issue at the right time, as these groups were searching for a politically unassailable cause to break the Republican stranglehold on national policy activism.

Ironically, the enhancement of state and local political capacity so eagerly sought by the Reagan Administration indirectly advanced the case for federal action. In a national society with national media and national interest groups, state or local policy activism created programs that national policy activists tried to either extend or prohibit for the rest of the nation. State activism helped create the odd coalition favoring federal regulation—some to strengthen state and local policies, others to constrain unbridled state and local policy development.

Though these factors help explain how the issue gained a place on the federal policy agenda, they do not by themselves explain the absence of overt political conflict. Rather, the consensual status attained by the legislation can be largely attributed to the withering of traditional restraints on federal action: Both the regulated community and the conservatives became bystanders, watching the legislation move inexorably toward unanimous passage. The advocates succeeded in defining the issue and their bill in unassailable valence terms by which public opposition would be perceived to be illegitimate. The regulated community never successfully articulated a competing line of conflict that tapped widely held values by, for example, focusing on the impact of the mandate on property tax bills or other education programs. Lacking a publicly defensible position, the regulated community and the conservatives had no choice but to bow to the prevailing consensus as defined by the advocates. Politically paralyzed and crosspressured by the way the issue was defined, they could no longer brake federal action.

The outcome of the asbestos in schools policy also tests the assumptions behind the Court's *Garcia* decision, which held that state and local governments had sufficient political resources to fight mandates in the congressional arena without the protection of the 10th Amendment. The actions and inactions by the school lobbies suggest that the schools were too paralyzed to use their political resources to defeat the mandate itself, even though a unified state and local alliance might have derailed the asbestos policy juggernaut. The schools were not really bested in a political duel on this issue; rather, they were defeated from within, thanks to the way the issue was defined. This outcome contradicts the Court's rather confident projection of state and local political prowess in the national arena and suggests that mandate outcomes may be more reflective of conflict within rather than between opposing interest groups.

The schools did gain some concessions, including increased grant and loan funds, deadline extensions, and flexibility on how the standards were to be implemented. However, these ostensible concessions to federalism values only paved the way for acceptance of the more fundamental federal mandate in the 1986 legislation. Accordingly, federalism considerations did not affect the basic decision of *whether* to mandate, but only *how* to implement the mandate.

Consensus has its casualties. Latent conflicts can surface once the policy is implemented, as the implementors focus more clearly on their roles in the program. But Congress also showed itself open to policy reversal once the shoe began to pinch. Rather than modify the legislation at the outset based on speculative cost estimates, Congress chose to act first and then await political reaction to decide on postadoption policy corrections. This style of policymaking resembles the "politics of speculative augmentation" that Charles Jones found to characterize the nation's clean air policy.[84] In such areas, Congress is under pressure to take bold action to respond to public bandwagons, even if the policy is not firmly grounded in the capability of implementors. Although such policymaking is responsive to broad public moods, it invites later disillusionment with the policy and even with government itself once the mismatches between policy goals and implementation realities become apparent.

NOTES TO CHAPTER 6

1. Theodore Lowi predicts intense intergroup conflict for regulatory policy in his article "American Business, Public Policy, Case-Studies, and Political Theory," *World Politics* 16 (1964), pp. 677–715.

2. See National Institute for Occupational Safety and Health, *Workplace Exposure to Asbestos: Review and Recommendations* (Rockville, Md.: National Institute for Occupational Safety and Health, 1980), DHHS (NIOSH) Publication No. 91–103.

3. Cited in report by U.S. General Accounting Office, *Asbestos in Schools: A Dilemma*, GAO/CED–82–114 (Washington, D.C.: U.S. General Accounting Office, 31 August 1982).

4. For construction, the current asbestos standard is at Title 29 CFR Part 1926.58; for other workplace environments, the standard is at Title 29 CFR Part 1910.1001. OSHA standards apply to all private-sector employees, but only to those public-sector employees such as school workers in the thirty-four states that have approved plans for OSHA enforcement. The EPA subsequently issued a worker protection rule extending OSHA's asbestos standard to all public-sector workers on 12 July 1985; see Title 40 CFR Part 763, Subpart G (Worker Protection Rule).

5. See James S. Kakalik, *et al.*, *Costs of Asbestos Litigation* (Santa Monica, Ca.: RAND Corporation, Institute for Civil Justice, 1985). For an analysis of the issues involved in the suits, see Paul Brodeur, *Outrageous Misconduct* (New York: Pantheon Books, 1985).

6. Committee on Nonoccupational Health Risks of Asbestiform Fibers, National Research Council, *Asbestiform Fibers: Nonoccupational Health Risks* (Washington, D.C.: National Academy Press, 1984), p. iii.

7. John Kingdon, *Agendas, Alternatives, and Public Policies* (Boston: Little, Brown, 1984), p. 99.

8. William K. Stevens, "Despite Asbestos Risk, Experts See No Cause for 'Fiber Phobia,' " *New York Times*, 5 September 1989.

9. H. Seidman, R. Lilis, and I. J. Selikoff, "Short-Term Asbestos Exposure and Delayed Cancer Risk," 1976 paper cited in Environmental Defense Fund, *Petition to the Environmental Protection Agency to Control Asbestos Emissions from Spray-On Materials Which Have Been Applied in Public School Buildings for Insulation, Fireproofing, Decorative or Other Purposes* (Washington, D.C.: Environmental Defense Fund, 21 December 1978).

10. Environmental Defense Fund, *Petition to the Environmental Protection Agency*, p. 20.

11. House Education and Labor Committee, *Asbestos School Hazard Detection and Control Act of 1979*, Report No. 96–197, 96th Congress, 1st Session (15 May 1979), p. 5.

12. Eugene Bardach and Robert Kagan, *Going by the Book: The Problem of Regulatory Unreasonableness* (Philadelphia: Temple University Press, 1982), p. 19.

13. Mancur Olson would argue that they would not be well organized due to the free-rider problem, whereby the benefits of organization affect all beneficiaries regardless of whether they belong to the organization. See his *The Logic of Collective Action* (New York: Schocken Books, 1965).

14. Interview with Ron Outen, staff to Senator Stafford.

15. W. J. Nicholson, "Control of Sprayed Asbestos Surfaces in School Buildings: A Feasibility Study" (Washington, D.C.: National Institute of Environmental Health Sciences, 1978).

16. James L. Sundquist with David W. Davis, *Making Federalism Work* (Washington, D.C.: Brookings Institution, 1969), p. 11.

17. New York Education Law, Section 430, *et seq.* (McKinney 1983–1994).

18. U.S. General Accounting Office, *Asbestos in Schools: A Dilemma.*

19. Environmental Protection Agency, *Asbestos-Containing Materials in School Buildings*, 44 Federal Register 158, 23 March 1979.

20. Environmental Protection Agency, *Toxic Substances Control Act; Grant of Petition to Initiate Rulemaking Proceeding to Regulate Sprayed Asbestos in Schools*, 44 Federal Register 136, 13 July 1979, p. 40900.

21. U.S. General Accounting Office, *Asbestos in Schools: A Dilemma.*

22. In this regard, it was similar to many other public interest lobbying organizations. See Jeffrey M. Berry, *Lobbying for the People: The Political Behavior of Public Interest Groups* (Princeton: Princeton University Press, 1977).

23. Richard A. Ginsburg, "TSCA's Unfilled Mandate for Comprehensive Regulation of Toxic Substances—The Potential of TSCA Section 211 Citizens' Petitions," *Environmental Law Reporter*, Vol. 16, pp. 10330–10337.

24. Another factor in the EPA's reversal was proposed legislation in Congress to establish a new assistance program to help local schools inspect and abate hazardous asbestos (see later in the text for further discussion). The legislation would have vested leadership responsibility not with the EPA, but with the Department of Education.

25. Environmental Protection Agency, "Friable Asbestos-Containing Materials in Schools: Identification and Notification," 40 CFR, Part 763.

26. Burdett Loomis, *The New American Politician: Ambition, Entrepreneurship, and the Changing Face of Political Life* (New York: Basic Books, 1988).

27. *Congressional Record,* House, 13 December 1979, p. H11941.

28. Interview with John Lawrence, staff to Congressman Miller.

29. Presentation by Aaron Wildavsky at the Annual Conference of the American Society of Public Administration, San Francisco, Ca., 1980.

30. E. E. Schattschneider, *The Semi-Sovereign People: A Realist's View of Democracy in America* (New York: Holt, Rinehard and Winston, 1960), p. 62.

31. David R. Beam, Timothy J. Conlan, and Margaret T. Wrightson, *Taxing Choices: The Politics of Tax Reform* (Washington, D.C.: Congressional Quarterly Press, 1990).

32. Congressional Record, House, 13 December 1979, H11942.

33. On the cost side, the EPA estimated that the rule would only add about $6 million to school budgets. This was based on their estimate of the costs to inspect the remaining 44,000 schools. However, these estimates failed to include the consequent costs of abatement actions set in motion by these inspections. The cost figures were so minimal that the EPA was able to exempt itself from the cost-benefit analysis required under the president's new Executive Order 12291. The Office of Management and Budget, however, did review this regulation, as it did all proposed federal regulatory actions.

34. U.S. General Accounting Office, *Asbestos in Schools: A Dilemma,* p. 15.

35. Matthew Kauffman, "The State Flunks Out," *New Jersey Reporter,* November, 1989, pp. 6–13.

36. U.S. General Accounting Office, *Asbestos in Schools: A Dilemma,* p. 19.

37. Hearings before the Subcommittee on Commerce, Transportation, and Tourism, House Energy and Commerce Committee, 98th Congress, 1st Session, *Asbestos Exposure,* 4 March 1995, p. 35.

38. Hearings before the Subcommittee on Toxic Substances and Environmental Oversight of the Committee on Environment and Public Works, United States Senate, 99th Congress, 2nd Session, *Hazardous Asbestos Abatement,* 15 May 1986, p. 67.

39. See Paul Brodeur, *Outrageous Misconduct.*

40. Cited in Plaintiffs' Pretrial Brief, *City of Berea; and* Berea Independent Board of Education vs. United States Gypsum Company, United States District Court, Eastern District of Kentucky, Lexington, Ky., Lexington Civil Action No. 86–172, p. 3.

41. Interview with Edward Westbrook, attorney with Ness, Motley, Loadholt, Richardson, and Poole, representing schools in product liability suits.

42. Grant McConnell, *Private Power and American Democracy* (New York: Alfred A. Knopf, 1966).

43. See Mel Dubnick and Alan Gitelson, "Nationalizing State Policies," in *The Nationalization of State Government,* ed. Jerome Hanus (Lexington, Mass: D.C. Heath, 1981).

44. Based on an interview with Daniel Guttman, Counsel, SEIU.

45. Reuben A. Guttman and Kathryn D. Wagner, "The Asbestos Model: Labor and Citizen Groups and a Multi-Pronged Approach to Regulatory Change" (paper delivered at the 1987 Annual Meeting of the American Political Science Association, Chicago, Illinois, 3 September 1987).

46. Richard A. Ginsburg, "TSCA's Unfilled Mandate for Comprehensive Regulation of Toxic Substances—The Potential of TSCA Section 21 Citizens' Petitions."

47. "Florio's Images Connect in Camden," *New York Times*, 12 September 1989.

48. "In Capital, Jersey Rivals Behave Like Statesmen," *New York Times*, 26 October 1989, p. B5.

49. Richard Fenno, *Home Style: House Members in Their Districts* (Boston: Little, Brown, 1978).

50. "Florio Attacks Asbestos-Removal Guidelines," *Camden Courier-Post*, 2 March 1986.

51. Burdett Loomis, *The New American Politician.*

52. Interview with Michael Lakat, Special Assistant to the Director, Asbestos Control Service, New Jersey Department of Health.

53. Matthew Kauffman, "The State Flunks Out."

54. Based on interviews with Congressman Florio's subcommittee staff present during bill development.

55. Robert C. Mitchell, "Public Opinion and the Green Lobby: Poised for the 1990's?" in *Environmental Policy in the 1990's*, ed. Norman J. Vig and Michael E. Kraft (Washington, D.C.: Congressional Quarterly Press, 1990), p. 83.

56. Henry C. Kenski and Margaret Corgan Kenski, "Congress against the President: The Struggle over the Environment," in *Ibid.*, pp. 97–120.

57. Hearings before the Subcommittee on Commerce, Transportation and Tourism, Committee on Energy and Commerce, U.S. House of Representatives, 99th Congress, 1st Session, *Asbestos Exposure*, 4 March 1986.

58. Dingell headed a coalition of Republicans and oil-state Democrats who pushed a version of the Superfund amendments through Florio's subcommittee against Florio's own position. See "House, Senate Pass Superfund Authorization," *Congressional Quarterly Almanac* (Washington, D.C.: Congressional Quarterly Press, 1986), pp. 191–197.

59. Burton Loomis, *The New American Politician*, p. 170.

60. Interview with Robert Summers, staff member, Subcommittee on Commerce, Transportation and Tourism, House Committee on Energy and Commerce.

61. The discussion of the House bill relies a good deal on the Report of the Committee on Energy and Commerce, U. S. House of Representatives, 99th Congress, 2nd Session, *Asbestos Hazard Emergency Response Act of 1986*, Report 99–763, 7 August 1986.

62. Hearings before the Subcommittee on Commerce, Transportation and Tourism, Committee on Energy and Commerce, U.S. House of Representatives, 99th Congress, 1st session, *Asbestos Exposure*, 4 March 1986, p. 203.

63. Interview with Teresa Gorman, minority staff member, House Energy and Commerce Committee.

64. Interview with Ron Outen, staff with the Senate Committee on Environment and Public Works, and Reena Steinser, Staff Director of the Florio Subcommittee on Commerce, Transportation and Tourism of the House Energy and Commerce Committee.

65. David Truman, *The Governmental Process* (New York: Alfred A. Knopf, 1951).

66. Interview with Robert Summers, staff member with the Subcommittee on Commerce, Transportation and Tourism, House Energy and Commerce Committee.

67. Interviews with Bruce Hunter, American Association of School Superintendents; and Edward Keely, National Association of School Boards.

68. See testimony of Governor Toney Anaya before the Subcommittee on Commerce, Transportation, and Tourism, House Energy and Commerce Committee, 99th Congress, 2nd Session, *Asbestos Exposure*, 4 March 1986, p. 345.

69. Interview with Bruce Hunter, Washington staff with the American Association of School Superintendents.

70. Interview with Ed Keely, National Association of School Boards. This is consistent with how Dexter describes the role of the Washington representatives as instructing their clients how to adapt, accommodate, and adjust to prevailing norms and values in Washington. See Lewis Anthony Dexter, *How Organizations Are Represented in Washington* (New York: Bobbs-Merrill, 1969), p. 103.

71. Interview with Jim Henderson, Executive Director, Wyoming Association of School Boards.

72. Statement of Lloyd A. Kelley Jr. on behalf of the American Association of School Administrators, Hearings before the Subcommittee on Toxic Substances and Environmental Oversight, Committee on Environment and Public Works, United States Senate, *Hazardous Asbestos Abatement*, p. 28.

73. Transcript of markup, Committee on Environment and Public Works, United States Senate, 99th Congress, 2nd Session, 12 August 1986, p. 52.

74. Interview with committee staff, Ron Outen.

75. Based on interviews with Ron Outen, Senate Environment and Public Works staff; Daniel Guttman, counsel to the Service Employees International Union; and Joel Packer, lobbyist for the National Education Association.

76. Interviews with Florio's two subcommittee staff members, Rena Steinser and Robert Summers.

77. Senator Stafford made it clear that the bill is not intended to prevent or discourage a local education agency from taking action beyond that required by EPA regulations. See his statement in *Congressional Record*, Senate, 3 October 1986, p. S13066.

78. Statement of Congressman Jack Fields in *Implementation of the Asbestos Hazard Emergency Response Act*, Joint Hearing before the Subcommittee on Hazardous Wastes and Toxic Substances and the Superfund and Environmental Oversight, Committee on Environment and Public Works, Senate, 100th Congress, 2nd Session, 15 March 1988, p. 7.

79. Statement of Senator John Melcher, *Implementation of the Asbestos Hazard Emergency Response Act*, Hearings before the Subcommittees on Hazardous Wastes and Toxic Substances and Superfund and Environmental Oversight,

Committee on Environment and Public Works, Senate, 100th Congress, 2nd Session, 15 March 1988, p. 3.

80. Statement of John A. Moore, Assistant Administrator, Office of Pesticides and Toxic Substances in *Ibid.*, p. 17.

81. Claudia Copeland, *Comparison of Bills to Amend the Asbestos Hazard Emergency Response Act: A CRS Report to the Congress* (Washington, D.C.: Congressional Research Service, 12 May 1988).

82. Jon D. Spengler, Haluk Ozkaynak, John F. McCarthy, and Henry Lee, *Summary of Symposium on Health Aspects of Exposure to Asbestos in Buildings* (Cambridge: Harvard University Energy and Environmental Policy Center, August, 1989).

83. Brooke T. Mossman and J. Bernard L. Gee, "Asbestos-Related Diseases," *New England Journal of Medicine*, Vol. 320, No. 26 (1989).

84. Charles O. Jones, *Clean Air: The Policy and Politics of Pollution Control* (Pittsburgh: University of Pittsburgh Press, 1975).

7

Education for Preschool
Handicapped Children

One of the most costly mandates passed by Congress over the past twenty-five years is the requirement for state and local governments to provide a "free and appropriate" education for all handicapped children. Traditions of local control of schools notwithstanding, this landmark piece of legislation imposed federal standards and protections on the entire field of special education with federal funds financing only a small portion of the costs of serving this new educational target group.

In 1986, bowing to pressures building from its own policy entrepreneurs and the disability community, Congress extended the mandated protections of this program from school-age children to preschool kids with disabilities. However, in doing so, it spurned a Senate-passed mandate in favor of a House bill that used grant subsidies and enriched funding in lieu of coercion. Given the broad support and public sympathy advocates of the handicapped had enjoyed at the federal level for the prior fifteen years, the restraint shown by Congress indicates at least conditional congressional concern for state and local costs and federalism values.

Unlike the asbestos issue, the schools mounted a vigorous and concerted grassroots lobbying campaign against the Senate mandate. They succeeded in convincing members of Congress and allies among the teachers' union that the pursuit of one consensual public value (service to preschool handicapped children) could jeopardize other widely held values (keeping property taxes down and financing educational reform activities such as higher teacher salaries and longer school days).

However, the schools succeeded in part because benefits were delayed, not denied. Not even the schools objected to the goals or a new federal program presence as long as appropriate funding was provided. Both schools and beneficiaries could heartily endorse an enhanced federal assistance program, an outcome that a Congress attracted to consensual solutions could easily embrace. The final outcome, although less coercive than the Senate bill, nevertheless established a new federal presence that promised to leverage significant new state and local programs and resources to serve handicapped children from birth through five years old. Thus, though a coercive mandate was averted, the final bill nevertheless promised to shift state and local spending priorities, thereby giving credence to Max Neiman's caution that those worried about the manipulative potential of coercion should be sensitive to how the carrot can be employed to one's detriment as well.[1]

THE GROWTH OF THE FEDERAL PRESENCE IN SPECIAL EDUCATION

The growth of the federal role in special education paralleled the shifts in the federal role for education in general. The 1960s saw a breakthrough in the federal role in elementary and secondary education. The federal government embarked on a strategy to use categorical grants to entice state and local education agencies to focus on such target groups as the disadvantaged and the handicapped, who were perceived to have been bypassed or excluded from the mainstream education system. The Elementary and Secondary Education Act of 1965 was the watershed legislation of the modern era and established the relationships between the federal government and local schools that influenced later initiatives on handicapped education.

The federal role in special education can also be dated to the 1965 passage of the Elementary and Secondary Education Act (ESEA). Using the precedents established in that legislation, Congress worked toward the landmark legislation mandating education for all handicapped children in 1975. The 1965 act authorized school districts to consider the handicapped as educationally deprived, thereby making them eligible for special programs funded under Title I of ESEA. This was followed in 1966 with a separate assistance program to the states for handicapped education projects. Congress added discretionary programs to fund training, research, and demonstration projects, culminating in 1970 legislation that created a separate law, the Education of the Handicapped Act, to consolidate legislative authority for the growing panoply of federal assistance programs.

This early congressional interest was prompted by several factors. One was the general political awakening of the disabled community. Following quickly on the heels of the civil rights revolution, the handicapped were swept up in the rights movement as well.[2] Public interest groups representing disabled people in Washington grew in both numbers and political diversity, paralleling the more general growth of public interest organizations headquartered in Washington during this period.[3] Some of these groups began to discard the service orientation of the past, which assumed that the disabled were clients needing protection from benevolent service providers, in favor of a civil rights orientation that viewed the disabled as self-sufficient people entitled to the same rights and privileges as nonhandicapped persons. Moreover, policy activists serving on congressional staffs and with other civil rights organizations saw the battle for the rights of the elderly, women, and the disabled as a logical extension of the civil rights struggles of the 1960s.

Just as the civil rights movement initially focused on integrating African Americans into the American mainstream, the disability movement sought to place handicapped children in regular classrooms, to move the mentally ill from oppressive state institutions into community-based mental health programs, and to require all public buildings and transportation vehicles to become accessible to the handicapped. However, defining the issue as a civil rights question drew Congress toward mandates and regulation to guarantee rights, a strategy used with other minority issues. Those drafting legislation and regulations extending these rights to the disabled viewed state and local cost concerns as an excuse to delay full recognition for disenfranchised groups, an excuse that had been used against civil rights programs in the 1960s. As Katzmann notes, "Rights tend to be viewed as absolutes, overriding considerations of cost effectiveness."[4]

The epitome of this pattern was the 1973 passage of Section 504 of the Rehabilitation Act, an apparently simple one-sentence provision that prohibited handicapped individuals from being discriminated against or being denied access to any program or activity receiving federal funds. This provision was added at the initiative of policy entrepreneurs within Congress, whereas the disabled groups remained largely on the sidelines.[5] Senator Javits' staff drew the language directly from Title VI of the Civil Rights Act but with no deliberation about the appropriateness of the policy for this new uncharted area. There was no discussion on the floor of either chamber, nor was there any statement of legislative history or intent in the conference report, which forced Congress to provide such interpretations the following year. The unanimous passage of such critical legislation with little or no deliberation illustrates how tempting handicapped rights had become as a symbolic issue for political entrepreneurs in Congress and how politically untenable it had become to publicly raise objections about costs or implementation concerns.[6]

When viewed against the rising political expectations of the disabled community, many state and local education programs were found to be seriously deficient. As one observer noted, special education had traditionally been regarded as a stepchild of public education.[7] Private charities and nonprofit organizations, not public school systems, provided most educational services for the handicapped. Wealthier families could afford to send their children to the best of these private facilities, often far from their own communities, whereas lower income families were unable to educate their children. Professional educators working with these children were often little more than caretakers.[8]

The states' variability also stimulated the advocates' appetite by suggesting models for federal programs among the best states to be spread to the worst states. New Jersey was the first state to mandate the public provision of special education at the local level in 1954. By 1970, only eleven states had adopted such laws, prompting cries that obtaining a public education should not depend on where one lives— a familiar rationale for federal action. One House Committee on Education and Labor report alleged that 60 percent of the total handicapped school-age population were not receiving special education services.[9] The best information available to Congress in 1975 indicated that of the over 8 million handicapped children in the country, over 1 million were excluded entirely from the public education system, while another 4 million were not receiving the most appropriate educational services. One author maintained that over 2 million disabled children were being denied a free public education.[10]

None of these forces would have been sufficient to pass the 1975 handicapped education mandate without two significant federal district court decisions making states responsible for serving their handicapped population.[11] In a 1972 decision, a federal court ruled that Pennsylvania must provide a free appropriate public education to its mentally retarded children, including due process protections.[12] In another 1972 class action suit, a court found that all handicapped children in the District of Columbia were constitutionally entitled to a public education, even if the city lacked the money.[13] Other lawsuits followed so that by 1974 over thirty-six cases were pending or had been resolved in twenty-four states; the resolved cases had been decided in favor of the handicapped child.[14]

These cases gave states and localities an interest in an expanded federal program in addition to the advocates. The courts' rulings were perceived as a judicial mandate by the states, prompting many to enact their own public special education programs; between 1970 and 1976, the number of states with a law mandating public education for disabled children grew from eleven to forty-nine.[15] However, states quickly realized that they and their local schools needed more federal money to carry out these programs; one study estimated that the average cost of educating a handicapped child was 1.9 times that for a nonhandicapped child.[16]

PASSAGE OF THE 1975 MANDATE

The early congressional proponents of an expanded federal presence used the court cases to argue for a major federal program with increased funding, with the support of state officials to obtain federal funds to implement court orders. Significantly, senatorial Republicans bore the major responsibility for the first major funding and mandates in the 1974 Education Amendments, (PL 93-380). Senator Mathias, a Republican from Maryland, successfully offered a floor amendment dramatically increasing assistance provided to the states, arguing that they needed support to fulfill court mandates. Senator Stafford, a Republican from Vermont, insisted that Congress add certain mandates on the states in return for the increased funding provided by Mathias.

The 1975 legislation adopted the framework of the 1974 amendment. The Senate Subcommittee on the Handicapped and the full Labor and Public Welfare Committee reported their version of the legislation unanimously. The full Senate passed the bill, with several relatively minor floor amendments, by a vote of 83 to 10.[17] The House Subcommittee on Select Education, chaired by Congressman John Brademas, a Democrat from Indiana, and the full Education and Labor Committee passed their version unanimously as well. Although fiscal conservatives attempted to limit federal funding, the House adopted the final bill by a vote of 404 to 7. Faced with these overwhelming margins, a strong grassroots letter-writing campaign mounted by disabled groups, and a forthcoming election, a reluctant President Ford signed the bill, despite his concerns over the unrealistic authorization levels and burdensome administrative mandates. Although he promised to propose amendments, the program has remained largely intact since its passage, and it is the only major federal education program that has not undergone a significant legislative revision since its inception.[18]

The final bill, known as PL 94-142, incorporated several key mandates and funding features that were to remain controversial even to this day. The bill:

- required each state to provide a free and appropriate education to all handicapped children from age six to seventeen by 1978. Children ages three to five and eighteen to twenty-one would be covered where not contradictory to state law or court order.
- required that, where appropriate, such children be "mainstreamed," that is, educated with nonhandicapped children.

- required that an individualized education plan be prepared for each child setting forth goals and services to be provided and established due process protections for parents aggrieved by local actions.
- provided for grants to the states equal to 40 percent of the average national per pupil expenditure by 1982 for each child served (up to a maximum of 12 percent of all children in the state), resulting in an authorization of $3.16 billion for fiscal year 1982 and beyond.

In the years since the passage of the act, the consensus among program administrators, evaluators, and handicapped advocates has appeared to be that the law is working well to effectively expand education for the handicapped. Major evaluation studies by the Stanford Research Institute and the General Accounting Office concluded that the quality and quantity of services provided to handicapped children had improved and that many who had been either unserved or underserved were now receiving an appropriate education.[19] The number of children served increased from 3.7 million in 1976 to 4.4 million in 1986.[20] The proportion of handicapped children as a percentage of total school enrollment increased as well, from 8.3 percent in 1976 to 10.9 percent in 1984.[21]

CONSENSUS DISSOLVES DURING IMPLEMENTATION

However, the consensus and harmony that marked the passage of the bill were not reflected in the history of the program's implementation. Considerable intergovernmental conflict arose from the program's prescriptive procedural requirements, from the rights accorded to parents to bring actions against schools, and from the low funding actually appropriated by Congress to defray state costs.

The act placed significant new financial and administrative burdens on local schools. Districts had to assess and test children with complex medical and psychological histories, develop an individualized education plan for each student in consultation with often anxious parents, arrange for related health and social services where deemed necessary to permit the child to attend school, and place disabled children in regular classrooms where possible. Districts confronted shortages in special education teachers as well as lawsuits from parents. Some states had to change their fundamental relationship with local school districts; Florida, for example, had to alter its state law prohibiting state officials from intervening in local school decisions to accommodate the new appeal process in the law.[22] Several states initially refused to participate in the program in order to avoid complying with the new mandates, but pressures by advocates and the lure of federal funds ultimately brought New Mexico—the last holdout—into the program in 1983.[23]

Teachers, principals, and elected school superintendents worried that special education took resources from other school priorities. A RAND study found that it cost 2.7 times the cost of a nonhandicapped child to educate a handicapped child. Spending on related services also proved expensive; one state spent 25 percent of the transportation budget on bussing handicapped children, who made up only 3 percent of enrollment.[24] Teachers and principals found having handicapped children in regular classrooms proved to be taxing and sometimes disruptive to normal routines.[25]

For states and localities, the most egregious issue was the federal government's failure to provide appropriations levels sufficient to provide all the money promised in the original 1975 legislation. As a result, states and localities were left to largely foot the bill for implementing the federal mandate. Although funding had increased nearly fivefold between 1977 and 1986, the federal government did not fund more than 12 percent of the average per pupil expenditure, and this constituted an 11.1 percent real decrease in program funding between fiscal years 1979 and 1984, using constant 1984 dollars.[26] Nevertheless, as one measure of the continuing popularity of handicapped education programs, the appropriation for PL 94-142 fared better throughout fiscal year 1984 than appropriations for compensatory education for the disadvantaged, the bilingual education program, and the vocational education program.[27]

Nonetheless, special education remained one of the most burdensome unfunded mandates in the view of state and local officials. One survey of state and local education boards indicated that 73 percent said the mandate was placing a financial burden on them, and 27 percent reported they had been sued under the program.[28] City officials surveyed in 1980 by the National League of Cities ranked the handicapped mandate as one of the most costly federal requirements they faced, with 58 percent saying that alleviating the burden was important.

The burdens of special education mandates also paralleled more general state and local concerns over the restrictive framework of categorical grants and their intrusive conditions. Beyond the myriad of administrative grant requirements, critics attacked more substantive requirements that mandated particular educational approaches and methods, such as the provisions of the Title VII bilingual assistance program, which required schools to use the bilingual-bicultural approach in teaching children with limited English proficiency. Similar mandates from the 1970s included the Title IX amendment, which required equal access for women to educational programs and the Education Rights and Privacy Act of 1974, which controlled access to student records. The federal courts also expanded federal controls over the schools, mandating services to disabled children and to non–English proficient students in their native tongues. One study found that federal court rulings involving schools increased from 112 in 1946–1956 to 1,277 in the five-year period between 1967 and 1971.[29]

The growth in regulatory mandates prompted calls for block grants and deregulation to restore state and local discretion over the schools. Although they defeated block grant proposals in the 1970s, Congress finally approved an education block grant at the behest of President Reagan in 1981 consolidating over forty categorical programs, as well as loosening federal grant requirements for maintenance of effort and recordkeeping. Broader Reagan proposals to consolidate compensatory and special education into a special-needs block grant with little federal control or oversight failed to gain congressional approval. In fact, as Peterson, Rabe, and Wong observed, the two major federal redistributive education programs—compensatory education and handicapped education—both expanded in the Reagan era while retaining their regulatory features.[30]

PRESCHOOL HANDICAPPED COVERAGE MAKES THE AGENDA

One issue that proved somewhat contentious in the congressional deliberations on the 1975 program was the question of coverage for preschool children. Some schools had provided on their own for preschool programs for handicapped and normal children between three and five years of age. Handicapped programs focused on such educational activities as language, speech, and emotional and learning development.[31] A smaller group of states had taken the initiative to mandate comprehensive early intervention services, including health, education, and social welfare, to all infants from birth to age two with either a demonstrable handicap or at strong risk of developing such a handicap or developmental disability.

The mandate in the 1975 act required states to provide a free public education to handicapped children of six to seventeen years of age. States were to extend such coverage to their three- to five-year-old population only if not contradictory to state law and practice. For example, if state law did not require nonhandicapped children to be served, then nothing in federal law would mandate an education to be provided for the handicapped preschool group.

A bipartisan group of senators—Republicans Stafford, Javits, and Schweicker, and Democrats Kennedy and Hathaway—provided additional views in the 1975 committee report calling for extension of the mandate to the three- to five-year-old group. These members argued that dealing with the child's needs in the early years could prevent or mitigate many later problems. Senator Stafford did get Congress to approve a floor amendment providing incentive grants for states serving preschool children ages three through five. States serving such children were given up to $300 per child covered.

Several factors explain why Congress chose in 1975 to rely on permissive incentives to encourage states rather than a mandate to serve the preschool group. First, recall that the 1975 legislation sought to end discrimination against handicapped children when compared to education provided to nonhandicapped children. Though certainly true for school-age children, such a rationale could not be legitimately articulated for the preschool group since many states did not provide nonhandicapped children three to five years old with a free public education.

Second, it would be difficult to apply the framework of the 1975 program to the birth-to-five-year-old group due to their vastly different needs—differences that made many educators reluctant to take on the preschool handicapped in 1975. As noted by James Gallagher, the health professions, rather than the schools, had far more contact with this group of disabled children, particularly those from birth to two years of age.[32] Schools and the teachers' unions urged Congress to look elsewhere besides the schools to serve the youngest handicapped children since the children's parents and family play a more central role in the successful intervention for very young children, and treatment is often provided in the home setting.

The definition of handicapped is by no means clear at the younger ages since handicapping conditions hampering children in school are sometimes latent at earlier ages. It is therefore common practice to identify children in need of services as those "at risk" of developing disabilities. Three types of risk are commonly identified: children with known disorders such as Down's syndrome; children at biological risk with a history of prenatal or neonatal problems, such as low birthweight, that increase the probability of later dysfunction; and children at environmental risk whose family and social backgrounds, such as child abuse or neglect, suggest a high probability of delayed development.[33] Accordingly, the broader the risk criteria, the larger the program, thereby increasing the chances of treating children who in fact are normal in spite of their risk factors and increasing resistance from parents who deny disability in what appears to be a normal child.

Yet, in the ten years following the 1975 act, pressures mounted for an expanded federal role in promoting state and local services to preschoolers that ultimately succeeded in placing the issue on the congressional agenda once again in 1986. Factors that brought the issue to the federal agenda included a growing consensus among researchers in human development on the importance of early intervention, an increasingly supportive political climate following the high watermark of deregulation in the early 1980s, and the variability of the states in addressing the needs of this group.

According to one prominent expert in early childhood special education, one factor that promoted early intervention was the publication of two important works on human development: J. McV. Hunt's *Intelligence and Experience* in 1961 and Benjamin Bloom's *Stability and Change in Human Characteristics* in 1964. Both books emphasized the critical importance of the early years to latter development.[34] Studies by Jean Piaget and others took up this point, stressing that the most rapid rate of cognitive, physical, and neurological growth occurs in the first three years of life.[35] A number of studies found that stimulation programs for infants ameliorated a child's impaired development.[36] One study, for example, showed that mentally retarded preschoolers given nursery school training increased their IQ scores by thirty points, whereas the control group's scores declined.[37] These studies grew so numerous by 1980 that the *Journal of Childhood Special Education* devoted three issues to reporting the results.[38] Other work suggested that intervention could save public money by preventing disabilities. One study in four Colorado school districts with preschool programs for three- to five-year-old handicapped children found improvements that saved a net of over $1,500 per child, due to reductions in special education costs.[39]

Researchers also participated in the policy process, thereby helping to absorb and transform this body of professional work. Specifically, S. Gray Garwood—a prominent and well-published researcher in the field—was staff director of the House Subcommittee on Select Education during the period when the 1986 legislation was developed and enacted. Senator Weicker's key staff person who drafted his bill was Lonnie Florian—also a special education researcher.

To affect policy, ideas must connect with real-world concerns and interests. Expanding federal support for the preschool handicapped was always attractive, given the broad mass appeal that public support for the handicapped, particularly vulnerable children, had acquired. The logic of regulatory expansion provided a publicly compelling case for extending the protections of the 1975 act to at least the three- to five-year-old group. Justifying a preschool mandate as a cost containment strategy also provided a rationale, if not a compelling argument, for state and local schools to join the promandate coalition when it became politically expedient.

However, the tides of deregulation swept Washington in the late 1970s and early 1980s, and the climate for additional regulation worsened considerably during that period. Disability groups focused on defending their gains from the 1970s rather than on striving for new programs. As Richard Scotch observed, the disability movement itself peaked in 1978, followed by a period in which the cost burdens of implementing disability mandates emerged as a more potent political issue.[40] The Reagan Regulatory Relief Task Force, chaired by Vice President Bush, proposed to reform the regulations for the 1975 Education for the Handicapped program to provide state and local school districts with more flexibility in reporting, recordkeeping, and developing individualized development plans. Among the more controversial changes proposed in 1982 were removing requirements for placement in schools as close as possible to the student's home, for participation of handicapped children in extracurricular activities, for parental consent prior to initial placement, and for provision of certain related health and social services to handicapped children. The proposal also eliminated certain data and reporting requirements for states and permitted schools to apply normal disciplinary standards to handicapped children.[41]

However, these proposed changes aroused a storm of protest from the disability community, forcing the Department of Education ultimately to withdraw them.[42] According to some informed advocates, this caused the administration to become wary about proposing more deregulation in this area and of vetoing laws passed by Congress in 1986 expanding these programs.[43]

This improved the climate for considering preschool mandates as the mid-1980s drew near. In 1983 Congress passed a new program that provided planning and development grants to help states enhance coverage and management of preschool programs. And in 1986, immediately preceding the passage of the preschool program, Congress passed the Handicapped Children's Protection Act, which authorized payment of attorney's fees to parents who prevailed in administrative or court proceedings regarding the 1975 program.[44] Responding to a 1984 Supreme Court ruling denying attorney's fees for parents prevailing in court suits, Congress not only reversed this ruling, but expanded parents' ability to recoup fees for representation at administrative hearings as well.[45] Its passage was hailed as a triumph for an expansive view of the civil rights of the disabled.[46]

In an increasingly supportive political environment, the research findings on the value of preschool programs discussed earlier found fertile ground. Although Charlotte Fraas of the Congressional Research Service wrote that studies had not definitively made the case for either cost savings or effectiveness of early intervention for the handicapped, advocates nonetheless used the research to argue for a federal mandate requiring all states to serve the preschool handicapped.[47] Senator Kerry proclaimed on the Senate floor that Senator Weicker's 1986 preschool handicapped bill would save $3 for every $1 invested.[48] Such savings had become the conventional wisdom, accepted by both advocates and those state and local representatives concerned about the cost impact of a mandate.

Another factor promoting interest in a greater federal role ironically can be attributed to the federal assistance provided both in the 1975 act for preschool education and in other planning and demonstration programs funded by the federal government. First, the federal government funded much of the research discussed earlier demonstrating the value of early intervention and preschool services, including providing funding support for Early Childhood Research Institutes. Second, the preschool incentive grants in the 1975 act increased state programmatic efforts for early special education. In the first year, fiscal year 1977, only half the states participated in this incentive program, whereas all states were involved by 1986. This increased state participation is reflected in the 35 percent increase in the number of preschool children receiving special education over these years, from 197,000 to 261,000.[49] Thirty-five states mandated preschool education to at least some of their handicapped children in 1975, whereas forty-two did so as of 1986.

The 1983 legislation providing grants to states for the planning and management of preschool services also helped build a supportive state bureaucratic infrastructure.[50] State and local bureaucrats responsible for the preschool initiatives became an important lobby for federally mandated program expansions enhancing their roles.[51] Indeed, the national association representing state special education directors worked with Senator Weicker's staff in developing the 1986 mandate.

Federally funded state and local programs spurred the growth of in-state clientele served by the program, with a self-interest in lobbying for expanded state or local support. As program services awaken political awareness, parents and special education staff involved with these programs become a vital political force supporting new national legislation. Potentially, they can also make it politically expensive for elected state or local officials to mount a public campaign against a new federal mandate.

Notwithstanding the growth of state preschool programs, differences in coverage nevertheless continued, providing a rationale for national uniformity. For example, only twenty-one states required all handicapped children from three to five years of age to be served in preschool programs. Further, only seven states mandated early intervention services for infants up to two years old. Advocates used this state variability as an argument for a federal mandate.

In the 1986 House hearings, the Association of Retarded Citizens testified that since many states had not provided the services them-selves, they "must look to the federal government to provide that mandate."[52] House Subcommittee Chairman Pat Williams asked in these same hearings how long the American public should wait for states to provide preschool services and suggested that the public use the federal government to say to certain states, "That's it, time's up, let's go."[53] Once again, advocates could also use the experience of states with progressive programs as models to develop mandates to bring the uninvolved states up to these standards. In fact, Senator Weicker's staff used Texas as a model in developing their early intervention grant program for handicapped infants.

There was considerable uncertainty about how many children were unserved as a result of this state variability. As discussed before, handi-capping conditions or developmental disabilities among the very young are by no means self-evident. Accordingly, estimates varied. Using the rather expansive definition of eligibility in his bill, Senator Weicker estimated that 239,000 children were unserved.[54] However, based on a narrower definition of eligibility in the House bill, the Department of Education estimated that 70,000 children of the ages of three through five were not being served.[55] The number of unserved children would be important in estimating the costs of new legislated mandates, as discussed below.

THE SENATE PASSES A PRESCHOOL MANDATE

The disability community had been advocating a preschool program for years and were emboldened by their defeat of administration dereg-ulation and congressional passage of planning and development grants in 1983. What was needed, however, was a political entrepreneur strate-gically placed in Congress to move legislation.

Such leadership and a supportive political environment were forth-coming from the Senate Subcommittee on the Handicapped of the Senate Human Resources Committee. The subcommittee was a narrow-purpose, single-issue subcommittee. Originator of the 1975 legislation, it was structurally predisposed to serve as an advocate for handicapped causes. As one lobbyist put it, the subcommittee was a legislative backwater and without the support of handicapped groups, it would be out of business. In 1987 Senator Tom Harkin of Iowa, Weicker's chairman, noted:

> Let us face it—and again I will be very frank—this is not one of those subcommittees that necessarily helps a Senator, in the States; it is not one of those subcommittees in which you deal with the powerful influences

of high finance and other things around the country, but it is a subcommittee on which every person who sits on this subcommittee has an intense personal and professional interest in what happens to the handicapped of this country.

Most important, the subcommittee had in the mid-1980s a committed and stubborn chairman who had every personal and political reason to adopt preschool education as his own cause—Senator Lowell Weicker. Although a Republican, he was widely regarded as a liberal maverick who set his own agenda, irrespective of Reagan Administration positions. He had developed a prominent political profile on handicapped issues during his tenure as subcommittee chair, most recently steering passage of the Handicapped Children's Protection Act through a conflictual process. Given credit as the key leader in promoting more expansive rights for parents in that legislation, Weicker had developed close relations with the disabled community.[56] Weicker also had a mentally retarded son, which fueled his commitment to disability issues as well.

Weicker also was in an ideal strategic position to move legislation on preschool programs. He chaired both the authorizing subcommittee as well as the Appropriations Subcommittee, which would be responsible for providing funding for any new program Congress enacted. He was thus in an ideal position to defuse state and local concerns about the congressional commitment to funding any new mandate.

Given his strong personal incentives, Weicker took the initiative in early 1986 by introducing a bill. Several key lobbyists for the disabled, who became important players in mobilizing support once the bill was introduced, credit Weicker alone as the principal actor who put the issue on the agenda, against their own judgment about its political acceptability that year.[57]

Weicker was able to secure unanimous support of his subcommittee for this initiative, as most handicapped legislation enjoyed bipartisan consensus throughout the legislative process. True to this bipartisan tradition, the ranking minority member, Democratic Senator John Kerry from Massachusetts, signed on as a cosponsor. The next most senior Republican was Robert Stafford, a liberal Republican from Vermont, who also signed on as a cosponsor. Recall that he had joined with liberal Democrats in 1975 to protest the omission of three- to five-year-olds from the original mandate. For Stafford, the civil rights issue at stake in providing these children an equal educational opportunity far outshadowed its costs. Further, as Stafford's staff explained, Vermont would get more federal funds to serve the three- to five-year-olds they were already committed to serve.

Weicker's staff developed a bill in tandem with a number of groups in the disabled community. They also consulted with the state directors of special education, who Senate staff felt favored a mandate as a lever to obtain higher funding from their elected officials. Notably absent from prebill negotiations and subsequent Senate hearings were representatives of school boards, school administrators, governors, and state legislators. The Weicker bill sailed through the subcommittee without a formal markup or vote, thanks to the deference accorded the chairman and the informal input provided by other members' staff in drafting the bill.

The bill reported out of subcommittee established two new program initiatives addressed at the two age groupings of the preschool handicapped population. First, the bill extended the mandate of the 1975 legislation to the three- to five-year-old children, thereby requiring states and localities to provide them with a free appropriate education. The bill also mandated states to include all preschool children defined as being "developmentally delayed," a potential expansion in coverage from the 1975 definition keyed to specific categories of disability. The regulatory conditions of PL 94-142 would also be extended to this younger group, thus requiring preparation of individual development plans for each child, integration of these children in environments with their nonhandicapped peers where possible, provision of related medical and transportation services necessary for these children to participate, and procedural rights to parents aggrieved by school decisions. States failing to adhere to the mandate after two years would lose all federal funds for handicapped education, including those provided under PL 94-142 for the six- to seventeen-year-old group. Importantly, no new federal funding authorization was provided for this new mandate.

Second, the bill established a new grant program of $100 million to the states for early intervention services to handicapped infants from birth through two years of age. State participation would be voluntary, but states choosing to participate would have to provide all eligible infants comprehensive early intervention services from health, education, and social welfare agencies. An individualized plan of service would have to be developed for each infant, with the involvement of the parents, and the state would be mandated to provide the services specified in that plan. Services would have to be provided at no cost to the family, and parents would have procedural rights to appeal decisions made about their child. Regarding eligibility, handicapped infants were defined to include those who are "substantially developmentally delayed" and those with specific congenital conditions.

Interestingly, Weicker's staff was willing to accommodate some of the states' concerns about the early intervention program, but not the three- to five-year-old mandate. Because the early intervention program was to be an assistance program, state participation was voluntary. Moreover, only seven states had such comprehensive programs in 1986, and the amount of funding authorized was acknowledged to be only a minor share of the eventual costs of a program serving all eligible children.

Mindful of these constraints, Weicker's staff recognized that states were to be partners in this program, with the power to exit if the conditions proved to be too onerous. Unlike other major assistance programs, the limited support authorized for this program made non-participation a realistic option for states. Accordingly, Weicker's staff resisted pressure from advocates to mandate expansive eligibility rules that would require states to cover apparently nonhandicapped children who had biological or environmental risks of becoming disabled.[58] This is consistent with the work of Nathan and of Derthick, who both have argued that the federal reliance on states as partners in grant arrangements requires the cooptation and support of a "vertical coalition" of state and local service providers, introducing a decentralizing bias into program design and implementation.[59]

Weicker's staff, however, did not feel that such forbearance was in order in developing the three- to five-year-old mandate. Although states could technically sidestep the preschool mandate by relinquishing all federal handicapped education grant money, this was not a realistic option, given the large federal dollars provided to states. As discussed in Chapter 1, this mandate could be defined as a crossover sanction, whereby failure to comply with the requirement triggers the loss of a major grant that states have come to depend on. Given the choice of this mandating strategy, states would not have the exit option available to them, thereby depriving them of the leverage they could attain in a partnership program.

Once legislation has been placed on the congressional agenda by a subcommittee to provide benefits to the handicapped, conservatives have traditionally been wary of appearing to oppose such a consensual value. Any conservative concerns over costs or federalism typically have had to be addressed behind closed doors, either by quashing any attempt to keep it off the agenda entirely or in markup or private negotiation. When Chairman Hatch advised Senator Quayle during markup of the attorney's fees bill that he could always put a hold on the bill following committee approval, Quayle said that "no one is going to stop" such legislation once it gets going.[60] Moreover, conservatives were led to believe that no action would be taken in the House that term, so they could rely on House inaction to kill the bill without taking public positions that could later cause trouble with their state's disability groups.

One veteran lobbyist for the Council for Exceptional Children—a major disability interest group representing over a million parents and special education teachers—suggested another reason for conservative acquiescence on this kind of bill.[61] He views federally mandated services for the handicapped as a middle-class entitlement. Those families most likely to use the various procedural protections to fight for the best education for their children under PL 94-142 have been found to be middle- or upper-income families.[62]

Senator Orrin Hatch, a Republican from Utah, was chair of the full Human Resources Committee, so his concurrence was vital. As chairman, one would think that Hatch would be strategically positioned to either quash or significantly modify the bill. Practically, Hatch's staff felt his options were limited. Unlike chairmen in the days before the congressional reforms of the 1970s, Hatch did not have the power to stop Weicker from holding hearings or his own markup in subcommittee. Further, he recognized that conservatives were in fact a minority on the full committee on issues such as these because Republicans Weicker and Stafford could be depended on to vote with committee Democrats. Weicker had not even negotiated with Hatch's staff prior to the drafting of his bill or the subcommittee approval.

Once Weicker's subcommittee reported the bill, it became politically unstoppable, and even Hatch felt personally disposed to support it in principle. When first elected from Utah in 1976, Hatch came to Washington as an upstart conservative, but as he became chair of the committee following the 1980 elections, he proved to be surprisingly supportive of certain liberal-sponsored legislation, including that for the handicapped.[63] His state has a strong disability constituency as well, which he has attempted to organize for his political benefit, bolstered by the strong credo of the Mormon Church. His staff describe him as a fiscal conservative, except for elderly and handicapped issues. He supported the expansive attorney's fee bill in 1986 and opposed the 1982 deregulation effort by the administration to loosen regulations for the PL 94-142 program. He had previously organized a handicapped advisory committee from his own state.

Although Hatch supported Weicker's bill, he was also aware of the schools' objections to the new mandate from contacts with Washington lobbyists for the schools.[64] Accordingly, he held up the markup in full committee until Weicker agreed to modifications, but he did receive considerable mail protesting his delay.

Mindful of the need to pass a bill before the clock ran out on the 99th Congress and, in all likelihood, his chairmanship, Weicker was disposed to compromise. Accordingly, several substantive changes were made to ameliorate the impact of the mandate on schools at Hatch's behest, including a one-year delay in the mandates and a further delay if funding failed to increase. The funding increase was a proposal both advocates and schools could embrace and Weicker could help achieve this as chairman of the relevant appropriations subcommittee. Finally, Hatch bargained for several earmarked research and demonstration programs for Utah. Weicker was not averse to engaging in distributional logrolling to enhance support for the legislation. He had already earmarked funds for Hawaiian programs to obtain the cosponsorship of that state's two senators.[65]

The only conservative voice protesting the bill publicly at this stage was the administration, represented by Education Secretary William Bennett. Much like in 1975, the administration was the lone conservative dissenter on special education mandates, and for most of the same reasons. Expanding the PL 94-142 represented a "serious encroachment" on local and state control of education, according to Bennett, and the new infant early intervention program was too prescriptive. Moreover, authorizing new domestic programs was felt to be inappropriate, given the large budget deficit.

Although senatorial conservatives, perhaps even Hatch to some extent, may have furtively agreed with Bennett, none felt that they could afford to be publicly associated with opposition to such laudatory and consensual public values. The bill obtained the unanimous approval of the full committee, and so confident were Weicker and Hatch of the bipartisan unanimity, they placed the bill on the unanimous consent calendar.

The particular advantage of this procedure in the Senate is that it thwarts efforts to attach nongermane amendments to legislation. Reflecting the consensual support, most disability legislation is passed on unanimous consent to avoid the temptation of members to attach politically odious amendments on issues like abortion to such politically irresistible legislation. Unanimous consent also permits quick movement with minimal debate. Despite the quiescence of conservatives, Weicker's staff was concerned about the potential political fallout from a CBO estimate that the bill's three- to five-year-old mandate could cost states and localities between $535 million and $2.7 billion. Notwithstanding this cost estimate, the bill passed unanimously, with the strongest plaudits from conservative Republican Whip Alan Simpson of Wyoming.

Shortly after passage, Weicker delivered on his funding promise. His appropriations subcommittee reported a fiscal year 1987 appropriations funding bill that included full funding for the new infant program and more money for the regular PL 94-142 to accommodate the new three- to five-year-old mandate, in spite of the recent passage of the Gramm-Rudman-Hollings deficit-reduction legislation. This action sought to defuse the concerns of schools about the costs of the new provisions and to heighten the enthusiasm of disability groups to press for action in a reluctant House.

THE BILL BREAKS THROUGH TO THE HOUSE AGENDA

The relevant House subcommittee was the Subcommittee on Select Education of the Education and Labor Committee. Its chairman, Pat Williams, and the entire subcommittee had just finished the Handicapped Children's Protection Act of 1986, whose passage was marked by unprecedented divisions and bitter rivalries among the organizations representing the disabled. Following the Supreme Court's decision overturning the award of attorney's fees to parents of handicapped children for court cases challenging local decisions under PL 94-142, the established groups representing providers such as special education personnel favored legislation awarding fees in court cases, whereas some of the more radical groups favored awarding fees to parents prevailing in administrative proceedings as well. The schools had vigorously opposed the broader legislation, summoning a grassroots effort. Williams had favored a more moderate approach, only to be overruled when the radicals joined forces with civil rights organizations and prevailed on the full committee chairman, Augustus Hawkins, to support the broader bill. Disability groups, having grown accustomed to controlling the subcommittee, called Williams' staff director a "traitor."[66] Harkening back to the era when handicapped legislation enjoyed consensus support and easy passage, the more recent split within the disabled coalition took the joy out of serving on this subcommittee.[67]

Having just been through the fight over the attorney's fees bill, Williams was ambivalent and reluctant to take up the Weicker bill. As chairman of the subcommittee, he was expected to be a friend of the handicapped and supportive of key legislation favored by the disabled community. However, he was a five-term Democratic congressman from the eastern part of Montana who had strong ties to the local schools. Although a union stronghold, his district did not have a strong grassroots network of disabled organizations. The head of the disabled coalition's education task force noted that they had to use other members and staff to persuade Williams to take up the Weicker bill since they lacked grassroots organizations in Montana.[68]

The schools, by contrast, did have a strong grassroots network in the state. School board members were important politicians in the district in their own right. The statewide association of school boards was led by Williams' brother-in-law. Williams himself was a former public school teacher. Accordingly, he was sympathetic to the schools' concerns about the burden of special education mandates.

There were, however, more fundamental reasons for the reluctance of the House to consider the Weicker bill. The Democrats stood a good chance of regaining control of the Senate in the 1986 elections. Rather than let Weicker take credit for such a politically appealing bill, they would have gained more advantage by delaying action until the next congressional term, thereby producing a fully Democratic bill. On a more personal level, Weicker would receive full credit for a bill passed in 1986, whereas Williams might get nothing but political flack from groups like the schools who were dissatisfied with the outcome. However, credit claiming also explains why Williams subsequently agreed to take up the bill.

Following the Senate's action, Williams became the target of considerable pressure, not only from Weicker himself, but from Democratic leaders such as Senator Edward Kennedy, as well as from the disabled community. But perhaps the most important influence came from an attempt by a House rival for leadership of the issue. Congressman Mario Biaggi, a Democrat from New York, had developed close ties to the disabled community and had earlier turned down the opportunity to chair the Subcommittee on Select Education. He was the champion of the radical position on the attorney's fees bill in the House. In the process, he alienated the school lobbyists; one suggested that he was an enemy of the public school system. Several lobbyists from the disabled community approached Biaggi and wrote a bill based on Weicker's bill, which he agreed to sponsor. Concerned with the preemption of his institutional leadership, Williams agreed to hold hearings on the issue, thereby forestalling Biaggi's initiative.

The House Subcommittee Seeks to Accommodate State and Local Concerns

The nature of the subcommittee and the full Education and Labor Committee also influenced the outcome. As with the Senate, the Subcommittee on Select Education was a noncontroversial subcommittee, accustomed to doing business by consensus on legislation that was difficult to publicly oppose. The subcommittee's jurisdiction was limited to disability education programs, and the disability groups came to feel that they "owned" the subcommittee.

Nevertheless, the schools were very much part of the effective constituency of the subcommittee. The ties of its chairman, Pat

Williams, to the school community were discussed earlier. Its ranking minority member—Congressman Steven Bartlett, a Republican from Dallas—proved to be supportive of the schools' concerns. Unlike his more liberal Republican counterparts in the Senate, Bartlett was a conservative Republican with concerns for state and local costs, partly arising from his local government roots as past member of the Dallas city council. (In 1991, Bartlett quit his seat to run for mayor of Dallas.) Nevertheless, Bartlett had asked to join the subcommittee because its size enabled him to become the ranking minority member as a freshman.

Bartlett hoped to help disabled children through federal subsidies to schools, not through mandates. Supporting federal assistance for special education enabled him to protect both the beneficiaries of these programs and the local taxpayers, whom he viewed as an integral part of his constituency. He gained credibility with the disability community, due to his willingness to modify and not obstruct legislative proposals. As he noted in an interview, any changes had to be articulated to help beneficiaries, and the state and local interest would be protected only in ways consistent with the interests of the beneficiaries.[69] His effectiveness on the subcommittee was enhanced by his reputation as a stalking horse for the administration's Assistant Secretary of Education, Madeline Will. He effectively held a veto on legislation when the subcommittee operated on a consensus basis, as it did with the preschool legislation.

Finally, the full House Education and Labor Committee served as a constraint on the subcommittee. The subcommittee enjoyed considerable autonomy from the full Education and Labor Committee as long as, in the words of one schools' lobbyist, "they don't screw it up."[70] The schools had become a key part of the full committee's constituency or issue network over the years. Congressman Goodling, the full committee's ranking minority member, was a former school superintendent and member of the American Association of School Administrators. In fact, one-third of the fifteen members of the full committee were former teachers or school officials. Although a bastion of federal categorical programs, the committee had become sensitized to the schools' demands for more federal assistance over the years.[71]

A lobbyist for the schools concluded that the House Education and Labor Committee members are more protective of the financial interests of the schools than their Senate counterparts. He attributes this to the broader constituencies of the average senator, resulting in the balancing of the schools against other advocacy groups active at the state level. In contrast, within the narrower confines of the average House district, the schools are likely to overshadow other groups, particularly those of handicapped organizations, which are more likely to be organized at the state rather than the local level.[72]

THE SCHOOLS AWAKEN TO THE COST IMPACTS OF THE SENATE BILL

Perhaps the most important factor responsible for favorable House attention to the schools' concerns, however, was the successful mobilization of the schools on this issue. Unlike the asbestos issue, their interest groups were able to mount an effective and unified campaign from the grassroots level. Given the generally supportive environment of the House committee discussed earlier, such an effort was bound to achieve some success.

Organizations representing the interests of the schools—the National Association of School Boards and the American Association of School Administrators—and the general-purpose governmental lobbying organizations were not directly involved in the Senate deliberations. Although Hatch did negotiate for a three-year delay in the legislation's effective date to give schools more time to adjust, the bill emerged from the Senate with little change from the version first introduced by Weicker. The lobbyist for the American Association of School Administrators said that every one of their suggestions for changes in the Weicker bill was ignored.[73]

Once raised on the congressional agenda by the Senate action, the schools were bound in their public positions to support the basic purpose of the legislation and the need for a program. As with the asbestos mandate, providing education for preschool handicapped children tapped a strong and compelling consensual value. Although they could not publicly urge defeat of the program on its merits, the schools made an argument for full federal funding in the form of a judicially enforceable entitlement supported by a dedicated funding source.[74] Given the federal budget deficit, Congress would be highly unlikely to even consider such an measure. Practically speaking, the schools were recommending that the bill be killed without publicly saying so.

The schools also argued against the Weicker bill's coverage of the "developmentally delayed," pointing out that this would expand the coverage of existing preschool programs to cover children prone to, but not actually suffering from, handicaps. Further, they alleged that the mandate would cause other funding sources, most notably Medicaid, to stop paying for related health services for the preschool group, due to the requirement placed on schools to provide for these services.

Unlike the asbestos mandate, however, the schools were unified in their position and could mobilize an intense grassroots campaign against the Senate bill by local school board members and administrators in the House. At the urging of their Washington associations, hundreds of schools wrote letters to Williams and Bartlett expressing their support for full guaranteed funding.

Why did this bill call forth such intense opposition from the schools? The answer lies in what Anthony Downs once called the "issue-attention cycle."[75] Unlike the asbestos issue, the schools had a twelve-year track record with unfunded or partially funded federal mandates for special education. The schools' support for the original 1975 legislation was of course heavily influenced by the promise of federal funding to help finance a mandate that judicial rulings had made inevitable. However, they subsequently had become painfully aware of the costs accompanying that mandate, a burden exacerbated by the federal government's failure to come even close to providing 40 percent of the costs as promised by that legislation. Intergovernmental conflict over such special education issues as health and transportation services for disabled children and attorney's fees had made schools wary of new federal mandates in the area.[76]

Schools had become aware of the painful trade-offs necessary to finance the new mandates in an era of declining public support for government and its programs. The Washington lobbyist for the Association of School Administrators attributes the militancy of their Federal Policy Committee to the experience of the committee's chair, the school administrator of Pittsburgh. Because urban districts have disproportionate concentrations of handicapped children, they are disproportionately affected. Funding for the special education mandate competes with, and sometimes crowds out, funding for disadvantaged children in these hard-pressed districts with limited fiscal capacity.[77]

Frank Machiarrola says that due to federal, state, and court mandates, special education had emerged as "the most protected of all educational services."[78] New York City was spending a quarter of its education budget on special education. However, thanks to federal and state mandates, these programs largely escaped budget cuts, forcing disproportionate reductions on regular class activities. For example, until the city obtained a waiver in 1991, it could not increase class size for the 70,000 learning-disabled students above 12 per class.[79]

One observer warned that the failure of special education to better integrate with the general educational program was eroding political support in the community and causing resentment by teachers and other school professionals.[80] This souring of support was manifest in 1983, when legislation was introduced in fourteen states to curtail special education entitlements or reduce protections.[81] Frank Machiarrola, former chancellor of the New York City school system, observes that the growing public ambivalence about special education was partly due to the heightened skepticism toward government, epitomized by the tax limitation movement and the election of President Reagan, and partly due to the inevitable uncertainties surrounding the implementation of a major new social venture. He aptly quotes Wallace Sayre: "The benefits of reform are immediate; the costs cumulative."[82]

These trade-offs permitted schools to mount publicly defensible arguments against new special education mandates by suggesting that other widely valued programs or clientele would suffer as a result. Schools could thus change the lines of conflict by transforming the definition of the issue. This argument proved to be telling in gaining the political support of a key ally—the teachers.

The school lobbyists anxiously sought the support of the two principal organizations representing teachers—the powerful National Education Association and the smaller American Federation of Teachers (AFT). Such appeals failed on the asbestos issue, partly because asbestos was still a proposed mandate with no cost record and partly because teachers, as workers in school buildings, were direct beneficiaries of asbestos abatement. However, on the preschool mandates in 1986, the unions were split, with the NEA supporting quick passage of the Weicker bill and the AFT aligned with the schools and opposed to passage without federal entitlement funding. In their testimony before the House subcommittee, the AFT joined the schools in concluding that education reform programs would have to be cut to find the funds for the new mandate.[83]

Teachers reportedly had come to resent the status and resources enjoyed by special education teachers and programs, feeling that regular education programs were being shortchanged.[84] This reflects a broader shift in the education debate, as concerns for the quality of education had come to replace the concern over equity and access as the dominant issues facing schools in the 1980s.[85]

The Vice President of the National School Boards Association characterized the AFT position as one of two critical factors that prompted the House to modify the Weicker bill, the other being a supportive House Committee on Education and Labor.[86] The schools' position was also supported by the two organizations representing state elected officials—the National Governors' Association and the National Conference of State Legislatures (NCSL). Since the schools were not the primary service provider for handicapped infants, the committee solicited the views of the NGA and NCSL on this portion of the Weicker bill. The NGA indicated that a new mandate must be accompanied by adequate assurances of funding and that it could not support the Weicker bill, which lacked such guarantees.[87] The NGA also argued that the infant program be delayed, pending study of critical implementation issues such as the definition of infants and conditions covered. Nevertheless, the NGA was supportive of the goals of early intervention, as expanding early childhood education and social service programs became a key strategy for governors in responding to the problems of the underclass.

One sign of the success of the intergovernmental lobby in raising the salience of the cost issue was the House reaction to the CBO cost estimate of the Senate bill, which projected additional costs ranging from $530 million to $2.7 billion from the three- to five-year-old mandate alone.[88] The CBO projected that an additional 265,000 to 600,000 children would have to be served under the expansive mandate and definition under the Senate bill. Though the estimate did not affect the Senate debate, the staff director of the House subcommittee could not ignore it, given the sensitivity of Pat Williams, Steve Bartlett, and the broader committee to school costs.

Accordingly, once Williams decided to do a bill, the House staff met with the CBO estimators to discretely lobby them to lower the estimate. The CBO's cost estimate was partly reflective of the impact of including preschoolers with developmental delays. A new estimate was produced by the Department of Education that projected that the Senate bill would cause only an additional 70,000 children to be served, rather than the higher number used by the CBO. Ultimately, the CBO used this smaller figure in preparing a lower cost estimate for the House bill's reduced mandates, estimating state and local costs to be $575 million.[89]

THE HOUSE BILL: THE POLITICS OF CONSENSUS

Although Pat Williams was pressured to take action by the advocates, he and his staff realized that precious little time remained until the end of the session. Holding "emergency" hearings in July 1986 and facing a pending September adjournment for elections, Williams felt that quick passage would be guaranteed only with a consensus bill that could pass on the House floor under suspension of the rules procedures. Consequently, he had to satisfy the schools' concerns, as well as those of Congressman Bartlett. These latter two actors enjoyed perhaps their greatest leverage at this point, given both the need for consensus and the fact that they did not require or want a bill.

To engineer consensus, Williams adopted an innovative strategy tailored for someone caught between two conflicting constituencies.

Rather than get himself in the middle between the advocacy groups and the schools, as happened with the fees bill, he decided to convene negotiating sessions, chaired by his staff director, S. Gray Garwood. Participants included the key interest groups involved—the National Association of School Boards and the American Association of School Administrators from the schools and several groups representing the disabled community, ranging from the more moderate Council for Exceptional Children to the more radical Association of Severely Handicapped, who represented the severest mentally retarded and whose director chaired the education task force of a forty-organization umbrella group of disability associations. Congressman Bartlett's and Congressman Goodling's staff from the full committee also participated.

Following five days of negotiations, a consensus bill to replace the Senate bill emerged. A major reason for the success was that each party feared the worst if they walked out of the talks. The disabled community could not leave for fear of jeopardizing chances for a bill that could pass the House. The schools could not risk seeing a bill developed without their input, a bill that might gain full approval from a House loathe to vote against the handicapped. The Republicans recognized that they had unique leverage as long as they were needed to form a consensus and feared that a bill drafted without their input might nevertheless come to the floor in a manner that could not be publicly opposed. For his part, Williams did not have the appetite to risk another bruising conflict with the disabled groups and schools.[90]

All parties to the negotiations, including the more radical disability organizations, realized that the mandate in the Senate bill for three- to five-year-old coverage would have to be withdrawn to gain the support of the schools. Recognizing that this new group of beneficiaries could not be entirely denied, the schools sought to convert what they perceived to be a Senate mandate into a voluntary assistance program. The House bill accomplished this by removing the sanction in the Senate bill that would withhold all federal funding for handicapped education if states failed to serve all three- to five-year-olds within three years.[91] Instead, the House created a new preschool assistance program and gave states up to five years to fully cover all three- to five-year-old children; states choosing to opt out would simply not be eligible for this more limited pool of money, and they would lose a small share of the portion of their basic handicapped education grant based on the number of preschool children served. The school groups also developed a formula for this new program that promised to provide significant funds for each child served if fully funded in the appropriations process.

Schools also succeeded in eliminating the developmentally delayed language for the new three- to five-year-old program. Instead, states choosing to cover this new group of children would use the eligibility definitions for the regular handicapped education program. The new early intervention program that covered infants from birth through two years of age would, however, be geared toward children with developmental delays, provided that each state would be permitted to define that term as it saw fit.

Subcommittee staff felt that the early intervention program would prompt the greatest disagreement and be the most difficult to include in a consensual bill. After all, only seven states had such a program covering all infants from birth through age two, and the schools were only one of several state and local services that would be engaged. States choosing to participate would have to comply with an extensive and potentially expensive new mandate that could well exceed the limited funding authorization. They would also be obligated to provide health, education, and social services called for by an individualized family service plan tailored to each child.

However, neither Bartlett nor the NGA fought the need for a basic program. The NGA's own platform called for stepped-up early intervention services, and Bartlett's home state of Texas had one of the most advanced early intervention programs in the country. Rather, the debate centered around the extent to which states would be free not to opt out of the program. Bartlett's strategy was to convert mandates into a grant, which was calculated to gain the support of both the beneficiaries and the states. He argued that a voluntary program does not penalize states, but has financial incentives sufficient to "fuel local advocates" seeking to gain the benefits of early intervention for their states.[92]

Although the Senate bill provided for a voluntary assistance program with a limited $50 million authorization, states participating would be mandated to cover all eligible children after the first three years. The House negotiators agreed to give states five years, and states could still opt out of the program before they had to implement benefits for all covered eligibles.

The negotiations concluded successfully with a bill that gained unanimous passage at subcommittee, full committee, and House floor, where it passed under a suspension of the rules. Facing the end of the session and the disabled community's support for the House bill, Weicker had no choice but to agree with it. Accordingly, the Senate adopted the House bill without a conference. President Reagan's signature might have been questionable, given the administration's earlier opposition to the bill. However, the Council for Exceptional Children mobilized a letter-writing campaign that tapped its 1,000 chapters throughout the country. Moreover, the White House, rebuffed in the 1982 effort to deregulate the basic handicapped education program, had become weary of taking on the disabled community, particularly when the schools felt their concerns had been addressed. Consequently, the bill was signed, albeit absent a signing ceremony.

THE POISONED CARROT?

The passage of time permits us to briefly examine how the schools' political success affected state and local decisionmaking. Although avoiding a mandate, federal goals and standards nonetheless came to dominate the priorities and budgets of state and local governments. The achievement of some level of national uniformity and new services in the absence of a direct mandate attests to the impacts that grant programs can have in promoting national goals.

States have now adopted the federal standards for the three- to five-year-old program. The additional funding appropriated for the program provided sufficient incentive for most states to either start a program or extend existing programs to cover all preschool children. Although the new program funds enticed state participation, the program came at a price for states. Federal standards similar to the basic special education program, which covered such issues as individualized plans and comprehensive services, had to be adopted as well. The federal subsidy, moreover, did not go far in some states in covering the additional costs. For instance, in the early years of implementation, the federal payment of $1,200 per child fell far short of average per child costs, ranging from $5,800 per year in Iowa to $14,000 in New York.[93]

The Part H early intervention program had a more tumultuous implementation history. All states received grants the first three years of the program for planning and capacity building, but a number threatened to exercise their option to drop out after the fourth year, when they were scheduled to accept responsibility for implementing a full-scale program. States faced a daunting set of mandates and requirements should they agree to this final program adoption. They would have to provide parents of all eligible children the opportunity to develop individual plans for covered children from birth to two years of age, and they were obligated to provide the services called for in that plan. States were particularly anxious about being sued by parents when local providers failed to deliver. Moreover, only a small portion of these costs would be covered by new federal Part H money. For instance, Maryland's application estimated a $52 million total cost, with only $1.4 million coming from this program.[94]

To gain participation of these states, Congress gave them more time to develop a program before the full responsibilities were triggered. Eventually, all states accepted full responsibility for the program and its mandates.[95]

To explain the states' participation, one must go beyond financial incentives to look at the impact of such a program on advocacy groups and parents within each state. Research on other federally assisted programs tells the same story: Federal seed money increases the action and influence of political forces within each state.[96] This is what Congressman Steven Bartlett had in mind when he assured disability advocates that a grant would ultimately accomplish the same goals as a mandate by fueling the interests of parents and advocates of the disabled. Bartlett articulated what McCubbins labelled the "fireman's" theory of federal influence, that is, that third parties at the state and local level with vested interests in achieving federal goals and standards would oversee implementation more effectively than hard-pressed federal bureaucrats could accomplish alone.[97]

IMPLICATIONS

This case shows what can happen when states or localities attain sufficient unity and intensity on federal mandate issues. Given that disability issues are politically untouchable, transforming the proposed mandate into a federal grant was a state and local lobbying success.

Why did the schools succeed? In the issue attention cycle, the costs of special education mandates in general had become more salient over the years, facilitating the mobilization of local schools. The schools were able to shift the terms of the debate and lines of conflict away from the compelling goals served by the mandate and toward the compelling goals that the mandate threatened—including school reform and property tax levels. This shift enabled them to attract an important ally in the American Federation of Teachers, a chink in the armor of the beneficiary coalition supporting the mandate. Finally, unlike on the asbestos issue, the House committee considering this legislation was disposed to view schools as a vital part of their issue network, a part instrumental to achieving many of the other program goals of the committee.

Yet, this political victory delayed rather than denied the claims of those pressing for a mandate, and it is doubtful whether state and local interests would have been successful if they had sought to totally defeat new preschool initiatives. The incentives of the grant program induced states to participate and thereby nationalized the educational priorities of states and localities with most of the attendant fiscal and political consequences of a mandate. Although avoiding a mandate, federal goals and standards nonetheless came to dominate the priorities and budgets of state and local governments throughout the country.

NOTES TO CHAPTER 7

1. Max Neiman, "The Virtues of Heavy-Handedness in Government," in John Brigham and Ken W. Brown, ed., *Policy Implementation: Penalties or Incentives?* (Beverly Hills: Sage, 1980), p. 28.

2. Richard Scotch, *From Good Will to Civil Rights* (Philadelphia: Temple University Press, 1984).

3. See Jeffrey Berry, *Lobbying for the People: The Political Behavior of Public Interest Groups* (Princeton: Princeton University Press, 1977).

4. Robert A. Katzmann, *Institutional Disability: The Saga of Transportation for the Disabled* (Washington, D.C.: Brookings Institution, 1986), p. 189.

5. *Ibid.*, p. 76.

6. See Timothy J. Conlan and Stephen L. Abrams, "Federal Intergovernmental Regulation: Symbolic Politics in the New Congress," *Intergovernmental Perspective* (Summer, 1981), pp. 19–26.

7. Laurence E. Lynn Jr., "The Emerging System for Educating Handicapped Children," *Public Policy* 2 (January, 1983), pp. 26–34.

8. Paul E. Peterson, Barry G. Rabe, and Kenneth K. Wong, *When Federalism Works* (Washington, D.C.: Brookings Institution, 1986).

9. U.S. Congress, House, Committee on Education and Labor, *Elementary and Secondary Amendments of 1969*, report to accompany H.R. 514, 91st Congress, 1st Session, Report No. 91–114 (Washington, D.C.: U.S. Government Printing Office, 1969), p. 5.

10. S. Gray Garwood, "The Role of Theory in Studying Infant Behavior," in *Educating Handicapped Infants: Issues in Development and Intervention,* ed. S. G. Garwood and R. R. Fewell (Rockville, Md.: Aspens Systems, 1983).

11. Paul E. Peterson, Barry G. Rabe, and Kenneth K. Wong, *When Federalism Works*, p. 56.

12. *Pennsylvania Association of Retarded Citizens (PAR) v. Commonwealth of Pennsylvania*, 334 F. Supp. 1257 (E.D. Pa. 1972).

13. *Mills v. Board of Education of the District of Columbia*, 348 F. Supp. 866 (D.D.C. 1972).

14. Charlotte J. Fraas, *PL 94-142, the Education for All Handicapped Children Act: Its Development, Implementation, and Current Issues* (Washington, D.C.: Congressional Research Service, Library of Congress, 10 February 1986), p. 10.

15. *Ibid.*, p. 11.

16. "Aid to Education of Handicapped Approved," *Congressional Quarterly Almanac* (Washington, D.C.: Congressional Quarterly Press, 1985), pp. 651–655.

17. The one significant amendment adopted on the floor provided for a preschool incentive grant to states, sponsored by Senator Stafford. This will be discussed in the next section.

18. Charlotte Fraas, *PL 94–142, the Education for All Handicapped Children Act*, p. 32.

19. Stanford Research Institute International, *Local Implementation of P.L. 94-142* (Menlo Park, Ca.: Stanford Research Institute, December, 1982). Comptroller General of the United States, *Disparities Still Exist in Who Gets Special Education*, IPE-81-1 (Washington, D.C.: U.S. General Accounting Office, 1981). *Topics in Early Childhood Special Education*, 8, No. 1 (1988).

20. U.S. Department of Education, *Tenth Annual Report to Congress on the Implementation of the Education of the Handicapped Act* (Washington, D.C.: U.S. Government Printing Office, 1988), p. 23.

21. Charlotte Fraas, *PL 94-142, the Education for All Handicapped Children Act*, p. 40.

22. Paul E. Peterson, Barry G. Rabe, and Kenneth K. Wong, *When Federalism Works*, p. 154.

23. New Mexico's participation was influenced by a successful suit brought by parents on the grounds that the state was violating Section 504 of the Rehabilitation Act, which provides for access to programs assisted with federal dollars. See Edwin W. Martin, "Lessons from Implementing PL 94-142," in *Policy Implementation and PL 99-457: Planning for Young Children with Special Needs*, ed. James J. Gallagher, Pascal L. Trahanis, and Richard M. Clifford (Baltimore: Paul H. Brooks, 1989).

24. Charlotte Fraas, *Education of the Handicapped* (Washington, D.C.: Congressional Research Service, 16 October 1986), p. 13.

25. Edward W. Martin, "Lessons from Implementing PL 94-142," pp. 155, 172–173.

26. Charlotte Fraas, *PL 94-142, the Education for All Handicapped Children Act*.

27. *Ibid.*, p. 49.

28. Roberta Weiner and Maggie Hume, . . . *And Education for All: Public Policy and Handicapped Education* (Alexandria, Va.: Capitol, 1987).

29. John C. Hogan, *The Schools, the Courts, and Public Interest* (Lexington, Mass.: D.C. Heath, 1974), p. 7.

30. Paul E. Peterson, Barry G. Rabe, and Kenneth K. Wong, p. 224.

31. Charlotte Fraas, *Preschool Programs for the Education of Handicapped Children: Background, Issues, and Federal Policy Options* (Washington, D.C.: Congressional Research Service, 17 March 1986), p. 5.

32. James J. Gallagher, "Implications of Social Policy: A Policy Analysis Challenge," in *Policy Implementation and PL 99-457*, p. 207.

33. Theodore Tjossem, "Early Intervention: Issues and Approaches," in *Intervention Strategies for High Risk and Handicapped Children*, ed. Theodore Tjossem (Baltimore: University Park Press, 1976).

34. S. Gray Garwood and Robert Sheehan, "Designing a Comprehensive Early Intervention System: The Challenge of Public Law 99-457," unpublished manuscript.

35. See literature summary in Terese J. Lilly and Jay R. Shotel, "Legal issues and the Handicapped Infant: From Policy to Reality," in *Journal of the Division for Early Childhood* 12, No. 1 (1987), p. 4.

36. *Ibid.*, p. 4.

37. S. A. Kirk, *Early Education of the Mentally Retarded* (Urbana: University of Illinois Press, 1958).

38. S. Gray Garwood and Robert Sheehan, "Designing a Comprehensive Early Intervention System: The Challenge of Public Law 99-457," p. 14.

39. *Effectiveness of Early Special Education for Handicapped Children*, Report Commissioned by the Colorado General Assembly, 1982.

40. Richard Scotch, *From Good Will to Civil Rights*, p. 164.

41. See Angela Evans, *Summary of the Proposed Regulatory Changes to Selected Provisions of the Education of the Handicapped Act-State Grant Programs* (Washington, D.C.: Congressional Research Service, 18 August 1982).

42. See Angela Evans, *Analysis of the Proposed Regulatory Changes to Major Provisions of the Education of the Handicapped Act-State Grant Program* (Washington, D.C.: Congressional Research Service, 3 September 1982).

43. The fallout from this episode included a reluctance to finalize transportation accessibility rules for the handicapped, resulting in 1982 legislation offering congressional guidance.

44. "Legal Fees for the Handicapped," *Congressional Quarterly 1986 Almanac* (Washington, D.C.: Congressional Quarterly Press, 1987), pp. 271–272.

45. *Smith v. Robinson*, 468 U.S. 992.

46. Jane E. West, *The Handicapped Children's Protection Act of 1986: A Case Study of Policy Formation* (doctoral dissertation, University of Maryland, 1988).

47. Charlotte Fraas, *Preschool Programs for the Education of Handicapped Children*.

48. *Congressional Record*, 6 June 1986, p. S7038.

49. U.S. Department of Education, *Tenth Annual Report to Congress on the Implementation of the Education of the Handicapped Act*, p. 81.

50. U.S. Department of Education, *Tenth Annual Report to the Congress on the Education for All Handicapped Children Act,*

51. The tension between state and local program bureaucrats forming vertical alliances with their federal counterparts to expand federal program initiatives and their more skeptical generalist leaders within state and local government is a manifestation of what is commonly called "picket fence" federalism. See Deil Wright, *Understanding Intergovernmental Relations* (North Scituate, Mass.: Duxbury Press, 1978), p. 145.

52. Testimony of Carol Reedstrom, Hearings before the Subcommittee on Select Education of the House Committee on Education and Labor, *The Education of the Handicapped Amendments of 1986*, Washington, D.C., U.S. Government Printing Office, 99th Congress, 2nd Session, 23 July 1986, p. 112.

53. Pat Williams' discussion in *Ibid.*, p. 134.

54. *Congressional Record*, 14 April 1986, p. S4196.

55. Unpublished data provided to the Congressional Budget Office.

56. Jane West, *The Handicapped Children's Protection Act of 1986*.

57. Interview with Fred Weintraub, Vice President, Council for Exceptional Children.

58. Interview with Loni Florian, staff assistant to Senator Weicker.

59. Richard Nathan, "State and Local Governments under Federal Grants," *Political Science Quarterly* 98, No. 1, (1983); Martha Derthick, *The Influence of Federal Grants* (Cambridge: Harvard University Press, 1970).

60. Transcript of full committee markup, Handicapped Children's Protection Act of 1986.

61. Interview with Fred Weintraub, Assistant Executive Director, Council for Exceptional Children.

62. One study concluded that most appeals under the act originated from well-to-do parents fighting school districts for expensive services for their handicapped children. See Joel F. Handler, *The Conditions of Discretion: Autonomy, Community, Bureaucracy* (New York: Russell Sage Foundation, 1986), p. 6.

63. See Julei Kisterlitz, "Tough to Typecast," *National Journal*, 19 August 1989, pp. 2088–2092.

64. Interview with Christine Lord, minority staff, full Senate Labor and Human Resources Committee.

65. Madeline Will, the Assistant Secretary of Education for Special Education, subsequently decided to award the Western grant to Alaska.

66. Interview with S. Gray Garwood, former Staff Director, Subcommittee on Select Education.

67. Interview with Fred Weintraub, Council for Exceptional Children.

68. Interview with Celane McWhorter, The Association of Severely Handicapped.

69. Interview with Congressman Steve Bartlett.

70. Interview with Bruce Hunter, American Association of School Administrators.

71. Advisory Commission on Intergovernmental Relations, *Intergovernmentalizing the Classroom: Federal Involvement in Elementary and Secondary Education* (Washington, D.C.: ACIR, 1981).

72. Interview with Bruce Hunter, American Association of School Administrators.

73. Interview with Bruce Hunter, Association of School Administrators.

74. National Association of School Boards, *Federally Mandated Pre-school Services for Handicapped Children* (Alexandria, Va., 13 August 1986).

75. Anthony Downs, "Up and Down with Ecology—The 'Issue-Attention Cycle,' " *Public Interest* (Summer, 1972).

76. Fearing that the fees bill would promote a more litigious relationship with parents, the National Association of School Boards took an intransigent position, rejecting Congressman Bartlett's attempted compromise that would have required a showing of bad faith on the part of schools for fees to be paid.

77. Interview with Bruce Hunter, Washington representative, American Association of School Administrators.

78. Frank J. Machiarrola and Robert W. Bailey, "Special Education: The Costs of Experimentation," *Policy Studies Review* 2, Special No. 1 (1983), p. 137.

79. Joseph Berger, "New York Special Education: Aiding Some with Little Need," *New York Times*, 30 April 1991, p. 1.

80. Tom Joe and Frank Furrow, "Guides for Future Special Education Policy," *Policy Studies Review*, 2, Special No. 1 (1983), p. 222.

81. *Ibid.*, p. 217.

82. Frank J. Machiarrola and Robert W. Bailey, "Special Education," p. 137.

83. Jacqueline Vaughn, Testimony before the Subcommittee on Select Education, House Committee on Education and Labor, 99th Congress, 2nd Session, 29 July 1986, p. 138.

84. Tom Joe and Frank Farrow, "Guides for Future Special Education Policy."

85. David Stedman, "Can Special Education Be Coordinated with Other Service Systems?" *Policy Studies Review* 2, Special No. 1, (1983), p. 123.

86. Interview with Michael Resnick, National Association of School Boards.

87. Statement by Alicia Smith, representing the National Governors Association, in Hearings before the Subcommittee on Select Education of the Committee on Education and Labor, House of Representatives, 99th Congress, 2nd Session, *The Education of the Handicapped Amendments of 1986* (Washington, D.C.: U.S. Government Printing Office, 24 July 1986), p. 123.

88. Letter from Rudolph G. Penner, Director of the CBO, to Senator Orrin G. Hatch, 29 May 1986, published in Senate Committee on Labor and Human Resources, 99th Congress, 2nd Session, *Education of the Handicapped Amendments of 1986*, Report No. 99-315, p. 19.

89. Letter from Rudolph G. Penner, Director of the CBO, to Congressman Augustus Hawkins, Chairman of the House Committee on Education and Labor, published in House Committee on Education and Labor, 99th Congress, 2nd Session, *Education of the Handicapped Amendments of 1986*, Report No. 99–860, 22 September 1986, p. 40.

90. The account of the negotiations is drawn from interviews with the key participants, including Fred Weintraub, Council for Exceptional Children; Celaine McWhorter, Association of Severely Handicapped; Michael Resnick, National Association of School Boards; Bruce Hunter, American Association of School Administrators; S. Gray Garwood, Staff Director of the subcommittee; Robert Silverstein, staff member with the subcommittee; and David Esquith, staff to Congressman Bartlett.

91. Some might argue that, technically, the Senate bill's provision for coverage is not a mandate because states can choose to opt out of the entire federal handicapped education program to avoid the new mandate. However, given the relatively large dollars at stake and the clientele that had come to depend on these funds within each state, the states would have practically had little choice but to comply with the new mandate.

92. Statement by Congressman Steven Bartlett, *Congressional Record*, House, 22 September 1986, p. H7904.

93. Michael deCourcy Hinds, "Nationwide Revolution in Education Is Giving Handicapped a Headstart," *New York Times*, 17 July 1991, p. A19.

94. Interview with James Hamilton, federal program official, Office of Special Education, U.S. Department of Education.

95. Interview with Bobbie Stetner Eaton, Part H Liaison, Office of Special Education, U.S. Department of Education.

96. U.S. General Accounting Office, *Federal Seed Money*, (Washington, D.C.: GAO, 1978).

97. Matthew D. McCubbins and Thomas Schwartz, "Congressional Oversight Overlooked: Police Patrols and Fire Alarms," *American Journal of Poitical Science* 28 (February, 1984), pp. 165–179.

8

The Politics of Mandate Reform

Amid much intergovernmental fanfare, Congress passed the Unfunded Mandates Reform Act (UMRA) in March 1995.[1] The first plank of the Contract with America to pass Congress and be signed by the president, it marked the culmination of a concerted effort by state and local governments and their allies within Congress to stem the increasing reliance on mandates by federal policymakers. It was hailed as both symbol and substance of a renewed congressional commitment to federalism.

The passage of mandate reform certainly constituted an important victory for state and local interest groups, and for the new Republican congressional leadership as well. The nature of the debate was transformed, as the costs imposed by mandates became just as important as the benefits realized. The passage of mandate reform illustrates how federalism values can become politically compelling in our system, at least for a time. The real question is whether such commitment would be sustained when individual mandate proposals are considered.

MANDATE REFORM ACHIEVES AGENDA STATUS

Mandates rose to federal agenda status in the early 1990s on the heels of the regulatory resurgence chronicled in earlier chapters. As noted in Chapter 1, the mandate issue has exhibited a dialectic character since its first appearance on the federal agenda in the late 1970s; mandate concern and reform is followed by mandate resurgence, which ushers in another period of federal remorse and reform.

Policy and Fiscal Pressures

The first wave of mandate concern was addressed in the early 1980s. In 1981 Congress passed legislation requiring the CBO to prepare state and local cost estimates for proposed bills reported out of committees.[2] Mandate burdens also prompted the 1980 congressional passage of the

160

Paperwork Reduction Act, establishing a paperwork budget and OMB clearance process for new federal information requirements, and the Regulatory Flexibility Act, requiring federal agencies issuing new regulations to consider less burdensome alternatives for small communities and businesses.[3] Perhaps the most important hope for regulatory relief was offered by the incoming Reagan Administration, which required OMB clearance for the first time of federal regulations proposed by the agencies and convened a Task Force on Regulatory Relief to review and modify the most burdensome private and intergovernmental regulations.

When it ended in 1983, the task force, headed by Vice President Bush, had revised such burdensome mandates as handicapped access to transportation and Davis-Bacon prevailing wage requirements, which it estimated would save states and localities $2 billion in annual costs and $4 to $6 billion in capital costs.[4] Moreover, the administration could also point to reduced burdens brought about by the congressional passage of nine new block grants, consolidating over eighty categorical grants.

Ironically, these reforms appear to have set the stage for a regulatory resurgence in the 1980s and early 1990s that ultimately prompted the most recent wave of mandate reform. First, state and local groups and other reform advocates were assuaged, and they moved on to new concerns, content that the mandate problem was being visibly addressed. One major study of the Reagan regulatory relief program, for instance, declared state and local governments to be the big winners.[5] Moreover, the deregulation initiatives of the early Reagan years prompted advocates of those programs to intensify their own lobbying and seek to recoup their losses in other forums, including Congress and the courts. Congress, seeing its legislative handiwork threatened by administration regulatory retrenchments, funding cuts, and unsympathetic political appointees, proved to be a receptive audience. By seeking regulatory change primarily through executive channels, the administration helped prompt a congressional backlash.

This backlash, in fact, helped form the policy backdrop for the reemergence of mandates as an issue. As documented in prior chapters, the reliance on mandates continued. Although the early Reagan Administration succeeded in reducing regulatory burdens administratively for such areas as handicapped transit, Congress succeeded in passing a new round of mandates in the 1980s and early 1990s, an ostensibly conservative era, that surpassed those enacted earlier.[6] As noted in prior chapters, state and local officials found it difficult to arouse grassroots concerns when these mandates were passed since the benefits of mandate legislation at the time of passage were visible and compelling.

The costs, in contrast, appeared to be vague and distant until the federal agency promulgated regulations some years later.

Major mandates that passed in the 1980s with state and local acquiescence or support later served as catalysts, arousing state and local cost concerns when agencies promulgated the accompanying regulations several years later. Regulations take time to develop, however, so the actual costs associated with the mandates of the 1980s were not perceived as salient by states and localities until the early 1990s. For instance, the safe drinking water amendments of 1986, passed with state and local support, became an intergovernmental issue once the EPA's regulations were developed several years later, requiring specific local actions on various contaminants. Many communities, particularly smaller ones, noticed these mandates for the first time when faced with specific regulatory compliance responsibilities. The earlier consensus supporting the mandate's passage dissolved, which was reflected in a 1992 amendment sponsored by Senator Domenici to reduce safe drinking water regulations that was defeated by only ten votes.

Medicaid followed a similar progression, with the enactment of new federal mandates for services to children and pregnant women from 1984 through 1990, supported by the governors. Medicaid costs grew in the late 1980s and early 1990s to comprise 13 percent of state budgets. Although higher state Medicaid costs were only partly fueled by these mandates, governors and state legislatures asked for a moratorium on Medicaid mandates and greater flexibility beginning in 1990 to help them address these health-care cost pressures.[7]

The mandates of the 1980s, then, created a bow wave of costs that crested in visibility in the early 1990s. At the same time, the resources available to state and local governments came under renewed pressure. The expansion of mandates in the 1980s corresponded with a period of relative fiscal stability and even expansion in a state and local sector rebounding strongly from the recession of the early 1980s. Although it is difficult to determine a causal relationship, it is clearly possible that stronger state and local fiscal positions may have reduced the visibility and perceived state and local cost consequences to national officials.

This period of relative state and local fiscal prosperity was followed by fiscal pressures brought on by the national recession of the late 1980s and early 1990s. Pressed to balance budgets with shrinking resources, most states engaged in spending cuts and tax increases to close budget gaps, and several states were left with deficits that had to be carried over to subsequent years.[8] In 1991 alone, states raised taxes by $14 billion.

Moreover, federal aid to states and localities was constrained by federal budget deficit pressures. Medicaid and other open-ended entitlement grants to states did increase in the 1980s and early 1990s, and states were able to use Medicaid funds for a time to free up their own spending for other purposes.[9] However, federal grants supporting state and local service delivery and operating costs fell in constant dollars during this period. From a peak of $53 billion, these grants fell to $34 billion in 1985, and dropped further to $28 billion in 1990 (in constant 1987 dollars).[10] The largest general-purpose grant to state and local governments—General Revenue Sharing, which provided over $4 billion per year to local governments—was terminated in 1986. Again, although causal linkages are difficult to define, the renewed state and local fiscal pressures most likely played a role in heightening state and local sensitivities to mandate costs while increasing the visibility of these cost concerns to national officials as well. Similarly, a study of the "fluctuating" national fortunes of American business found that the influence of business concerns in national policymaking tends to increase during periods of perceived weakness in the private economy.[11]

The Politics of Agenda Change

The latest round of reform, culminating in the passage of UMRA, then, was prompted by growing federal regulatory burdens, as well as by fiscal pressures at all levels of government. However, problems by themselves do not get placed on the agenda without a convergence of political forces that articulate the problem as a policy issue that is resolvable through federal action.[12] As noted by Conlan and Beam, ironically, some of the same forces responsible for the rapid adoption of mandates themselves also helped the mandate reform issue achieve agenda status in relatively short order.[13]

As previous chapters documented, the passage of mandates themselves was propelled by a political system that had become far more open to new ideas and rapid policy change than had previously been thought possible. Major new federal regulatory programs were often passed on the heels of the "issue attention cycle" discussed by Anthony Downs. New ideas quickly took the policy system by storm as elites and the public became alarmed by the discovery of a new problem or issue.[14] These issues took on a valence quality where it became illegitimate to openly oppose the issues as defined by advocates, thus facilitating their rapid embrace and adoption by Congress. As Baumgartner and Jones observe, major policy decisions are taken that overturn established interests and policy subsystems within a relatively short period of time, as waves of enthusiasm sweep over policymakers with little public opposition. Established policy monopolies and iron triangles weaken or disintegrate as new images of issues and problems take hold.[15]

Ideas and their rapid dissemination by an increasingly diverse and assertive set of interest groups and media outlets play a central role in producing this more open, fluid, and dynamic system. As was noted in Chapter 2, classic views of the policymaking process emphasized the dominance of interests, reinforcing an incrementalist view of a system locked into established policies and loathe to change. More contemporary views, in contrast, highlight the role of ideas and experts as agents initiating and reinforcing change. A politics based on ideas is more fluid and unpredictable than a politics based on interests.[16] Images undergirding major policies are more vulnerable to change since each policy proposal can be associated with contending views that various policy actors seek to promote.[17]

The emergence of mandate reform as an issue in the 1990s was in part grounded in a shift in ideas and policy images. The policy images giving rise to the creation of mandates took root without competition, thanks to the valence nature of the benefits purported to be fostered. As discussed in previous chapters, it was difficult to muster a politically legitimate case against asbestos in schools, handicapped education, or federal safe drinking water mandates. In the 1990s, however, a competing set of policy images were fostered, as state and local governments and their allies sought to join the struggle over defining the issues at stake.[18] These emerging images were grounded in the burdens and costs associated with the implementation of mandates and in the purported threat that these mandates posed to other policies and commitments held dear by state and local governments and their publics. Thus, for instance, the image of public health hazards played a key role in promoting federal safe drinking water mandates in the 1970s and 1980s, but competing images advanced in the 1990s of hard-pressed local taxpayers and water customers struggling to pay for these mandates have taken root in terms also compelling to policymakers.

Making the cost side of the mandate policy equation as compelling as the benefits side involved the development of convincing data to demonstrate the scope and magnitude of the problem. As Deborah Stone has argued, quantifying the size of a problem is an important way for advocates to highlight the face of an issue or policy image that helps define that issue in favorable and persuasive ways.[19] Measurement can help promote broader awareness of an issue by both policymakers and members of the group themselves.

State and local governments adroitly used estimates of the aggregate costs of mandates to fortify their image of the mandate problem. In one key study that gained national attention, Columbus, Ohio, discovered that the costs associated with unfunded mandates would grow to comprise one-fourth of their budget by 1996.[20] Other jurisdictions followed suit with their own studies. Finally, in 1993 the U.S. Conference of Mayors (USCM) and the National Association of Counties (NAACO) commissioned Price Waterhouse to survey the total costs of mandates across major jurisdictions. The USCM study reported 1993 costs for 10 major mandates of $6.5 billion for 314 responding cities; the NAACO study found $4.8 billion in costs for 12 major mandates in the counties.[21]

These estimates had their detractors—the studies did not determine whether many of these costs would have been incurred anyway by states and localities already implementing mandated functions under their own laws, and the studies did not consider offsetting federal grant funds or tax expenditures helping to reduce state and local tax bite and bond financing costs.[22] Nonetheless, the state and local estimates received wide circulation, as did more qualitative "horror stories" of state and local officials' struggles with unreasonable or inflexible mandates that caused seemingly nonsensical actions. A widely exposed story involved safe drinking water requirements for the local testing and control of an agricultural pesticide currently used only on pineapples in Hawaii. (The EPA countered that past use of this chemical in other states could pose water supply hazards for years to come and that waivers were available.)

The state and local attack on mandates received legitimacy by research undertaken by the Advisory Commission on Intergovernmental Relations. Starting with reports in the 1970s, the ACIR has traced the growth of mandates and preemptions and has documented their collective impact on state and local governments and the vitality of our system of federalism. The 1984 report entitled *Regulatory Federalism: Policy, Process, Impact and Reform* traced the growth in mandates as an intergovernmental problem, and an influential 1993 report updated that study. Its findings that the pace of new mandates enacted in the supposedly conservative devolutionary era of the 1980s had actually surpassed that of earlier decades received front-page coverage by the *New York Times* and gave new legitimacy to state and local concerns.[23] The commission also provided a body of recommendations to steer national policy consideration of the mandate issue. Over the years, for example, ACIR has recommended full federal reimbursement for additional costs imposed by mandates, a two-year moratorium on new mandates, and the establishment of preemption analyses within both

Congress and the executive branch. In the mid-1990s, ACIR helped guide consideration of the mandate reform by issuing reports charting the range of what it defined as "federally induced costs" and, at the request of the Office of Management and Budget, guidance on the development of federal mandate relief legislation.[24]

Other forces were also at work in elevating mandate reform to national agenda status. A competitive and increasingly diverse range of media outlets helps to spread new ideas and issues across different policy institutions and levels of government with remarkable speed. Always searching for new ideas and new slants on issues, the media proved to be a receptive vehicle for the transmission of mandate protests and problems experienced by various states and localities to a national stage.

The key focusing event that brought the issue to national attention in a compelling way was the first National Unfunded Mandates Day, a quintessential media event staged by state and local interest groups. On 23 October 1993, state and local governments held news conferences, public forums, and other events in Washington, as well as in other locales across the country. It was here that the national studies of mandate costs were released to the press. A study by Conlan, Riggle, and Schwartz showed that this event succeeded in transforming the mandate issue from specialized intergovernmental discourse to the broader public agenda. Their research shows a significant increase in media coverage leading up to and following the National Unfunded Mandates Day. The number of newspaper articles on unfunded mandates rose from 22 in 1992 to 836 in 1994.[25]

This catalytic event capitalized on a public mood that had grown increasingly conservative. Polls showed a growing public mistrust of Washington and a propensity to view state and local governments more favorably than the federal government. These trends accelerated during the early 1990s, according to an ACIR study. Specifically, a 1994 poll showed that 46 percent of the public felt that the federal government provided the least value for their tax dollar, up from 36 percent in 1989. State and local governments, in contrast, improved in the public perception during this period; only 21 percent of the public felt that they got the least value from states and 19 percent felt the same way about local governments.[26] Some suggested that mandate reform rode the wave of the "devolution revolution," during which elites and the broader public had reached a consensus on the need to devolve greater responsibilities to states and communities.[27]

However, as many of these polling studies are careful to note, Americans are in fact ambivalent about government. Although increasingly voicing conservative views about federal power in general,

Americans are at the same time supportive of specific programs by large majorities. As one study observed, opinions about big government exist in "splendid isolation" from views on specific aspects of governmental involvement in our society.[28]

Though a more open policymaking process surely helped promote the unfunded mandates movement, perhaps the most important factor was the mobilization of a more traditional source of policy development—state and local governments and their interest groups. Previous chapters have shown that these organizations were often crosspressured and immobilized when individual mandates with wide appeal attained agenda status. Although gaining important concessions on money and mandate flexibility, state and local groups found it difficult to mount a frontal assault against most mandates. As a result, they were often unable to effectively defend their jurisdictional prerogatives.

Although ambivalent on individual mandates, state and local groups were nonetheless able to lead the movement to place unfunded mandates on the public and governmental agendas. Actually, the unfunded mandates movement was as much led from the grassroots by individual state and local governments as it was steered by the Washington intergovernmental interest groups. As noted above, Columbus, Ohio, was but one of a number of jurisdictions estimating the costs of mandates for their own public budgets. Missouri created a Federal Mandate Auditor, whose responsibility was to inventory the costs of unfunded federal mandates. Some states went beyond estimates to pass resolutions asserting state sovereignty under the 10th Amendment to highlight the mandate issue. Other states passed laws inviting their congressional delegations to appear before state legislatures to discuss unfunded mandates. Alabama's legislature succeeded in meeting with all nine congressmen from the state, and all of them endorsed far-reaching mandate relief bills. Several states were reported to actively resist implementing federal mandates, ranging from Virginia Governor Allen's refusal to impose centralized auto emission inspections required by the EPA, to California Governor Wilson's announcement that the state would not implement "motor voter" mandates without federal funding.[29]

State and local interest groups in Washington were able to form a unified coalition whereby states, cities, and counties joined forces to highlight the unfunded mandates issue and, ultimately, support congressional allies in passing the UMRA of 1995. The ability of those groups to reach across party and jurisdictional lines to mount a concerted effort to achieve policy victory was unusual, similar to their equally successful campaign to gain adoption of general revenue sharing in 1972.[30]

Defining the issue of mandates as a general problem neatly sidestepped the political conflicts inherent in confronting broad coalitions of beneficiaries on specific mandates. Shifting the focus of the debate toward the more aggregate impacts on state and local budgets and priorities took advantage of the public's ambivalence toward government by highlighting the drift toward federal power that Americans dislike in the abstract. The question was not whether each mandate was beneficial on its own merits—a question that had stymied state and local groups before. Rather, the question became whether mandates collectively were eroding the fiscal flexibility of states and localities to satisfy the unique needs of their electorates. This was an issue that their own membership could rally behind without being crosspressured by the pull of mandate goals and beneficiaries. In fact, in advancing their cause, leaders of state and local groups were careful to articulate their support for the purposes of each mandate. As Louisville Mayor Jerry Abramson, the president of the mayors' conference said, "We're all in favor of cleaning the environment, helping the disabled and making the world a better place. What we object to is this ham-handed, one-size-fits-all approach that costs huge amounts of money and often accomplishes very little."[31]

ACTION IN CONGRESS

Reaching the public agenda was an important step for the unfunded mandates issue, but it would be futile if reforms were not adopted by the federal government. Initial signs were encouraging. The day before the National Unfunded Mandates Day, President Clinton signed executive order 12875 directing federal agencies to avoid promulgating new regulations that imposed mandates without state and local consultation and funding. Streamlining of waiver processes was also included in this order. However, the order lacked enforceability in one view since state and local governments were not given rights to seek judicial review of federal agency failures to comply.[32]

State and local governments, however, had learned from the Reagan deregulation initiatives that lasting reform must begin in Congress, not in the executive branch. As the ACIR has observed, the basic impetus for mandates comes from Congress, and mandate statutes are often far too prescriptive for administrative reform to significantly modify.[33] Moreover, the earlier administration initiatives actually may have served to exacerbate regulatory problems when Congress reacted to what it considered administration subversion of congressional priorities by initiating a new round of even more prescriptive regulatory programs.

Just as the focus of mandate reform shifted to Congress, so did the leadership. In fact, members of Congress vied with each other for leadership of the issue. In the 102nd Congress (1991–1992), twenty mandate reform bills were introduced, increasing to thirty-four bills in the 103rd Congress (1993–1994), both in Congresses with Democratic majorities.[34] In February 1993, a new Congressional Task Force on Federal Mandates was organized by Republican congressmen to develop a legislative strategy to reform mandates.

The congressional reform proposals proceeded from the same premise—that Congress had, in the words of Justice O'Connor, an "underdeveloped capacity for self-restraint" in considering mandates.[35] A breach of accountability occurs when one government can experience the joy of legislating benefits without having to recognize the costs. Since mandate programs appear to be free to Congress, the financial discipline that ordinarily constrains policy decisions is absent, perhaps permitting greater mandating than is necessary or appropriate. The congressional proposals incorporated several different approaches to institutionalize greater self-restraint within Congress in considering mandate legislation:

- *Estimation and transparency.* Some bills would have expanded the CBO's existing cost estimates to include a broader range of bills, such as budget reconciliation, appropriations, and conference legislation. Several bills would have required an annual report on the aggregate amount of additional state and local costs associated with new mandates.
- *Points of order.* This approach provides for a point of order to be raised against proposed legislation imposing unfunded mandates on the state and local sector. Mandates could still be passed by overcoming a point of order with a majority or supermajority vote of each chamber, but such a provision could help ensure a debate on the mandate itself.
- *Reimbursement.* A "no money, no mandates" approach would require full federal funding for state and local compliance costs associated with mandates and would excuse state and local noncompliance for mandates without full funding. Bills had differing definitions for mandates and for costs that would have to reimbursed.

It took several years for Congress to sift through these proposals and pass the final UMRA legislation in 1995. This was not wasted time, for important issues were at stake in designing a workable approach to mandate reform. It is sometimes not enough for a problem to be placed on the federal agenda; a solution must also be proposed that is workable and legitimate to the policy community.

Of the three approaches listed above, cost estimates alone were the most feasible but offered the least potential impact on congressional incentives or behavior. Earlier studies of the existing CBO state and local cost estimates found that they had limited impact on the course of mandate legislation, absent a prior legislative commitment to address mandated costs.[36]

Mandate reimbursement, alternatively, offered the greatest prospects for incentive shifts within Congress, but it raised a host of conceptual, political, and methodological concerns that could have derailed the mandate reform movement. When concerns over regulatory federalism first arose in Washington in the early 1980s, state and local groups as well as the Advisory Commission on Intergovernmental Relations seized on mandate reimbursement as the appropriate federal policy response.[37] As implemented in selected states, this approach would have required Congress to provide full reimbursement every time it passed a mandate, permitting state and local governments to ignore mandates passed without full funding.

Reimbursement raises a number of problems and objections in the minds of many observers. Providing a new open-ended claim on the federal treasury for state and local governments threatened federal budget policy and opened the door for protracted litigation and implementation delays, as courts would invariably be invited to decide whether the full costs were in fact reimbursed.[38] Should fiscal policy prevent full congressional funding, states and localities would be free to ignore the mandate, a prospect that some viewed as undermining the federal government's responsibility to promote a uniform level of service across the nation.[39] Moreover, some objected to the notion that state and local governments would be paid to implement constitutionally based rights and federal rules such as minimum wage or family and medical leave that private companies must bear from their own resources. Economists argued that though mandates contain benefits that are external to individual jurisdictions, they also carry benefits to the taxpayers of those communities that should rightfully be paid by them, not by the rest of the nation—full federal reimbursement would violate this principle of cost sharing.[40]

Determining reimbursement formulas would also be difficult and fraught with painful trade-offs. If scarce funding were provided only for additional costs incurred due to the mandate—an approach designed to avoid providing a fiscal windfall for existing state programs—perverse incentives would be provided by penalizing states who took the initiative prior to federal action and rewarding states and localities who chose to delay their commitment. Reimbursement would also

prove cumbersome in Congress since legislation authorizing most mandates is separate from appropriations and other funding bills that
would provide reimbursement. Perhaps due to some of these same
problems, it is not surprising that "automatic" restraints on legislative
mandating often proved to be ineffective in the states, as state legislatures felt free to ignore or circumvent reimbursement provisions,
whether based in statute or state constitutions.[41]

Given the pitfalls of both the estimating and reimbursement approaches, Congress ultimately chose to focus serious legislative attention on the point of order approach, which was to become the
centerpiece of mandate reform. This approach proved to be more workable within the congressional environment, as well as more appealing
to the bipartisan majorities necessary to pass the legislation. In essence,
the point of order approach does not *require* congressmen to respect
state and local interests on mandate issues, but rather *reminds* them to
do so.[42] This process offers a new tool to state and local interests to
shift the focus of the debate away from the benefits of the proposed
mandate to the cost implications, and it could be effective as long as
members of Congress felt that they could be politically vulnerable by
ignoring state and local cost concerns. Experience with points of order
in the congressional budget process suggests that they can be useful
when they serve the interests of a congressional majority, but are often
violated when they do not. And that is to be expected because, by their
very nature, points of order are designed to promote accountability
for certain decisions, not to prevent those decisions from being made.[43]

The key to eventual passage of this approach was the emergence
of congressional entrepreneurs who had both the motivation and the
legislative skills needed to gain congressional adoption. The dispersion
of power within Congress has opened up leadership opportunities for
many junior members who are anxious to claim credit for championing
issues of importance to their electorate, and earlier chapters have shown
how members have often chosen in the past to champion individual
mandates.[44]

Several members emerged as leaders on mandate reform. House
members such as Congressman Rob Portman were important. Senator
Dirk Kempthorne emerged as a key player. A former mayor of Boise,
Idaho, Senator Kempthorne was a freshman Republican who worked
with the Democratic majority in control of the Senate in 1993 to achieve a
pragmatic solution to a problem that had faced him as mayor. Although
initially backing a mandate reimbursement bill, he chose to craft a
bipartisan bill that could gain the acceptance of the Democratic majority
and signature by a Democratic president.[45]

Senator Kempthorne was able to find Democratic members interested in mandate reform to team with as legislative partners. It is not

unusual in our system for both parties to compete for leadership on publicly compelling issues, accounting for the wide majorities often achieved on the final passage of important legislation.[46] Senator John Glenn, a Democrat from Ohio, proved to be a willing player. Working with Ohio's governor and other state and local officials to do something about the mandate problem, he used his position as Chairman of the Senate Governmental Affairs Committee to develop the leading Senate bill.

The bipartisan bill, S993, included a stronger cost estimation provision and provided for the point of order while at the same time excluding civil rights, conditions of aid, and several other types of mandates from its purview. It received the endorsement of President Clinton and was reported out unanimously by the full committee in June 1994. However, opposition gathered from a broad-based coalition of nearly 100 health, labor, environmental, and civil rights groups and from some committee chairs in the House.[47] The House companion measure was reported out too late in 1994 to be considered on the floor and the Senate bill was pulled from the floor in the last days of the session, after it became the vehicle for a number of nongermane amendments offered on the floor.[48]

But this was only to be a temporary delay, for the 1994 elections ushered in a Republican Congress anxious to prove their federalism mettle. Republicans gained a majority in the House for the first time in forty years and won a smaller majority in the Senate as well. The Contract with America embodied their ambitious agenda, including a restoration of federalism principles through block grants and through mandate reform and relief. Initially, mandate reform was not highlighted in this platform but was subsumed as part of a bill involving capital gains tax cuts.

Several developments served to accelerate the timetable for passing mandate reform in 1995. First, though many proposals embodied in the contract were highly partisan and controversial, mandate reform had already gained bipartisan support in a Democratic Congress. Moreover, the Kempthorne-Glenn bill had emerged from the Senate, which was proving to be less enthusiastic in their embrace of the contract agenda, partly because Republicans lacked the sixty-vote margin needed to move legislation through that body. A new congressional leadership eager to show early policy achievements would find the potential for achieving passage and presidential signature of an important piece of legislation to be an attractive proposition.

Second, mandate reform took on greater urgency because the states' support would be necessary to confirm the balanced budget constitutional amendment that Republicans championed as one of their most important goals. State leaders warned, however, that their support of the amendment would be jeopardized by the failure to pass meaningful federal constraints on mandates. This threat was reinforced by leaders of the Republican Governors Association, a group that had gained significant early access and influence with congressional leadership on the heels of the Republicans' capture of a majority of the nation's governorships as well in 1994.[49] At a meeting with these governors immediately following the November 1994 elections, Speaker Gingrich and Majority Leader Dole promised to make mandate reform the first piece of legislation introduced in the Senate.

There was some debate between House and Senate Republicans about what kind of bill to offer. House Republicans wanted a stronger bill, including a so-called agency backstop provision to prohibit federal agency enforcement of mandates unless full federal funding was appropriated for state and local governments' direct costs.[50] This provision was designed to address the fragmentation between congressional authorization and appropriations. Proposed mandates might authorize full funding, thereby escaping a point of order, but Congress might subsequently refuse to appropriate the funds. Proposals were also advanced to increase the votes needed to overcome a mandate point of order from a majority to three-fifths, similar to many points of order protecting congressional budget resolutions and rules. Senate Republicans, however, won the argument to proceed with the Kempthorne-Glenn bill as the basis since Democrats were likely to filibuster a significantly stronger bill with reimbursement and supermajority points of order.[51]

As promised by the leadership, the mandate reform bill was first introduced in the Senate as S1. The bipartisan consensus enveloping mandate reform in the prior Congress quickly dissolved, as some Democrats saw the mandate issue as an opportunity to challenge the new Republican majority on their Contract with America. Forty-four separate amendments were offered on the Senate floor, many of which would exempt additional policy areas or programs from the scope of the bill.

Republicans defeated most with unanimous party line votes. One amendment that was accepted, however, was Senator Byrd's revision to the bill's proposed agency backstop provision. The Senate bill had been strengthened by adding a federal agency backstop requiring agencies to either void the mandate if appropriations were not provided or scale it back to fit the appropriations provided. Fearing excessive delegation of congressional power to the executive, Byrd's amendment required agencies to come back before Congress with proposals prior to implementing such plans. This amendment remained in the final bill.

The companion House bill was reported to the floor without hearings. A blizzard of amendments were offered here too. The final bills passed, however, with bipartisan majorities in both houses. A difficult conference ensued, since the House bill retained a stronger agency backstop provision and a judicial review of federal agency performance under the act. The conference bill retained judicial review, limited only to whether the agency prepared the written mandate cost analysis, and adopted the Senate's backstop incorporating the Byrd amendment to maintain congressional control. The final bill was passed by near unanimous margins in both houses and was signed by President Clinton in March 1995.

Provisions of the Final Bill

The UMRA was widely praised by intergovernmental officials and students of federalism alike as a responsible attempt to institutionalize congressional self-restraint on mandates. Title I of the law focused on legislative accountability and will be the focus of this discussion.[52] The final act also contained regulatory review, analysis, and consultation requirements that applied to federal agency intergovernmental regulatory rulemaking and a requirement for the review of existing unfunded mandates by the Advisory Commission on Intergovernmental Relations.

The heart of the new process was the new point of order. Any unfunded mandate defined by the law with an uncompensated cost determined by the CBO greater than $50 million a year, can be stopped by a point of order raised on the House or Senate floor. (The $50 million threshold is net of state and local savings and direct federal funding contained in the bill). A majority of the membership can override the point of order and pass the mandate, but at least the provision ensures the potential for a debate about the issue of mandating itself. Congressional actions covered include direct orders that require additional state and local spending, provisions that preempt state and local revenue sources, and reductions in authorizations for federal aid to defray state and local compliance costs.

Bills with mandates can not be challenged if they identify funding sources that CBO estimates would fully cover the additional state and local costs for a ten-year period. Funding can be provided either by direct entitlement spending included in the legislation itself or, as is most likely, by authorizations for subsequent appropriations sufficient to meet the costs. The bill must also provide backstop guidance to the federal agency for terminating or scaling back the mandate should appropriations fall short of the authorization.

As some are quick to note, certain types of mandates are excluded from UMRA, including those enforcing constitutional rights, preventing discrimination, conditions of grants, and preemptions of state and local authority to regulate or provide services that do not carry state or local fiscal implications exceeding the $50 million threshold. Moreover, mandates associated with emergency assistance and national security are also exempt from UMRA. Of the four types of intergovernmental mandates identified by ACIR as most intrusive, only direct orders are covered, whereas three—crosscutting requirements, crossover sanctions, and partial preemptions—would generally be exempt from UMRA.[53] The points of order also do not apply to appropriations bills, except for legislative provisions imposing mandates exceeding the threshold. However, new grant conditions or funding caps for major entitlement grant programs exceeding $500 million annually, such as Medicaid, are defined as mandates under the act if state and local governments lack authority to adjust to these changes. Except for the ACIR study discussed above, existing mandates are not addressed by UMRA, but the act does apply to changes in existing mandates that CBO projects will increase uncompensated state and local costs by more than the $50 million threshold.

Committee reports must identify and submit mandates in reported bills to the CBO, as they did before UMRA, and a point of order can be raised against a bill without a CBO estimate. Committee reports are also to include information on funding mechanisms to defray the costs. The CBO is required to determine if there is an unfunded mandate in a committee reported bill, along with an estimate of costs if they exceed the $50 million threshold. Although similar to the CBO's existing responsibilities, UMRA extended cost estimation requirements, where practicable, to conference agreements and amendments containing mandates not previously considered. Despite the fact that the CBO had been doing state and local estimates since 1981 under earlier legislation, UMRA prompted the agency to enhance its role by creating a separate unit devoted exclusively to state and local estimation. The CBO has consulted routinely with state and local groups to identify mandates and sources for assessing cost impacts.[54]

IMPLICATIONS

The passage of UMRA reflected the emergence of new forces in the mandate debate. State and local governments became more vigilant on these issues, and mandate reform dovetailed nicely with the desire of the new Republican Congress to demonstrate its commitment to reduce the federal role in domestic policy. For a time, state and local governments had succeeded in preempting the same kind of bandwagon politics that had facilitated consensual passage of mandates in the years before. Just as the passage of mandates had become a valence issue whereby opposition was not legitimate, mandate reform became a valence issue as well. Both parties clambered aboard this fast-moving legislative juggernaut, and it became difficult to stop.

The adoption of mandate reform showed that federalism values still could tap congressional allegiance, at least as a general government reform issue. The most important questions remained: Could the high-minded principles embodied in reform be consistently applied to the consideration of proposed new mandates, and could this renewed commitment to federalism be sustained over the longer term? It is to these questions that we now turn in Chapters 9 and 10.

NOTES TO CHAPTER 8

1. Public Law 104-4, 109 Stat. 48.

2. Public Law 97-108.

3. Public Law 96-511 and Public Law 96-354.

4. Presidential Task Force on Regulatory Relief, *Reagan Administration Achievements in Regulatory Relief for State and Local Governments: A Progress Report* (Washington, D.C.: Executive Office of the President, 1982).

5. Michael Fix, "Regulatory Relief: The Real New Federalism," *State Government News* (27 January 1985), p. 7.

6. Advisory Commission on Intergovernmental Relations, *Federal Regulation of State and Local Governments: The Mixed Record of the 1980's*, (Washington, D.C.: ACIR, 1993), A–126.

7. Jocelyn M. Johnston, "The Medicaid Mandates of the 1980's: An Intergovernmental Perspective," *Public Budgeting and Finance* (Spring, 1997), pp. 4–34.

8. See Steven D. Gold, ed., *The Fiscal Crisis of the States* (Washington, D.C.: Georgetown University Press, 1995). Also, see United States General Accounting Office, *Balanced Budget Requirements: State Experiences and Implications for the Federal Government*, GAO/AFMD-93-58BR (Washington, D.C.: GAO, March, 1993).

9. Steven Gold reports that although state general fund contributions to Medicaid went up during the early 1990s, nearly 40 percent of the increase was attributable to taxes and donations from providers that were used to generate an additional $11 billion of federal aid to states. See Steven Gold, *The Fiscal Crisis of the States*, p. 30.

10. Office of Management and Budget, *Analytical Perspectives: Budget of the United States Government, FY 1997* (Washington, D.C.: Office of Management and Budget, 1996), p. 169.

11. David Vogel, *Fluctuating Fortunes: The Political Power of Business in America* (New York: Basic Books, 1989).

12. John Kindgon, *Agendas, Alternatives and Public Policies*, 2nd edition (New York: Harper Collins, 1995).

13. See the excellent article on the politics of mandate reform by David R. Beam and Timothy J. Conlan, "The 1995 Unfunded Mandates Reform Act: The Politics of Federal Mandating Meets the Politics of Reform," *Public Budgeting and Financial Management* 7 (1995), pp. 355–386.

14. Anthony Downs, "Up and Down with Ecology—The 'Issue Attention Cycle,' " *Public Interest* 28 (Summer, 1972), pp. 38–50.

15. Frank Baumgartner and Bryan Jones, *Agendas and Instability in American Politics* (Chicago: University of Chicago Press, 1993).

16. Martin Shapiro, "Of Interests and Values: The New Politics and the New Political Science," in *The New Politics of Public Policy*, ed. Marc K. Landy and Martin A. Levin (Baltimore: Johns Hopkins University Press, 1995), pp. 3–22.

17. Frank Baumgartner and Bryan Jones, *Agendas and Instability in American Politics*, p. 8.

18. Rochefort and Cobb refer to this as the struggle for problem ownership. See David A. Rochefort and Roger W. Cobb, "Problem Definition: An Emerging Perspective," in *The Politics of Problem Definition*, ed. David A. Rochefort and Roger W. Cobb (Lawrence: University Press of Kansas, 1994), p. 14.

19. Deborah Stone, *Policy Paradox: The Art of Political Decision Making* (New York: W. W. Norton, 1997), pp. 163–187.

20. Margaret Kriz, "Cutting the Strings," *National Journal* (21 January 1995), p. 167.

21. U.S. Conference of Mayors/Price Waterhouse, *Impact of Unfunded Federal Mandates on US Cities: A 314 City Survey* (Washington, D.C.: U.S. Conference of Mayors, 1993); National Association of Counties/ Price Waterhouse, *NAACO Unfunded Mandates Survey* (Washington, D.C.: National Association of Counties, 1993).

22. See Senate Committee on Environment and Public Works, *Analysis of the Unfunded Mandates Surveys Conducted by the U.S. Conference of Mayors and the National Association of Counties* (Washington, D.C.: 14 June 1994); Jim St. George, *Mandate Relief for State and Local Governments* (Washington, D.C.: Center for Budget and Policy Priorities, 17 May 1994).

23. Advisory Commission on Intergovernmental Relations, *Regulatory Federalism: Policy, Process, Impact and Reform*, A-95 (Washington, D.C.: ACIR, 1994); and *Federal Regulation of State and Local Governments*.

24. Advisory Commission on Intergovernmental Relations, *Federally Induced Costs Affecting State and Local Governments*, M–193 (Washington, D.C.: ACIR, December, 1994); and *Development, Implementation, and Evaluation of Federal Mandate Relief Legislation* (Washington, D.C.: ACIR, 13 January 1995).

25. Timothy J. Conlan, James D. Riggle, and Donna E. Schwartz, "Deregulating Federalism? The Politics of Mandate Reform in the 104th Congress," *Publius: The Journal of Federalism* 25, No. 3 (1995), pp. 23–39.

26. Advisory Commission on Intergovernmental Relations, *Changing Public Attitudes on Governments and Taxes*, S–23 (Washington, D.C.: ACIR, 1994).

27. Richard Nathan, "The Role of States in American Federalism," in *The State of the States*, 3rd edition, ed. Carl E. Van Horn (Washington, D.C.: Congressional Quarterly Press, 1996), pp. 13–32.

28. Linda L. M. Bennett and Stephen Earle Bennett, *Living with Leviathan: Americans Coming to Terms with Big Government* (Lawrence: University of Kansas Press, 1990), p. 107.

29. Thomas Atwood and Chris West, *Home Rule: How States Are Fighting Unfunded Federal Mandates* (Washington, D.C.: Heritage Foundation, 28 December 1994).

30. David R. Beam and Timothy Conlan, "The 1995 Unfunded Mandates Reform Act."

31. William Tucker, "Are Unfunded Regulations at Flood State?," *Washington Times*, 21 February 1994.

32. Joanne Desky, "States, Locals Protest Unfunded Mandates," *PA Times* 16, No. 12 (1 December 1993), p. 2.

33. Advisory Commission on Intergovernmental Relations, *Federal Regulation of State and Local Governments*, p. 27.

34. Sandra Osborne, *Mandates and the Congress* (Washington, D.C.: Congressional Research Service, 16 April 1993), p. 39.

35. Justice O'Connor's dissenting opinion, *Garcia v. San Antonio Metropolitan Transit Authority*, 105 S. Ct. 1005 (1985).

36. U.S. General Accounting Office, *Legislative Mandates: State Experiences Offer Insights for Federal Action*, GAO/HRD–88–75 (Washington, D.C.: GAO, September, 1988).

37. The ACIR report called for full reimbursement of only direct and incremental costs associated with new mandates, a definition similar to UMRA. See Advisory Commission on Intergovernmental Relations, *Regulatory Federalism: Policy, Process, Impact and Reform*, p. 265.

38. Jim St. George, *Mandate Relief for State and Local Governments* (Washington, D.C.: Center for Budget and Policy Priorities, 1995).

39. U.S. General Accounting Office, *Legislative Mandates: State Experiences Offer Insights for Federal Action*.

40. See U.S. Department of Treasury, Office of State and Local Finance, *Federal-State-Local Fiscal Relations* (Washington, D.C.: Department of the Treasury, September, 1985), pp. 80–92.

41. U.S. General Accounting Office, *Legislative Mandates: State Experiences Offer Insights for Federal Action*.

42. See Robert E. Goodin, "Institutionalizing the Public Interest: The Defense of Deadlock and Beyond," *American Political Science Review* 90, No. 2 (1996), p. 341.

43. Congressional Research Service study of budget points of order.

44. David Mayhew, *Congress: The Electoral Connection* (New Haven: Yale University Press, 1974); Burdett Loomis, *The New American Politician* (New York: Basic Books, 1988).

45. Timothy J. Conlan, James D. Riggle, and Donna E. Schwartz, "Deregulating Federalism?"

46. David Mayhew, *Divided We Govern: Party Control, Lawmaking and Investigations 1946–1990* (New Haven: Yale University Press, 1991).

47. "Unfunded Mandates Battle Pauses," *OMB Watcher* XII, No. 4 (Washington, D.C.: 25 October 1994).

48. Dan Morgan and William Claiborne, "Bid to Curb Unfunded Federal Mandates Bogs Down," *Washington Post*, 8 October 1994, p. A13.

49. Andrew Tailor, "Governors: Don't Balance Budget without Ending Mandates," *Congressional Quarterly* (26 November 1994), p.340.

50. Job Creation and Wage Enhancement Act, Title X, Section 10502, cited in Advisory Commission on Intergovernmental Relations, *Federal Mandate Relief for State, Local, and Tribal Governments*, A–129 (Washington, D.C.: ACIR, January, 1995), p. 21.

51. Timothy J. Conlan, James D. Riggle, and Donna E. Schwartz, "Deregulating Federalism?" p. 32.

52. Unfunded Mandates Reform Act of 1995, Public Law 104–4, 22 March 1995.

53. Advisory Commission on Intergovernmental Relations, *Regulatory Federalism: Policy, Process, Impact and Reform.*

54. Congressional Budget Office, *The Experience of the Congressional Budget Office During the First Year of the Unfunded Mandates Reform Act* (Washington, D.C.: CBO, January, 1997).

9

The Impact of Mandate Reform

The passage of the Unfunded Mandates Reform Act in 1995 occasioned high expectations. Congressional sponsors hailed it as the vehicle that could replace years of coercive federalism with a renewed commitment to cooperative federalism. Analysts also suggested that it would help reduce the number of ill-considered requirements enacted into law.[1]

The effectiveness of UMRA would, however, ultimately rest with the commitment within Congress itself to sustain the act's objectives of mandate self-restraint. There is very little about the new process that is automatic. First, a member of Congress must formally raise a point of order to trigger the act's presumption that covered mandates are unsuitable in each chamber. These mandate opponents must then defeat efforts by mandate advocates by mustering a majority in one chamber to sustain the point of order, thereby preventing further congressional consideration of the mandate. As previous chapters have shown, proposed mandates can often be quite compelling, particularly when defined by advocates as valence issues for which costs are not perceived as legitimate issues.

Past may not be prologue, however. The 104th Congress came to Washington pledging to turn over a new federalism leaf and indeed raised fundamental new issues about the federal role in domestic policy. Republican governors were welcomed to the inner policy circles of the congressional leadership[2] and had a major role in crafting early 1995 proposals to block grant more than 70 percent of federal assistance to state and local governments.[3] State and local governments showed a unified and intense lobbying presence in gaining the passage of UMRA itself.[4] Indeed, these two key variables—party as well as state and local interest group support—would be critical in determining whether the general support for mandate reform translated into specific victories on individual mandate legislation.

The first year of UMRA's implementation, 1996, thus should provide the most favorable test for the act. The same Congress which had in 1995 originally passed the law could be expected to be vigilant in applying the act's protections against new mandates. We would expect, then, that at least for this one year, the act would serve as a deterrent in preventing congressional consideration of mandates proposed by advocates or as the spur to provide federal funding for whatever mandates were adopted. This chapter reviews Congressional mandate decisions in 1996 to explore the act's impact.

OVERVIEW OF MANDATES ENACTED IN 1996

The only systematic inventory of mandates covered by UMRA is prepared by the Congressional Budget Office, pursuant to its responsibilities under the act. The CBO tracks bills for which it provides estimates, generally at the committee report stage. So, for a given mandate issue, the CBO would generally count each estimate it provided for all relevant bills reported by committees during the legislative process, both in the House and in the Senate.[5] The CBO's data also includes estimates for bills that never became law.

For 1996, the CBO's tally indicates that, when compared to the total number of intergovernmental mandate estimates it provided, the number of significant mandates exceeding the $50 million threshold in UMRA were quite small, as shown in Table 9.1. The eleven bills exceeding the $50 million UMRA threshold addressed five distinct mandates: minimum wage increase, parity for mental health in health insurance, preemption of state securities fees, mandated use of Social Security numbers on driver's licenses, and extension of federal occupational safety and health to state and local employees. According to the CBO, four of these mandates were passed, but only one—the increase in the minimum wage—exceeded the $50 million UMRA threshold once it was considered on the floor. The others were modified to reduce their costs, as discussed later.

TABLE 9.1
Congressional Budget Office Mandate Statements, 1996

Total Estimates Prepared	718
Estimates Identifying Mandates	69
Mandates Exceeding $50 Million	11
Mandates That Could Not Be Estimated	6

Numbers refer to CBO estimates transmitted to Congress on bills defined as intergovernmental mandates by UMRA.

Source: Congressional Budget Office, *The Experience of the Congressional Budget Office During the First Year of the Unfunded Mandates Reform Act* (Washington, D.C.: CBO, January, 1997), p. 5.

At first examination, the CBO data would suggest that, at least with regard to major mandates covered under UMRA, 1996 was a year of restraint for Congress, as could be expected. How does this compare with previous years? Comparable data are not readily available for other periods, but data reported on mandates enacted between 1983 and 1990 in Chapter 4 can provide some insights. Of the thirty-one major mandates passed between 1983 and 1990—the era that the ACIR describes as witnessing a resurgence of major mandates surpassing even that of the 1970s—twelve would probably be covered by UMRA's definition of a mandate, or an average of less than two covered major mandates that passed per year during this period. It is likely, however, that this earlier listing does not capture additional mandates passed in the 1983–1990 period exceeding the $50 million threshold that nevertheless were not considered major mandates using ACIR or CBO criteria at the time.[6] Thus, when defined by the UMRA criteria, major mandates in earlier periods may have passed somewhat more frequently than in 1996, although the differences in pace are not striking.

However, the 1996 indicator of UMRA mandates excludes important mandating activity that should be accounted for. First, it excludes the passage of mandates not covered by UMRA, such as laws protecting against discrimination and grant conditions. The CBO identified more than seventy-five additional bills reported by committees in 1996 that would impose increased costs to state and local governments in this category alone. (Examples of these will be discussed later.) Preemptions of state and local authority not imposing additional direct state or local costs are also excluded. Moreover, since CBO estimates record the net costs of mandates, major mandates contained within legislation that have offsetting savings for the state and local sector are not included either; examples of these mandates include welfare reform and safe drinking water, to be discussed later in this chapter.

MANDATE RESTRAINT AND MODIFICATION

What influence did UMRA itself have on legislative mandate decisions? This is a difficult question to answer since the factors responsible for legislative outcomes are intertwined and covariant. Congressional mandate decisions are most assuredly a product of both the UMRA mechanism itself and various political forces active in Congress in 1996. Certainly among these political forces was the commitment by many in the Congress to reduce the intrusiveness of the federal government's role in our system. The 1996 experience suggests that this generalized political commitment and UMRA itself were mutually reinforcing and were principally responsible for whatever mandate restraint occurred during the Congressional term.

The design of UMRA would suggest that mandate opponents would rely on the point of order to stop the passage of major mandates. However, the point of order was raised only a handful of times during the entire year. Congressional opponents of the minimum wage hike used the point of order unsuccessfully several times in the House, as House majorities voted to override UMRA to consider and subsequently pass the mandate. Minimum wage advocates accused opponents of cynically using the unfunded mandate vehicle in a dilatory fashion to gridlock the House when their objections had little to do with intergovernmental impacts.

The primary impact of UMRA came not from the blockage of legislation, however, but rather from its effect as a deterrent to mandates in the drafting and early consideration of legislation. Sponsors of legislation feared that their carefully crafted coalitions might come undone if faced with a point of order vote on the floor of either chamber.

Accordingly, potential mandates were sometimes modified when sponsors learned that they might prompt a point of order. In some cases, this happened informally in the initial drafting stages, as congressional staff consulted with CBO staff on the possible application of UMRA to proposed legislation.[7] On other occasions, important legislation was modified following its formal introduction. When learning of a CBO cost estimate that could trigger a point of order, sponsors made significant modifications that brought the costs below the $50 million threshold. This occurred in three prominent cases in 1996:[8]

Telecommunications reform
Years in the making, this massive bill deregulating the industry was pending in conference committee when UMRA went into effect in early 1996. State and local governments were able to adroitly use the threat of a point of order to gain a seat at the table in conference deliberations. The pending bill appeared to preempt state and local taxes and fees covering franchises and licenses given to cable and other communications companies, and it also appeared to prohibit state and local authority over the zoning of communications infrastructure, including the siting of communications towers used in wireless communications. Sponsors, sensing a threat that could potentially unravel their compromise, modified the legislation to address state and local concerns and head off a point of order, even though one local government lobbyist felt that the sponsors could have easily beat back the point of order on a floor vote. Specifically, the legislation permitted state and

local governments to continue tax and fee collections and steered clear of an absolute preemption of zoning and siting authority.

Immigration reform

As part of his perennial immigration reform, Senator Simpson's (R-Wy) initial bill would have required states to use Social Security numbers on driver's licenses to promote a more secure way for the public and private sector to enforce prohibitions against illegal aliens' access to jobs or benefits. States would also be required to adhere to new federal standards for issuing birth certificates as well as driver's licenses that would limit tampering or counterfeiting. Because the new mandates would have been effective immediately, the CBO estimated that the original bill would have cost between $80 million and $200 million to states in the first year, clearly well above the UMRA threshold.[9] Concerned about the potential use of UMRA's point of order by those opposing the bill, Simpson modified the legislation to delay the phasing in of the these mandates over a ten-year period, stretching out and limiting the state and local costs to a level below the threshold in any one year.

Securities reform

This legislation responded to the interests of large national investment firms by preempting state regulatory authority over the registration of mutual funds and large investment advisors, transferring exclusive jurisdiction to the Securities and Exchange Commission. The CBO estimated that the committee-reported bill would have increased state and local costs by over $125 million annually through the preemption of states' authority to collect fees from these entities.[10] The legislation was modified subsequently to preserve the states' authority to continue their fees for a specified period, while retaining the preemption of state program and legal authority.

In these cases, the point of order represented a credible threat because federalism issues associated with mandates had become an issue of importance to members of Congress. Past Congresses had also raised concerns about coercive federalism, but federalism concerns were typically eclipsed, as other dimensions of issues were defined as being more salient and important. In the dispute over what the conflict is about, the social problems or benefits addressed by proposed mandates had in those earlier years become more politically compelling than the impacts of those initiatives on state and local authority and costs.[11]

Against this backdrop, the UMRA point of order became a tool that raised the salience of federalism issues in certain cases. Sponsors, moreover, feared that the point of order would become useful not only to state and local groups, but to other interests and congressmen opposed to the legislation for different reasons. The new point of order enabled states and localities potentially to create new allies in the business community and elsewhere opposed to the legislation for other reasons. In general, successful coalition leaders must not only mobilize supporters, but avoid prompting significant opposition that, even as a minority, could threaten to slow down the legislative process or arouse latent publics in ways that could embarrass the supporters at some future time. Much congressional scholarship, accordingly, suggests that risk-averse and consensus-seeking behavior characterize much legislative activity within Congress.[12]

THE MARCH OF MANDATES CONTINUES

The modifications reducing the costs of mandates were certainly a noteworthy development, but such apparent state and local victories occurred in legislation that nevertheless succeeded in imposing substantial new mandates or preemptions on the state and local sector. Essentially, intergovernmental concessions were won not in deciding whether to mandate, but how and when to mandate.

The securities legislation, for instance, although retaining states' authority to continue fees, nevertheless constitutes significant preemption of state authority to register and regulate mutual funds and larger investment advisors with assets over $25 million. The changes to the immigration reform bill reduced the near term costs below the $50 million threshold by delaying the effective date of the mandate, but new federal mandates were still imposed for the first time on state-issued driver's licenses and birth certificates. Just as with congressional budget scoring, decision processes linked to estimates can prompt legislative actions to adroitly delay or phase in changes that are calculated to avoid triggering action-forcing thresholds, whether they be UMRA limits or congressional budget scoring windows.

Similarly, the telecommunications legislation preempted major areas of state regulation of the industry, often in the name of deregulation. States were prohibited, for instance, from preventing the resale of local telephone companies. The FCC acquired new authority, with state input, to define requirements for universal service, including deciding what services had to be offered to schools and libraries, and states were prohibited from adopting conflicting service policies. States and localities were preempted from regulating cable technology, customer equipment, and "decency" standards for computer networks. Federal preemption occurred even in the zoning area, where UMRA prompted last-minute changes—state and local governments were preempted from regulating smaller satellite dishes or TV antennas. Local authority to regulate siting of wireless transmission towers was also constrained—they could determine placement of towers but could not prohibit the siting of towers within their boundaries, nor could they use health considerations as the basis for zoning decisions. The telecommunications reform act was also used in 1997 in a court case by cable companies to contest local franchises and fees for cable companies entering into telephone service—the argument was that such local provisions cause a barrier to entry and competition, thereby frustrating the deregulatory thrust of the reform.

In addition to these three laws, there were a number of other major new federal mandates and preemptions enacted in 1996, some covered by UMRA and some not covered. The author used the CBO's database, information supplied by state and local governments, and a comprehensive review of the *Congressional Quarterly* weekly reports for the year to identify some additional areas where one or more new mandates or preemptions were enacted in 1996:

Minimum wage
As noted earlier, this was the one mandate covered by UMRA exceeding the threshold that Congress passed. Covering state, local, and private employers alike, the increase in the minimum wage was estimated by the CBO to raise state and local costs by over $1 billion within five years.[13]

Criminal justice
A range of new federal initiatives were passed that impose new duties on the state and local sector. Some were direct orders, such as the requirement for states to amend their laws to require restitution to victims of international terrorism (PL 104-132). Others consisted of federalization of such crimes as interstate stalking (PL 104-201). Others of more consequence for local governments were enacted as conditions of aid for federal criminal justice grants that excluded them from UMRA's purview. "Megan's Law" was enacted, requiring state and local law enforcement agencies to notify citizens when a sexual offender has been released to live in the community, building on an earlier 1994 mandate requiring states to maintain registries of such offenders. One provision of an omnibus appropriations bill required states to test all prisoners and parolees for substance abuse, pursuant to Justice Department guidelines. Congress also passed a new federal law banning the possession of guns in local schools, attempting to reverse the

Supreme Court's recent *Lopez* decision, which overturned a similar congressional mandate.[14]

Health care

Several preemptions and mandates were passed that affected the state and local sector. The Kennedy-Kassebaum legislation enacted new federal standards for health insurance, preventing plans from denying coverage for preexisting conditions and allowing continued coverage for workers losing or leaving jobs. States were given the option of enforcing the new requirements, but this legislation extended new federal standards to an area traditionally under the purview of states. A requirement for minimum forty-eight-hour hospital stays for mothers delivering babies preempted state laws regulating health care and will increase state costs under Medicaid. Congress also passed a new standard for group health insurance plans to prevent lower limits on coverage for mental illness. Other health requirements were imposed, such as a provision mandating states to test all newborns for HIV as a condition for receipt of Ryan White grants. Significantly, none of these health provisions is covered by UMRA, either because they are pure preemptions, enacted as part of appropriations bills, or conditions of aid.

Pesticides

After many years of controversy, Congress preempted state and local governments in regulating pesticides in the production, shipping, or handling of food. Some states had exceeded federal standards for many years, which prompted the pesticides and food industries to seek a single federal standard (PL 104-170).

Local cost sharing for federal water projects

Congress decided to increase the cost share for flood control projects conducted by the Corps of Engineers from 25 percent to 35 percent of costs (PL 104-303). The administration had proposed a 50 percent cost share. The fiscal impact remains to be seen, for the higher match may discourage certain projects from being undertaken.

MANDATE ROLLBACKS

One of the continuing concerns about UMRA is that it formally does nothing about the significant intergovernmental mandates currently on the books, the ones that prompted Congress to pass UMRA in the first place.[15] The difficulties of changing existing mandates were illustrated by a 1996 draft report considered and rejected by the ACIR.

That report recommended the modification of thirteen politically sensitive mandates, such as those for the Davis Bacon prevailing wage rules and handicapped education, and sparked a political firestorm that helped pave the way for ACIR's termination in late 1996.[16] Ironically, earlier ACIR reports endorsing broad, sweeping changes in the federal system, including mandate reimbursement, received widespread support.[17]

Notwithstanding these obvious political obstacles, the 104th Congress did eliminate some of the most annoying highway grant conditions, including the federal speed limit, the mandate for states to use crumb rubber in highway reconstruction, the metric signage requirement, and the motorcycle helmet requirement. In 1996 Congress passed safe drinking water and welfare reform, two measures with significant deregulation provisions that promised to reduce costs and increase authority for states and localities. Yet, both of these measures also included some significant new federal mandates.

In the case of safe drinking water, the 1996 drinking water reform provided important relief from some of the most burdensome regulations by slowing down the pace of EPA regulations, giving the agency authority to consider costs in developing standards, permitting less costly alternatives to filtration, and reducing monitoring requirements, particularly for smaller communities. A new federal loan fund was provided to states to help communities obtain low-cost financing for compliance costs. However, new mandates were added that required water systems to notify the public of contaminant levels and to require systems operators to comply with new certification provisions, and the CBO estimated annual costs to be between $30 million and $40 million.[18]

Nonetheless, recent data suggest that safe drinking water standards will continue to mandate major costs for the nation's communities. The nation's water systems will need to invest $126 billion over the next twenty years to replace aging systems and comply with new standards, an amount that dwarfs the new loan fund, which must be repaid by local tax and rate payers.[19]

The welfare reform bill has to be viewed as a mixed outcome from the mandate perspective. On the one hand, the block grant eliminated the federal entitlement to benefits and gave states major new authority to determine eligibility and payment levels. Whereas the old open-ended matching programs penalized states by reducing benefits with a loss of federal matching funds, the new block grant provides a fixed grant and allows states to reduce their own funds to 75 percent of previous spending. In the CBO's estimate, the repeal of existing mandates is likely to reduce state spending by more than the new mandates.[20]

On the other hand, welfare reform introduced a host of new mandates on the states. In addition to the five-year cap on family eligibility and a variety of other limitations on recipients, states must place 50 percent of welfare recipients in jobs by 2002, a target that the CBO estimates will cost $10 billion for such activities as child care and job training. With regard to immigrants, the new law bans welfare for new legal immigrants by requiring states to "deem" new legal immigrants before granting them welfare and to track down and consider their sponsors' income and resources in determining eligibility.[21] State and local officials are also to report illegal aliens to the federal Immigration and Naturalization Service. Both provisions prompted New York City Mayor Guiliani to file court suits, charging that the new restrictions would impose added state and local costs by shifting these persons to state-local-financed general assistance programs.

The child support enforcement provisions of the new law mark a high point in the federal commandeering of state laws and bureaucracies to achieve national child support goals. States are essentially directed to track new hires by employers, match them against parents with child support orders, and then obtain and process withholdings of support payments from employers. Moreover, states are required to suspend driver's and other occupational licenses of individuals overdue in support payments. Because states would realize savings from increased collections and federal payments for installing tracking systems, the CBO indicates that the changes will actually produce savings to states of over $1.5 billion over five years.

THE POLITICS OF FEDERAL MANDATES REVISITED

The congressional commitment and heightened state and local interest group attention to mandate issues bore some fruit in the initial passage of UMRA and the subsequent modification of major proposed mandates. Nevertheless, Congress passed costs or authority limitations on the state and local sector in 1996 as well. It is important to understand what forces prompted the passage of mandates in this new era to assess whether the mandate restraints embodied by UMRA will be sustainable over the longer term.

As earlier chapters have chronicled, the passage of federal mandates in prior years reveals that they were an outgrowth of fundamental changes in the nature of our policymaking process. Significant changes in our party system, interest group formation, and Congress itself enabled mandates to emerge as a major tool of national policy. Mandates more easily attained agenda status, thanks to more open congressional institutions, more entrepreneurial members seeking to champion new policy claims, an interest group system that broadened to include newer groups representing mandate beneficiaries, a growing Washington-centered media fueling the propulsion of new policy ideas, and the growth of government itself, which created clientele and bureaucracies with an interest in improving and expanding federal programs.

At the same time that these forces bolstered mandate advocates, traditional restraints on congressional regulatory activity appeared to erode, as allegiance to federalism principles lost its central role as a constraint on federal actions. The underlying electoral ties that used to bind state, local, and national officials in firm political alliances were severed, replaced with a competitive or even antagonistic relationship between independent political entrepreneurs in search of public visibility. Although federalism still captured rhetorical support in the new era, more specific policy goals often took precedence, even among Republicans and conservatives, who were traditionally viewed as a bulwark against federal activism.

The consequences for congressional action were profound. Although the new congress displayed a renewed commitment to federalism principles, UMRA did not repeal other nationalizing forces. Thus, it is not surprising that the passage of mandates in 1996 followed some familiar political patterns established earlier. In some cases, congressional entrepreneurs and interest groups continued to have success defining mandate goals in valence terms, by which only the benefits supported by the mandate were perceived to be legitimate.[22] These proposals appeared to be unassailable and were ushered in on a wave of enthusiasm that state and local governments and others in Congress were obliged to support as well. In other cases, mandates were enacted to carry out the distinct party agendas of both Democrats and Republicans. Finally, other proposals promoted the objectives of strong national interest groups, while state and local groups were too crosspressured or ambivalent to mount effective opposition to the mandates themselves.

Valence Politics

Several mandates that were passed in 1996 illustrate how mandates continue to be defined in valence terms, fueled by extensive media coverage of issues. For instance, Megan's Law was passed following the tragic slaying of young Megan Kanka by a released sex offender living near her home in New Jersey. Following extensive national media coverage, the bill mandating notification to communities of released sexual offenders was championed and introduced by Congressman Richard Zimmer, a conservative Republican from New Jersey. Neither members who fashioned themselves as protectors of UMRA nor members who had civil liberties qualms about the bill felt that they could vote against it, so the bill passed quickly and by acclamation. Defined in symbolic and valence terms, objections were not politically in order.

The drug testing of state and local prisoners and parolees was also defined opportunistically by political entrepreneurs in valence terms that enabled quick and consensual adoption. In this case, President Clinton conceived of the proposal during his presidential campaign as a way to counter Senator Dole's criticism of the effectiveness of his antidrug programs. Announced on 11 September, the proposal was attached to an omnibus appropriations bill and passed three weeks later.[23] Congressional Republicans were outflanked by the way the issue was defined, and opposition would have enabled the president to suggest that it was they, not he, who was soft on drugs.

A number of other mandates and preemptions discussed earlier also passed on voice votes at nearly all stages of the process. Though considerable conflict and bargaining occurred behind the scenes, once placed on the agenda, these bills did not engender any opposition. They included the increased local cost sharing for flood control, pesticides preemption, and securities preemption legislation.

Potentially, mandate reform and relief can also be defined in valence terms, as the lines of conflict are redefined from the benefit to the cost side of the policy equation. In these cases, the reduction of state and local costs and burdens could take on the character of a politically unassailable idea. The burdens of the EPA's safe drinking water standards on thousands of smaller communities made the regulatory relief in the 1996 bill politically compelling. Although environmentalists were able to gain several new mandates, the fact that they were forced to support the overall measure containing significant regulatory relief illustrated how compelling this idea had become. Once the political bargain was struck, the bill received unanimous support as it passed through the Congressional policy process.

Partisan Politics

Some mandates were proposed as tools to achieve partisan agendas and, as such, proved to be more contentious. However, as noted in Chapter 3, mandates as a tool of government did not constitute a stable basis for partisan division in voting on mandates and preemptions. Although Republicans championed the enactment of UMRA in 1995, the votes on specific mandates were driven more by the underlying policy goal supported by the mandate, rather than by the federalism issues posed by the mandate tool. Differences, however, emerged by chamber, with House Republicans being disposed to oppose mandates to a greater extent than Democrats or their Senate Republican counterparts.

The author reviewed all 1996 roll calls in both House and Senate and included in the study those involving mandate and preemption issues that prompted a division of at least 20 percent among members.[24] Of the fifty roll calls judged to involve mandate or preemption issues, forty-two were party votes whereby a majority of one party opposed a majority of the other party. For all roll calls, majorities of Republicans supported federal mandates and preemptions 54 percent of the time, whereas Democratic majorities supported mandates in 56 percent of the cases.

If, in fact, mandate voting is driven by underlying policy goals, then this seemingly counterintuitive result can be explained when the roll calls are disaggregated by policy dimension. The results in Table 9.2 show that Republicans supported mandates to achieve national welfare, social policy, immigration, and business preemption goals. Democrats, on the other hand, supported mandates to support the party's labor and housing agendas.

Immigration offers a good example of how programmatic policy issues eclipsed federalism positions as primary drivers of congressional voting behavior. Republicans supported greater restrictions on states to prohibit welfare for legal immigrants but supported measures to empower states to exclude illegal aliens from public education. These Republican immigration positions illustrate how mandates are a secondary voting dimension that calls forth support when it advances the

---

TABLE 9.2
Party Support for Mandates by Policy Dimension*

Mandate Policy Type (n = no. of roll calls)	Whole Congress, Republican for (n)	Whole Congress, Democrat for (n)
Welfare (17)	47 (8)	53 (9)
Immigration (13)	69 (9)	31 (4)
Labor (4)	0	100 (4)
Housing (5)	20 (1)	80 (4)
Other Services (6)	67 (4)	100 (6)
Business Preemption (2)	100 (2)	0
Social Policy (3)	100 (3)	33 (1)
TOTAL	54 (27)	56 (28)

*Numbers in each cell are percentages and frequencies of the roll call votes in each dimension in which a majority of the party supported the mandate. Percentages are computed based on total number of roll calls on each dimension.

party's more primary policy objectives and opposition when it detracts from the party's policy goals.

Other Republican-supported mandates and preemptions included supporting the interests of national business, who were seeking to promote a single national standard to preempt different states' rules on product liability—a bill passed by the Republican Congress but vetoed by the president. The social policy agenda of Republicans was advanced by votes prohibiting states from using Medicaid funds for abortion and by votes prohibiting states from departing from the federal definition of marriage, which proscribes recognition of same-sex marriages.

The Democrats supported mandates to back the party's labor agenda, principally to pass the minimum wage increase. They supported welfare and housing mandates that advanced their policy goals of protecting certain beneficiaries, such as opposing an optional state food stamp block grant and backing a provision limiting monthly rent in public housing to 30 percent of income. Democrats also voted for mental health parity mandates for health insurance.

These findings are similar to those reported in Chapter 3 for mandate roll calls in the 1980s. As in Chapter 3, a linear regression model was used for the fifty votes to validate key variables influencing mandate voting behavior by members.

The dependent variable in the analysis was a promandate score. The score was measured in two ways. To assess overall voting behavior, the score represented the percentage of all fifty votes, where a member voted for mandates or preemptions. Voting behavior within particular policy dimensions was measured as the percentage of a member's promandate votes to all votes within each dimension listed in Table 9.2: welfare, immigration, business preemption, social policy, and "other services." This last dimension collapses votes on labor, housing, and other services from Table 9.2 to increase the sample size for the analysis.

Independent variables included party, ideology, region, and previous state and local office-holding experience of each member. It was hypothesized that Democrats, liberals, members from the Northeast, and the lack of prior state and local office holding would be associated with a higher mandate score.[25] A prior study of voting on passage of UMRA itself concluded that conservatism was the most important variable affecting roll call voting on mandate reform.[26]

The results are presented in Table 9.3 for the Senate and Table 9.4 for the House. The coefficients measure the extent to which mandate scores were increased or decreased by each of the independent variables presented, given the other variables in the model.

For the Senate, Table 9.3 shows that overall mandate voting was

TABLE 9.3
Senate Voting Model for Mandates

	All Votes	Welfare	Immigration	Business	Other services
Intercept	.6289**	.4685**	.9618**	.8751**	.4579**
	(.0218)	(.0318)	(.0458)	(.1132)	(.0662)
Party (Dem = 1)	-.0355	-.0085	-.1665*	-.3799*	.1557
	(.0358)	(.0523)	(.0755)	(.1860)	(.1087)
Ideology	-.0017**	-5.51632E-04	-.0055**	-.0035	.0033*
(100 = liberal)	(4.9238E-04)	(7.1924E-04)	(.0010)	(.0025)	(.0014)
South	.0205	.0748*	-.0654	.0340	.0102
	(.0234)	(.0341)	(.0914)	(.1215)	(.0710)
Midwest	.0224	.0259	-.0225	.1018	.0559
	(.0216)	(.0316)	(.0455)	(.1143)	(.0658)
West	.0108	.0268	.0011	-.0139	-.0282
	(.0214)	(.0313)	(.0450)	(.1113)	(.0651)
Prior state and local	-.0243	-.0087	-.0613	.0954	-.1230*
experience (1 = none)	(.0166)	(.0243)	(.0350)	(.0869)	(.0506)
R_2	.5643**	.0896*	.7702**	.4041**	.4519**

*significant at 0.05
**significant at 0.01
(Numbers in parentheses are standard errors. No social policy votes occurred in the Senate.)

significantly related only to ideology, with liberalism being modestly associated with lower mandate support. The coefficient for ideology indicates that every 10 percent increase in liberalism is associated with a 1.7 percent decrease in mandate support scores. Party shows the strongest overall relationship with mandate scores, with Republicans on average having 3 percent higher mandate support scores than Democrats, but the results are not statistically significant. (Since party and ideology are intercorrelated to a great extent [.89], their mutual influence is not reported in the model but will be discussed later.) Interestingly, prior state and local experience proved to be of no help to the state and local cause, as the state or local background of members was actually associated with higher mandate support, although again the results were not significant. Members from the South, Midwest, and West were also likely to have higher mandate support scores than Northeastern Senate members.[27]

As with the 1980s roll calls, the overall model masks the role of the separate policy dimensions, which are, to some extent, offsetting, as shown in Table 9.3. The overall relationships shift once separate policy dimensions are considered, reinforcing the point that underlying policy goals have a significant influence on mandate voting. The influence of party and ideology, suppressed for overall mandate voting, is heightened when votes are disaggregated by policy dimension.

Table 9.3 shows that being both a Republican and a conservative independently raised mandate support scores for welfare, immigration, and business policy dimensions. Average Republican mandate support was 16 percent higher for immigration and 38 percent higher for business issues than for Democrats; unlike the overall model, party was statistically significant for these two dimensions. On the other hand, being a Republican and a conservative independently lowered support for mandates in other service areas such as housing and labor, as would be expected. Region had a statistically significant effect only on welfare voting, wherein being from the South raised mandate support scores compared to scores for the Northeastern members.

Overall mandate voting in the House was different. Unlike in the Senate, being a Democrat and a liberal actually raised mandate support for all votes, as hypothesized. As shown in Table 9.4, being a Democrat raised mandate scores about 3 percent higher than Republicans. For every 10 percent increase in liberalism, mandate scores jumped by about 4 percentage points. Prior state and local experience, like in the Senate, reduced members' propensity to oppose mandates, although the results were not statistically significant.

Again, the patterns differed for separate policy dimensions. Republicans and conservatives were more likely to support business

TABLE 9.4
House Voting Model for Mandates

	All Votes	Welfare	Immigration	Business	Social Policy	Other Services
Intercept	.3076**	.3034**	.2738**	1.061**	.4178**	.2117*
	(.0110)	(.0178)	(.0209)	(.0345)	(.0225)	(.0172)
Party (Dem = 1)	.0279	.0105	-.0056	-.1687**	-.0185	.0913**
	(.0179)	(.0292)	(.0340)	(.0566)	(.0365)	(.0279)
Ideology	.0041**	.0024**	.0036**	-.0092**	.0025**	.0066**
(100 = liberal)	(2.5463E-04)	(4.1421E-04)	(4.8284E-04)	(8.0261E-04)	(5.1910E-04)	(3.9672E-04)
South	-.0094	.0159	.0441*	-.0089	-.0463	-.0285
	(.0117)	(.0190)	(.0222)	(.0366)	(.0240)	(.0183)
Midwest	-.0188	.0063	.0133	-.0060	-.0959**	-.0240
	(.0119)	(.0192)	(.0226)	(.0370)	(.0243)	(.0185)
West	.0014	.0079	.0665**	-.0177	-.0316	-.0187
	(.0122)	(.0198)	(.0232)	(.0383)	(.0249)	(.01901)
Prior state and local						
experience (1 = none)	-.0065	-.0092	.0140	.0383	-.0013	-.0182
	(.0088)	(.0142)	(.0166)	(.0276)	(.0179)	(.0137)
R_2	.7908**	.3129**	.3854**	.7203**	.2214**	.8279**

*Significant at .05
**Significant at .01
(Numbers in parentheses are standard errors.)

preemptions than were Democrats or more liberal members of the House. Republicans, although not conservatives, were more likely to support social policy mandates as well. Like their Senate counterparts, House Republicans and conservatives were associated with stronger opposition to mandates in other service areas such as labor and housing. However, unlike their Senate colleagues, being a House Republican or a conservative was not as strongly associated with support of immigration and welfare mandates. On immigration, House Republicans were only marginally more supportive of mandates than were House Democrats, and conservatives were actually more prone to vote against these mandates. On welfare, both House Republicans and conservatives were associated with lower mandate support voting scores; every 10 percent increase in a member's liberalism index was associated with a 2.4 percentage point increase in support for welfare mandates.

The differences between Senate and House voting among Republicans are obscured in the full regressions discussed above; the high degree of multicolinearity between party and ideology masks the joint influence of both these variables on voting. Dropping ideology in a separate regression analysis can be justified by its strong association with party, and this more clearly reveals the influence of party in each chamber. As Table 9.5 shows, the party variable in these new regressions is strongly associated with voting; it is statistically

TABLE 9.5
Influence of Party on Mandate Scores[a]

	House	Senate
All Votes	.2865**	−.1496**
	(.0103)	(.0159)
Welfare	.1642**	−.0449*
	(.0137)	(.0220)
Immigration	.2237**	−.5334**
	(.0164)	(.0361)
Business	−.7498**	−.6117**
	(.0294)	(.0793)
Social Policy	.1384**	NA
	(.0170)	
Other Services	.5101**	.3752**
	(.0163)	(.0468)

[a] Democrat = 1
*significant at .05 or below
**significant at .01 or below
(Numbers in parentheses are standard errors.)

significant and confirms differences in the influence that party played in each chamber.

On average, Senate Republicans were stronger mandate supporters than their Democratic colleagues. Being a Senate Republican raised overall support scores by 14 percent, compared to being a Senate Democrat. Moreover, Senate Republicans had higher mandate support scores on each of the separate policy dimensions than did Democrats as well, with the exception of other services. Immigration and business preemption were the two dimensions for which being a Republican senator was most strongly associated with higher mandate support.

House Republicans, in contrast, tended to be less supportive of mandates than were their Democratic colleagues. For all votes, Republicans were linked to 28 percent lower mandate support scores. Furthermore, with the exception of business preemptions, House Republicans had lower mandate support for specific policy dimensions than did House Democrats. House Republicans tended to have lower mandate support for immigration and welfare mandates, in contrast to their Senate counterparts.

Thus, it is clear from Table 9.5 that House Republicans are less supportive of mandates than are Democrats, whereas Senate Republicans are generally more supportive. On first glance, it is tempting to ascribe these differences to the greater conservatism of House Republicans in the 104th Congress. House Republicans were a remarkably cohesive voting majority in 1995 and 1996 and supported a leadership that was pledged to return power to the states not only through mandate reform, but also through block granting entitlement and social welfare programs.[28] Although Senate leaders joined in championing mandate and welfare reforms, they faced the constraints of governing a more individualistic body, requiring moderate and crosspartisan support to pass legislation. One study concluded that the Senate, with its moderate Republicans and supermajoritarian rules, was less supportive of congressional passage of the Contract with America.[29]

It is tempting to conclude that House Republicans had displayed a consistency and fealty to federalism principles in their mandate voting that represented a sharp reversal from the policy-driven positioning of their fellow partisans in the 1980s and of their current Senate colleagues. Although continuing to support new national mandates and preemptions in business, their votes on other mandates seemed to be governed by the party's broader federalism goals to a greater extent than before.

Although Federalism principles may indeed have strongly influence House voting, the differential scores of House and Senate Republicans were also a function of the differing voting agendas in each chamber. Put simply, the two chambers faced dramatically different types of roll calls. The seemingly greater Senate Republican support for mandates is a reflection of the greater number of roll calls on proposed mandates favored by congressional Republicans of both chambers. With its more open voting rules, a greater number of roll call votes were prompted in the Senate by Republican advocates of conservative mandates in welfare and immigration bills or by Democratic opponents of those conservative mandates.

On the welfare issue, for instance, there were only three recorded roll calls on mandate issues in the House, with a majority of Republicans voting against mandates on two of them. In the Senate, alternatively, there were fourteen welfare mandate roll calls, with Republicans voting against mandates on only seven of them. Republicans supported amendments proposed by Republican senators themselves to increase restrictions on such issues as drug testing and time limits, while they opposed Democratic amendments to give states greater flexibility to extend benefits and avoid cutoffs to specific populations. Although we will never know for sure how House members would have voted on these precise roll calls, the votes of Senate Republicans to support conservative policies and deny states the flexibility to depart from them were consistent with at least the public position of leading House members as well.

In the House, amendments to pending legislation are restricted by the leadership operating through the House Rules Committee, so many of these issues never have a chance to come to a vote on the House floor.[30] Some of the mandates voted on separately by the Senate on such issues as welfare or immigration were already embedded in comprehensive bills presented for House floor votes.

Interest Group Politics

The balance of interest group pressures had a major influence on mandate outcomes in 1996 as well. Many of the mandates passed in 1996 were generated and supported by powerful national interest groups, in alliance with congressional entrepreneurs who realized that their national goals critically depended on either preempting or conscripting the states. State and local interests faced a formidable array of interest groups advocating mandates, including some of the most powerful business interests in Washington. For example, the telecommunications industry, although beset by internal differences, is united in pushing for preemption of state and local taxing and zoning authority, whereas national securities firms and pesticide firms have long sought preemption of state regulation. Ironically, when pressing for deregulation, businesses often seek to preempt state and local taxes, fees, and regulations as barriers to full market competition.

When not facing powerful business alliances, state and local governments had to face labor unions on the minimum wage and mental health parity mandates. And a host of "externality groups" has arisen to represent broader interests on environmental, public health, and consumer issues that have provided entrepreneurial skills to gain significant regulatory victories in the past thirty years.

In facing these groups, state and local governments have shown a renewed concern about the impacts of mandates in recent years, culminating in their successful mobilization behind mandate reform. In the early 1990s, their interest groups established a Mandate Monitor to alert their membership to pending mandate proposals. Although discontinued with the passage of UMRA, a new Preemption Monitor has been launched by the National League of Cities to keep track of pending proposals that threaten to preempt state and local legal authority.[31] Four major state groups, including the National Governors' Association and the National Conference of State Legislatures, convened a Federalism Summit in 1995 and a subsequent Federalism Steering Committee to provide periodic guidance to improve the "equilibrium" in our federal system.[32]

On individual mandates, the successful efforts of state and local groups to reform safe drinking water requirements and roll back onerous highway mandates have to be considered major victories, and they bear witness to the successes that state and local groups can achieve when they mount sufficient intensity and unity. Although some analysts might point to these efforts as a sign of increased state and local vigilance on individual mandates, the reforms of existing mandates are actually consistent with the experience of the 1980s. State and local groups have a far easier time mobilizing intensity once mandates are in place and the costs become more salient to their grassroots membership. The asbestos in schools and handicapped education stories in Chapters 6 and 7 illustrate this phenomenon well.[33]

Lobbying against new mandates has historically been more difficult for the state and local community since the benefits appear more salient at this stage than the costs, which continued to be a problem in 1996. New mandates and preemptions in criminal justice, health insurance, pesticides, welfare and child support, mental health parity, and minimum wage were either embraced or not strongly opposed by state and local groups. Opposition to many of these mandates was not politically possible to these groups due to the valence character of some of these policies or to the active support they engendered among at least some portion of the state and local community.

The same kinds of problems bedeviling their lobbying in the 1980s continued to crosspressure them in dealing with the mandates of the 1990s. First, as associations that represent elected political leaders, state and local groups had difficulty opposing mandates defined in publicly compelling terms. The nationalization of the media and political culture has probably increased the vulnerability of state and local leaders to the same publicly compelling causes as national leaders, neutralizing or even subverting their defense of their jurisdictional prerogatives. Thus, for example, state and local officials did not publicly oppose the minimum wage hike, nor could they publicly condemn the new federal health insurance standards embodied in the Kennedy-Kassebaum legislation.

Second, internal partisan and political differences also made it difficult for these groups to take unified positions on many mandates that were proposed to implement partisan agendas. For example, the National League of Cities (NLC) faced considerable internal partisan-based conflict over whether to support the Family and Medical Leave Act in 1993, which prevented the organization from mustering the required two-thirds vote needed to lobby against this mandate. One National League of Cities lobbyist indicates that national policy interests are asserting new pressures within the organization that could create greater internal conflict over mandates. The Christian Coalition has attempted to form a caucus of city officials within the NLC, and this faction is urging support for legislation on local prayer in schools and other moral mandates. Representatives of gay and lesbian organizations want similar recognition.[34]

Third, many proposed mandates have in fact been based on initiatives already in place in numerous states and localities. When supporting the direction in which state and local officials are headed anyway, they often garner state and local support, or at least ambivalence. As Elazar notes, many states have little problem adjusting to federal standards when they have themselves already often adopted these standards in similar form.[35] The new welfare mandates, for instance, were developed with the support of Republican governors whose states were already in the process of implementing work requirements and other welfare limitations. Mandates can help state and local officials protect these initiatives from opposing political constituencies within the jurisdiction.

Moreover, as was the case in the 1980s, mandates continue to be useful in helping state and local officials address problems resulting from intergovernmental competition, preventing a mutually destructive "race to the bottom."[36] The 1993 Brady Handgun Control bill that requires local police checks on gun purchasers is an example of a case in which a federal mandate helped localities that wished to control guns deal with the exporting of guns from the more lenient jurisdictions. The National League of Cities supported the mandate originally, as did other state and local organizations, and the NLC refused to endorse the court challenges to this mandate culminating in the Supreme Court's 1997 *Printz v. the United States* decision. The pending EPA air quality regulations to tighten particulate and ozone regulations would create new burdens for a number of states and localities, but they are nonetheless supported by many Eastern states as a way to deal with the exporting of air pollution from the Midwest.[37]

Thus, as in the 1980s, the roots of many national mandates continue to be intergovernmental. Although federal mandates are popularly thought to arise in response to state policy inaction, state policy activism, in fact, may itself lay the political basis for or at least reduce the barriers to new federal mandating among state and local officials. Moreover, state innovations in policy stimulate the interest of national interest groups for new federal policies by either mandating the benefits of these policies across the nation or limiting state policies through national preemption.

When they did mount intense lobbying campaigns on newly proposed mandates or preemptions, state and local groups achieved some success in modifying proposed mandates, as with telecommunications, securities, and immigration reform. Mandates are born in functionally based issue networks and congressional committees, environments in which geographically based interests are often viewed as outsiders.[38] As defensive actors seeking to influence policy proposals developed in functionally based arenas, state and local governments can obtain influence over the design and funding of the mandate, and the UMRA point of order may have enhanced this influence. Where UMRA became a viable threat, it helped state and local interests achieve modifications in proposed legislation. However, as in the 1980s, these groups had difficulty overturning the basic federal decision to mandate, and, in fact, concessions they won helped pave the way for easier passage of the underlying mandate or preemption.

OTHER INSTITUTIONAL DEVELOPMENTS

The implementation of unfunded mandate reform was also affected by important institutional developments at the national level. First, the Advisory Commission on Intergovernmental Relations was terminated in 1996, ironically during a time when interest in federalism had peaked in Washington. As the only truly intergovernmental institution operating at the federal level, it was assigned a prominent analytic role by UMRA to identify needed reforms for existing mandates, as well as to undertake other studies on cost estimation. In the 1970s and 1980s, ACIR made a number of broad-sweeping recommendations for reform of our federal system, including one in 1984 that recommended federal adoption of full-scale mandate reimbursement.[39] These reports were typically endorsed by the entire commission and greeted with respect, if not abiding interest, in Washington.

However, its 1996 report that recommended the modification of thirteen politically sensitive mandates, such as the Davis Bacon and that of handicapped education, sparked a political firestorm that helped erode whatever waning support the commission had, paving the way for its termination in late 1996.[40] The report prompted a coalition of handicapped, environmental, and other public interest programs to engage the White House in a concerted campaign to politicize the commission membership.[41] In an election year, the White House responded by mobilizing unanimous opposition by nearly all Democratic members of ACIR, causing the report to be defeated in one of the few events of its kind in ACIR's history. Among the many lessons that may be drawn from this, one is that broad-scale recommendations and even legislation such as UMRA may more easily garner support than proposals to eliminate specific regulations or programs—a lesson state and local groups know all too well.

The demise of ACIR corresponded with the rise of the CBO's intergovernmental capacity. Beginning with the State and Local Cost Estimation Act of 1981, the CBO had been required to estimate state and local costs of pending federal legislation. The agency had decided at the time to integrate these analyses with its estimation of federal budgetary costs. Since the CBO's federal budget cost estimates were an integral part of the enforcement of congressional budget resolutions, these estimates received priority within the CBO and Congress itself.[42]

With the enactment of UMRA, the CBO's state and local estimates became more central to the congressional process. Reflecting this heightened congressional priority, the CBO created a separate unit devoted exclusively to UMRA cost estimates. In addition to estimating costs for numerous legislative proposals (see Table 9.1), this group issued annual reports on UMRA, detailing the CBO's estimating activity.[43] The unit also met regularly with state and local interest groups to exchange notes about emerging mandates and to discuss other issues associated with UMRA implementation. Although differing with the CBO on specific cost estimation issues, state and local groups overall gave the CBO positive evaluations[44], even though they took issue with the agency's legal interpretation of certain provisions of UMRA.[45]

More Reform?

Several other federal regulatory reform initiatives were enacted in the 104th Congress that could be used in the future by those concerned about federal mandates. One such initiative affecting the congressional process, the 1996 Congressional Review Act (PL 104-102), requires all major federal agency regulations to be reviewed by Congress for sixty days prior to implementation. Congress has established expedited procedures to pass a resolution of disapproval that, if signed by the president, would prevent proposed regulations from going into effect. As of early 1998, this tool had not yet been used to object to any regulations.

In the same legislation, Congress enacted the Small Business Regulatory Enforcement Fairness Act, which required executive agencies to give special consideration to alternative ways to alleviate burdens on small businesses and communities when developing regulations, providing these entities with the right to enjoin regulations in court.[46] UMRA itself contained provisions that required broader federal agency consultations with state and local governments in promulgating intergovernmental regulations, exempting these consultations from the dictates of the Federal Advisory Committee Act and establishing a presumption that agencies would choose the least costly or burdensome regulatory approach. A 1998 GAO report concluded that UMRA had little direct impact on agencies' rulemaking in the first two years due to various exemptions as well as the similarity of these UMRA requirements to existing agency processes.[47]

Some feel that the UMRA process itself needs some patching to become a more effective bulwark against mandates. Proposals for strengthening the process include increasing the margin to overrule the point of order from 50 to 60 percent of members, covering preemptions with a new point of order provision, full reimbursement for federal mandate costs, and development of a regulatory budget to constrain the imposition of nonfederal costs.[48]

Perhaps the most notable gaps in the new process were the exclusions for the types of mandates typically used at the federal level to impose new duties or preempt old ones. Of the six types of mandates covered in this study, UMRA only directly covers direct orders. Grant conditions, crosscutting requirements, and crossover sanctions are excluded from the point of order, unless they increase state and local costs for major entitlement grants.[49] Partial preemptions and total preemptions are covered only if proposed legislation imposes costs exceeding the $50 million threshold, but measures are not subject to points of order if they primarily affect state and local authority rather than costs.

Many but not all, of the new mandates and preemptions enacted in 1996 fell into one of these exclusions. This was also the case in the 1980s. Of the thirty-one significant mandates of the 1980s discussed in Chapter 4, ten were direct orders that would have been covered by UMRA. The rest were either grant conditions, crosscutting requirements, crossover sanctions, preemptions, or direct orders, exempt from UMRA's reach because they dealt with civil rights, disability, or Social Security.

The limitations of UMRA's reach are in part premised on the act's conception of a mandate as an "enforceable duty" imposed by the federal government on state and local governments.[50] By excluding grant conditions for most programs, Congress essentially adopted the long-standing views of the courts that such conditions are not legal mandates or preemptions, due to the voluntary nature of grants themselves. As ACIR has said, the Court has seemingly found no area in which Congress might not spend its way around what would otherwise be the constitutional prerogatives of state power.[51] Under UMRA, Congress can do just that. Grants have served as a so-called Trojan horse, where federal compulsion is masked by the friendly and apparently almighty federal dollar.

The voluntaristic model of grants, although technically correct, ignores the fiscal reality that states and localities can rarely refuse to participate in major federal assistance programs, regardless of the perceived impact of their associated conditions. States and localities refusing federal aid make news, and they often are pressured to renege by constituencies and taxpayers who view federal grants as a return on their federal tax revenue that would otherwise be reallocated to neighboring states. Moreover, the voluntaristic model ignores the increasingly compulsory nature of many grant conditions, notably the crosscutting requirements and crossover sanctions that ACIR documented in the early 1980s. Congress has also not been reluctant to impose new conditions on ongoing grants, even years after states first exercised their choice to participate in the original program.[52]

At some point, it may be appropriate to reexamine the underlying theory relied on by the courts and Congress regarding grant conditions, particularly if mandate trends suggest that grants have increased their role as federal mandating vehicles. Consideration of new mechanisms to restrain intrusions on state and local authority through total preemptions might also be in order at some point. Indeed, legislation was introduced in 1996 that required explicit statements of congressional intentions to preempt state and local authority and that provided for a point of order to be raised against preemption legislation resting on insufficient constitutional authority.[53]

As much as reformers might be tempted to institute further process changes to "fix" the mandate problem, it should be recognized that the current process rests on a delicate political equilibrium. As noted in Chapter 8, UMRA's passage was in part grounded in the perception by all actors that the process represented a responsible way to make Congress more accountable for mandate decisions without putting it in a straightjacket that might jeopardize its capacity to respond to emerging priorities or to the political needs of the day. The exclusions and exemptions were formulated with an eye toward gaining the support needed to pass the legislation at the time. The apparent gaps and exclusions in UMRA thus reflect a political statement about the federal-state balance that Congress will revisit probably only when the underlying political equilibrium has shifted.

IMPLICATIONS

The first year of the Unfunded Mandates Reform Act was greeted with great expectations in the intergovernmental community. Although state and local governments did in fact realize some important victories in Congress, both in softening the impact of new mandates and in reversing some existing ones, 1996 did not prove to be the watershed year for which many had hoped. In fact, significant new mandates and preemptions were passed that year.

The passage of some significant new federal mandates and preemptions in such an intergovernmentally propitious time suggests that the forces supporting intergovernmental regulation are deeply embedded in our system. Shifting alliances continue to embrace mandates and preemptions as tools to achieve a variety of emerging goals placed on the federal doorstep in a national media culture. Ironically, two forces traditionally thought of as constraining national government—chronic deficits and private economic deregulation—can have the effect of increasing intergovernmental mandates and preemptions. Budget constraints can encourage the shift from grants to mandates, while federal deregulation of private businesses can prompt the preemption of state and local regulations and taxes that come to be viewed as barriers to full-market competition.

Though no longer structurally deferential to state and local interests, Congress does respond to state and local governments as interest groups when they are able to organize intense grassroots lobbying campaigns. State and local governments did, in fact, achieve notable rollbacks of existing mandates, even though these are not formally covered by the new mandate reform process. However, their effectiveness in forestalling new mandates continued to be compromised by internal conflicts and crosspressures.

The reforms ushered in by UMRA were not intended to reverse these fundamental political forces. Rather, they represented modest changes in procedure that could only work if backed by active defenders of state and local prerogatives and a supportive political climate in Congress. In this context, UMRA can be viewed as having achieved modest success in some important cases. Although not clearly reversing mandate decisions, the procedures facilitated efforts to modify mandates by highlighting intergovernmental costs, and the point of order may have deterred potential sponsors from introducing mandates for committee or floor consideration.

Since mandate advocates have so often been successful in defining the terms of the debate in publicly compelling ways, shifting the terms of the debate to emphasize costs and burdens is no small accomplishment. Particularly when viewed against the continuing appeal that mandates have in our national policymaking process, the achievements of UMRA can be best likened to what Samuel Johnson once said about the dog who walked on only his hind legs: What is remarkable is not how awkwardly he walks, but rather that he walks at all.

The last chapter of this book will discuss the sustainability of mandate reform over the longer term. UMRA could represent a new phase in a more devolved federal system or a pause preceding a new round of nationalization and centralization. The future outlook will hinge on broader trends in our political system.

NOTES TO CHAPTER 9

1. David Beam and Timothy Conlan, "The 1995 Unfunded Mandates Reform Act: The Politics of Federal Mandating Meets the Politics of Reform," *Journal of Public Budgeting and Finance Management* 7 (1995), pp. 355–386.

2. See Eileen Shanahan, "The Sudden Rise in Statehouse Status," *Governing* (September, 1996), p. 15.

3. See Paul L. Posner and Margaret T. Wrightson, "Block Grants: A Perennial but Unstable Tool of Government," *Publius: The Journal of Federalism* 26, No. 3 (1996), p. 88.

4. Timothy J. Conlan, James D. Riggle, and Donna E. Schwartz, "Deregulating Federalism? The Politics of Mandate Reform in the 104th Congress," *Publius: The Journal of Federalism* 25, No. 3 (1995), p. 37.

5. The CBO also included estimates done for individual members on proposed mandates.

6. Mandates were considered major by the author if they exceeded the $250 million threshold defined in the State and Local Cost Estimation Act of 1981 (PL 97–108).

7. Interview with Teresa Gullo, Congressional Budget Office, 29 January 1998.

8. The Congressional Budget Office indicates that a fourth piece of legislation mandating mental health parity for health insurance was also modified to fall below the threshold, but it is not clear that the UMRA provision itself was responsible for this. The original provision would have prohibited health plans from imposing more stringent financial and treatment limitations on mental health care, such as patient cost sharing and deductibles, which the CBO estimated would have increased state and local health insurance costs above the UMRA threshold. Extensive lobbying by private employers and the insurance industry was probably responsible for the bill's modification requiring parity only for lifetime and annual benefit limitations—which happened to reduce the state and local costs below the $50 million threshold.

9. Letter from Congressional Budget Office to Senator Simpson, 2 May 1996, transmitting cost estimates for Amendment No. 3855 to S. 1664.

10. Letter from the Congressional Budget Office to Congressman Bliley Jr., 6 June 1996, transmitting cost estimates for H.R. 3005.

11. For classic treatment of conflict definition and displacement, see E. E. Schattschneider, *The Semi-Sovereign People* (New York: Holt, Rinehart, and Winston, 1960).

12. See R. Douglas Arnold, *The Logic of Congressional Action* (New Haven: Yale University Press, 1990); John Kingdon, *Congressmen's Voting Decisions*, 3rd edition (Ann Arbor: University of Michigan Press, 1989); David Mayhew, *Divided We Govern* (New Haven: Yale University Press, 1991).

13. Letter from Congressional Budget Office to Senator Nancy Kassebaum, 25 March 1996.

14. This provision attempted to sidestep the Supreme Court's *Lopez* decision, overturning a previous federal gun ban by stipulating that the gun had to be shown to have traveled in interstate commerce. *Lopez v. United States*, 115 S. Ct. 1424 (1995).

15. Angela Antonelli, *Promises Unfulfilled: Unfunded Mandates Reform Act of 1995* (Washington, D.C.: Cato Institute, 1996).

16. Advisory Commission on Intergovernmental Relations, "The Role of Federal Mandates in Intergovernmental Relations," draft for discussion (Washington, D.C.: 23 July 1996).

17. Advisory Commission on Intergovernmental Relations, *Regulatory Federalism: Policy, Process, Impact and Reform*, A–95 (Washington, D.C.: ACIR, 1984), p. 265.

18. Letter from Congressional Budget Office to Congressman Thomas Bliley Jr., 25 June 1996.

19. Tom Arrandale, "The Price of Potability," *Governing* (December, 1997), pp. 67–78.

20. Letter from Congressional Budget Office to Congressman John Kasich, 26 June 1996.

21. Legal immigrants are barred from welfare for the first five years of residence.

22. See Frank Baumgartner and Bryan Jones, *Agendas and Instability in American Politics* (Chicago: University of Chicago Press, 1993), p. 150.

23. Burt Solomon, "Just Because of the Election, Parolees Face Testing for Drugs," *National Journal* (26 October 1996), p. 2304.

24. Duplicate votes in the same chamber, such as motions to reconsider a previous vote, were excluded.

25. Variables were defined in the same way as in Chapter 3. Party was a dummy, with Republicans = 0. Ideology was defined as scores given each member by Americans for Democratic Action, with liberalism = 100. Prior state and local office holding was a dummy recorded as 0 when any member had served in an elected or appointed state and local government position prior to his or her congressional term.

26. Timothy J. Conlan, James D. Riggle, and Donna E. Schwartz, "Deregulating Federalism? The Politics of Mandate Reform in the 104th Congress," *Publius: The Journal of Federalism*, 25, No. 3 (1995), pp. 23–40.

27. Although neither party, state and local experience, nor region is statistically significant, this is not a major issue for this analysis. Since the regression equations are based on the total population of mandate votes in 1996, we are not concerned here with questions of statistical inference. Accordingly, the relationships estimated by the coefficients are not attributable to sampling error.

28. Lawrence C. Dodd and Bruce I. Oppenheimer, "Revolution in the House: Testing the Limits of Party Government," in *Congress Reconsidered,* 6th edition, ed. Lawrence C. Dodd and Bruce I. Oppenheimer (Washington, D.C.: Congressional Quarterly, 1997), pp. 29–60.

29. John B. Bader, *Taking the Initiative: Leadership Agendas in Congress and the "Contract with America"* (Washington, D.C.: Georgetown University Press, 1996), p. 202.

30. One study found that 77 percent of the rules for considering major legislation in the House in 1995 were restrictive of amendments and debate time. See Barbara Sinclair, "Party Leaders and the New Legislative Process," in *Congress Reconsidered,* 6th edition, p. 239.

31. *Preemption Monitor* (Washington, D.C.: National League of Cities, 1997).

32. Memorandum from Dan Sprague, Council of State Governments, Lexington, Ky., 10 October 1997.

33. The tendency of our system to respond to state and local concerns following initial development of the program is illustrated by federal regulations on air pollution, for which federal standards have been continually modified and stretched out to accommodate state, local, and private concerns. Charles O. Jones, *Clean Air: The Policies and Politics of Pollution Control* (Pittsburgh: University of Pittsburgh Press, 1975).

34. Interview with Frank Shafroth, Director of Federal Relations, National League of Cities.

35. Daniel Elazar, *American Federalism: A View from the States,* 3rd edition (New York: Harper and Row, 1984), p. 111.

36. Susan Rose-Ackerman, "Does Federalism Matter? Choice in a Federal Republic," *Journal of Political Economy* 49, No. 1 (1981), pp. 152–163.

37. Joby Warrick, "Downwind States Welcome EPA Smog Plan," *Washington Post*, 16 March 1997, p. A16.

38. See Donald Haider, *When Governments Come to Washington* (New York: Free Press, 1974), p. 223.

39. Advisory Commission on Intergovernmental Relations, *Regulatory Federalism: Policy, Process, Impact and Reform.*

40. Advisory Commission on Intergovernmental Relations, *The Role of Federal Mandates in Intergovernmental Relations*, draft for discussion, 23 July 1996.

41. See Citizens for Sensible Safeguards, *Shirking Responsibility: ACIR's Call to Repeal Federal Protections* (Washington, D.C.: 5 March 1996).

42. General Accounting Office, *Legislative Mandates: State Experiences Offer Insights for Federal Action*, GAO/HRD-88-75 (Washington, D.C.: GAO, September, 1988).

43. Congressional Budget Office, *The Experience of the Congressional Budget Office During the First Year of the Unfunded Mandates Reform Act* (Washington, D.C.: CBO, January, 1997); *An Assessment of the Unfunded Mandates Reform Act in 1997* (Washington, D.C.: CBO, February, 1998).

44. National Governors' Association, *Issue Brief: Status of the Unfunded Mandates Reform Act of 1995, P.L. 104–4* (Washington, D.C.: National Governors' Association, 12 December 1996).

45. Letter to Speaker Newt Gingrich from the chairman and vice chairman, National Governors' Association, Washington, D.C., 16 May 1997, pp. 1–2.

46. Julie Kosterlitz, "Mom and Pop Get Even," *National Journal*, 8 March 1997.

47. General Accounting Office, *Unfunded Mandates: Reform Has Had Little Effect on Agencies' Rulemaking Actions*, GAO/GGD-98-30 (Washington, D.C.: GAO, February, 1998).

48. Angela Antonelli, *Promises Unfulfilled: Unfunded Mandates Reform Act of 1995.*

49. The Congressional Budget Office has interpreted UMRA to mean that additional grant conditions or funding caps for major entitlement programs are not covered if state and local governments have the flexibility to offset the increased costs or to lose federal funds by reducing their responsibilities or services. Congressional Budget Office, *The Experience of the Congressional Budget Office During the First Year of the Unfunded Mandates Reform Act*, p. 10.

50. Public Law 104-4, Sec. 421 (5).

51. Advisory Commission on Intergovernmental Relations, *Federal Regulation of State and Local Governments: The Mixed Record of the 1980's* (Washington, D.C.: ACIR, 1993), p. 78.

52. In one 1981 decision striking down ambiguous conditions, Justice Rehnquist warned that "though Congress' power to legislate under the spending power is broad, it does not include surprising participating states with post-acceptance or 'retroactive' conditions." *Pennhurst State School and Hospital v. Halderman*, 49 LW 4363 at 4369 (29 April 1981).

53. S. 1629, Tenth Amendment Enforcement Act of 1996.

10

Conclusions

Have mandates joined death and taxes as one of the inevitable certainties of life? It is hard to imagine, but before 1960, this question would have been greeted with puzzlement, as a presumption was shared by both parties against the national regulation of state and local governments. Yet, in the 1970s and 1980s, mandates came to be embraced by both parties as an efficient tool to achieve national objectives that leaders felt compelled to promote. The shift from voluntaristic to coercive tools of federal action marked a significant departure in our federal system.

The passage of mandate reform in the 1990s can be seen as a collective expression of national remorse over these trends and may presage a period where federalism casts a larger shadow over policy debates. However, mandates have deep roots in our political system. Many of the factors underlying the earlier shift to coercive federalism are still with us today, notably the continuing pressure on leaders to champion new national initiatives implicating state and local governments. Moreover, changes in our political system eclipsing congressional deference to state and local interests now require those governments to mobilize their membership to protect federalism interests in Congress, an uncertain prospect that is constrained by the ambivalence of state and local groups toward certain mandates. Thus, the passage of mandate reform, although signalling a renewed commitment to federalism, will require other changes in national political forces before a sustainable change in governance will emerge, characterized by a systemic forbearance and observance of federalism principles.

IMPLICATIONS OF THE NEW POLICYMAKING PROCESS

Classic notions of both federalism and policymaking suggested that Congress would show a great deal of deference to state and local governments in formulating national policy. Historically, state and local governments enjoyed considerable deference in the process, resting on the very real dependence of national office holders on state and local parties for their jobs.

This institutional deference was reflected in a presumption against coercive federal mandates and preemptions on the state and local sector that had been accepted as one of the rules of the game by all actors in the system prior to the 1960s. As discussed in Chapter 2, this influence was bolstered by a system that was widely viewed as stacked against major policy initiatives and grounded in policy incrementalism and the numerous veto points within Congress, and in the broader system as well, that tended to frustrate bold policy changes.

Classic political science literature suggested that mandate legislation would spark heated conflict within Congress. Major policy change was said to invariably prompt major conflict, with conflict rising as the stakes increase.[1] Consensus was expected in areas where the stakes were either small or where policy monopolies prevented the emergence of groups with conflicting perspectives, but regulatory policies were said to inspire a high level of conflict among interest groups.[2] As narrow interests facing concentrated costs from regulation, state and local governments would be expected to mobilize themselves more effectively than would advocates representing the more diffuse interest of regulatory beneficiaries.[3] The conflict could be expected to become partisan, as Republican allies of states and localities in particular would mobilize to oppose increased federal power over the states.

The congressional adoption of mandates and preemptions over the past twenty years is clearly at odds with these models of our system.[4] This study has indeed shown that mandates have become a major instrument of national policy, relied on by leaders of both parties at various times to support differing policy goals. The legitimation of mandates began in the 1970s and continued, surprisingly, into the 1980s and early 1990s, even in a purportedly conservative era of governance. Chapter 9 showed that notable mandate restraint and rollback occurred in 1996, but the record was mixed as Congress nonetheless enacted some significant new mandates and preemptions.

The rapid passage of many mandates chronicled in this study reflects the emergence of a new style of policymaking at the federal level. The adoption of far-reaching, nonincremental policy reforms became more commonplace during this period. Ideas that were purveyed by influential experts and policy entrepreneurs found increasingly fertile ground in a more open, activist Congress that was anxious to take credit for legislation appealing to broadly shared values championed by an all-pervasive media.

The change in congressional incentives was perhaps most important. Most studies suggest that members of Congress, freed from their state and local party moorings, became anxious entrepreneurs in search of new policy ideas and profiles to gain media attention and political support. The competition for policy leadership has had a profoundly nationalizing and centralizing effect on policymaking in Congress, as congressmen from both parties were compelled to sponsor national programs and policies, albeit serving different interests and ideas.[5] Most domestic programs embraced by national leaders, such as improving education or reducing crime, involve functions traditionally performed by state and local governments and thus invariably implicate them in new national initiatives.

Nationalization of policy became a logical response to this new environment, but why mandates? As noted in Chapter 1, we as a nation are loathe to empower federal bureaucracies to both fund and deliver domestic programs and services, particularly in well established areas of state and local jurisdiction. Accordingly, the federal government sought to either entice state and local involvement through grants or compel their participation through some form of mandate.

At the outset, the federal role often began with grants, reflecting in part the relative weakness of advocacy coalitions supporting new programs as well as diffuse resistance to the use of mandates as a policy tool.[6] Over time, however, the grant program served to strengthen the beneficiary coalitions and generate support from state and local bureaucracies and leaders as well. As these programs took root at the state and local level, the nation's tolerance eroded for differences among states' approaches and gaps in services to various groups, while the legitimacy of the federal role took hold. Accordingly, mandates came to be seen as a logical and appropriate tool to promote greater national uniformity.

But this logic was underscored by the growing political strength of beneficiary coalitions which enabled them to succeed in convincing policymakers to choose more coercive policy tools such as mandates. Remarkably, these coalitions were strong enough to gain both adoption of mandates and substantial federal funds to underwrite state and local compliance during a time when federal budget deficits reached peacetime highs in the 1980s and early 1990s. This pattern supports the conclusion of John Kincaid who argued that the era of cooperative federalism characterized by reliance on grants helped promote a more coercive federal role epitomized by the use of mandates.[7]

Perhaps more surprising than the passage of mandates was the frequent adoption of some of the most fiscally burdensome mandates in a consensual process rather than the kind of conflictual, deliberative process portrayed in traditional views of regulatory policymaking. State and local groups were not frequently mobilized to oppose this legislation, and Congress often proceeded to enact expensive mandates by unanimous acclamation or consensus. Far from a policymaking process paralyzed by gridlock, congressional policymaking, if anything, exhibited a race to claim credit on these issues.

A key factor was the success of mandate advocates in defining proposed mandates as politically compelling causes that could not be publicly opposed by either conservatives or state and local interest groups. Having successfully defined the scope of conflict in terms of benefit, not cost, the legislation moved through the congressional obstacle course at a rapid pace.

Recent literature suggests this pattern is not limited to intergovernmental mandates. Baumgartner and Jones posit a "punctuated equilibrium" model to explain how policy areas dominated by policy monopolies and seemingly unshakable programs suddenly can become unhinged and replaced by a new political and policy regime. Importantly, they suggest that major policy changes are often accomplished as waves of enthusiasm sweep over the system, typically driving out any serious opposition or countermobilization.[8] Such new policies are buttressed by an unassailable policy idea that legitimate political actors oppose only at their own peril. In Baumgartner and Jones' model, the political system "lurches" from one equilibrium to another, with the process of change often happening rapidly and by acclamation.[9]

This dynamic is similar to the issue-attention cycle posited by Anthony Downs. Downs wrote that nonincremental policy change occurs through a process of alarmed discovery and euphoric enthusiasm. Often after objective indicators of a problem have peaked, strong public pressure emerges to "solve" the problem.[10]

The types of issues in which "Downsian" mobilization are most likely to occur are what they call "valence" issues, for which only one side of the debate is perceived as legitimate.[11] As with many of the mandates examined in this study, it is difficult for affected interests to mobilize against these issues once they attain agenda status. But, as tempting as it is for politicians to vote for them, they are also difficult to solve, giving rise to the cycle observed by Downs in which politicians and the public lose interest over time.

Indeed, some suggest that national elected officials are more vulnerable to bandwagon politics than ever before.[12] Thanks to the erosion of allegiances to party or to state and local government leaders, members of Congress are said to be more atomistic and thereby feel less protected if they are on the wrong side of a publicly compelling issue. Furthermore, they are also increasingly operating in a transparent environment, with an increasingly omnipresent media feeding back images of their performance to their constituencies. Faced with this increasing pressure, public officials are increasingly anxious to avoid being perceived as being on the wrong side of issues, causing them to shun politically infeasible policies and support those that are politically compelling, regardless of ideology or party position.

What happened, though, to the constraints in our system that were thought to prevent this nationalization dynamic? The foregoing suggests that one of the major factors prompting rapid adoption of mandates in the 1980s and early 1990s was the neutralization or weakening of actors and constraints expected to limit the expansion of federal power in our system. Beginning in the 1930s, the Supreme Court provided the rationale for an expanded federal role in domestic policy and, until the 1990s, generally ruled that state and local governments had to look to the political process, not the 10th Amendment, to protect their jurisdictional prerogatives. Essentially, the Court's rulings enabled Congress to achieve its policy goals through mandates and preemptions.

During this period, Republicans, although supporting federalism principles, often engaged in a competition to avoid being blamed for defeating politically compelling mandates that were defined in valence terms or actually championed mandates when they implemented higher priority policy goals. Unless they could prevent mandate bills from coming to the agenda in the first place, Republicans often were consigned to the role of "reluctant mandators," supporting the overall mandate in formal votes but working behind the scenes to modify their stringency. In other cases, they endorsed mandates when other party goals and principles were at stake, as shown by the roll call analysis revealing Republican support for mandates that advance party objectives in such areas as moral policy, business preemption, and welfare.

This finding reinforces the views of Timothy Conlan, who observed that, like most Americans, national political leaders have a philosophical allegiance to federalism but are often unwilling to sacrifice more specific policy goals calling for federal action. He cites polling data that indicate public support for political conservatism on general issues of federal power but that also show public support for a wide range of new federal policy interventions.[13]

STATE AND LOCAL GOVERNMENTS AND MANDATES

State and local governments might have been expected to be the most significant restraint on the passage of mandates. After all, if they cannot defend their institutional interests and prerogatives, how can we expect other actors to speak effectively on their behalf?

In earlier eras, federalism enjoyed a presumptive status as one of the universal rules of the game, and the assertion of new federal powers required major mobilization of interests and ideas sufficient to justify departing from this political norm. The decline of the endemic political ties between federal, state, and local officials and the apparent erosion of federalism as a widely shared value has required the mobilization of state and local governments themselves to protect their interests through their interest group organizations in Washington. Unlike in earlier eras, federalism is no longer the default option, but rather it requires for its protection the active mobilization of state and local interests in orchestrated lobbying campaigns. Thus, in a very real sense, the protection of federalism values and positions rests in large part on whether state and local groups are effective guardians of their own prerogatives.

As we have seen, when state and local government interest groups marshalled an intense grassroots lobbying campaign, they enjoy some success in defending themselves on mandate issues, as Justice Blackmun's *Garcia* opinion envisioned.[14] In the mid-1980s, they launched a major mobilization that won key changes in the application of federal overtime standards following the *Garcia* decision and modified proposed mandates for preschool disabled children as well. In the mid-1990s they gained passage of mandate reform following a highly successful grassroots and media campaign. Moreover, they achieved some notable victories in rolling back onerous highway mandates, modifying safe drinking water, and protecting at least some of their powers in telecommunications, immigration, and securities reforms passed in 1996.

Internal Conflicts among State and Local Officials

However, all too often mandates disarmed state and local government interest groups and prevented the mobilization necessary for the protection of federalism interests in the current era. Frequently, state and local government interest groups themselves were not able to generate the requisite internal consensus needed to marshall active grassroots campaigns that were necessary to protect federalism interests in the face of politically compelling mandate goals.

The mandate goals proved to be compelling not only to congressional officials, but often to state and local officials as well. As shown in Chapter 5, state and local government groups were often neutral or even supportive of individual mandates and concentrated their lobbying on winning concessions or on federal funding to ease implementation. And, as illustrated by the special education story in Chapter 7, the federal funding carrot exerts a pervasive, albeit more subtle, nationalizing influence on state and local policy priorities.

Achieving unity on any contentious policy issue is not easy for organizations comprised of state and local elected officials of different political persuasions and parties. The broad political appeal of many mandates made it even more difficult for elected officials across the political spectrum to agree to oppose them. Like congressional conservatives, they risked public blame by opposing these programs. And, like members of Congress, some were policy entrepreneurs anxious to make a mark on the national stage. Absent a consensus, these organizations were often silent on the fundamental policy question pertaining to the need for a federal mandate. Instead, they chose to focus on the need for funding and flexibility in implementing mandates—issues that more readily garnered internal agreement among their politically diverse memberships.

The political appeal of most mandates was accentuated because the benefits of new mandates appeared immediate and concrete, whereas the costs and implementation challenges were difficult to visualize until the regulations specified the requirements. The asbestos in schools case discussed in Chapter 6 illustrates the pattern: Local schools initially could not publicly oppose the mandate, but later they became politically aroused when the EPA published regulations that prompted Congress to delay implementation. The Advisory Commission on Intergovernmental Relations concluded that this pattern of delayed state and local reaction is common for mandates with broad symbolic appeal, including the handicapped access requirements (Section 504 of the 1973 Rehabilitation Act) and Endangered Species Act.[15]

In contrast, state and local groups were likely to be more vigilant in attacking existing mandates whose costs have become salient to their members. As discussed in Chapter 7, the frustrations and problems experienced by schools in implementing the original special education mandate of 1975 enabled school boards to more easily mobilize against the 1986 extension of the mandate to preschool children. As noted in Chapter 8, the groundswell of support for mandate reform was prompted at least in part by the delayed impacts of the regulations issued a number of years after the passage of such legislation as the 1986 safe drinking water mandate and asbestos in schools mandate, which state and local groups initially did not oppose. Although public policy analysts would like costs and benefits to be considered together when major regulatory programs are established, often costs are dealt with serially and separately from benefits, as Congress uses the litmus test of experience to assess the need to modify regulatory statutes to deal with cost claims.[16]

Mandates also served a political function for state and local officials in gaining leverage—in policy struggles within their own governments, as well as in competition with other states or localities for economic development. Within their own governments, state and local officials found mandates to be a useful tool to accomplish their own policy agendas in the face of recalcitrant local political actors. As discussed in Chapter 5, states and localities also engage in competition with other jurisdictions for economic development, and federal mandates essentially provide a floor to prevent competition from degenerating. States or localities seeking to regulate in certain areas such as gun control or commercial truck drivers can see their efforts undermined if some jurisdictions benefit from inaction or refuse to adopt a common regulatory framework.

Intergovernmental Roots of Mandates

Ironically, as the foregoing suggests, state policy activism can prompt federal mandates every bit as much as can state policy inaction. This is a seemingly counterintuitive point since most advocates justify nationalization of policy to correct state policy inaction or inequities. In this view, the best way for states to ward off federal mandates would be to become policy activists and innovators.[17]

From this standpoint, states have earned greater federal forbearance by their modernization of administrative and fiscal systems and by their increased programmatic leadership over the past thirty years.[18] States threw off the yoke of segregation that for many years clouded their "states' rights" claims; revenue systems were expanded; bureaucracies became more professionalized; legislatures were reapportioned and became more responsive to policy demands; and interest groups representing a more diverse range of constituencies found their way to state capitols. Thanks in part to these trends, states have become policy activists, leaders, and innovators in many areas. States increased their spending in many programs that were originally started with federal grants to become senior fiscal partners, and they replaced many of the federal funding cuts of the early 1980s.[19]

However, in many cases the very policy maturity, activism, and diversity celebrated by federalism observers has helped lay the foundation for federal mandates. Most of the significant mandates passed in the 99th Congress were preceded by similar programs in a number of states, as both federal and state officials supported nationalization of policies initiated by the states for different reasons. Indeed, the growth of federal regulatory activism coincided with periods of state policy activism as well. This apparent puzzle can be resolved by accepting the view that state activism is positively linked to and prompts federal regulatory activism.

Traditionally, it has been acknowledged that state innovations sow the seeds for national adoption by testing policy ideas and approaches in "laboratories of democracy." However, state innovations also provide *political* incentives for nationalization of these policies. They inspire policy advocates to extend the policies of some states to all states. Similar to the logic of regulatory expansion from one protected class to another, inequities are perceived to exist when citizens of a national society have access to different services and benefits solely due to the state in which they happen to reside. Differences among the states in regulatory policies are also viewed with alarm by national businesses, who prefer a common national regulatory scheme with a single federal administrative entity in charge.[20]

The intergovernmental environment itself, then, came to be an important factor prompting policies' federal adoption. In an increasingly national political system, diversity among states' policies tends to be viewed not as a cause for celebration of the strengths of our federal system, but as a reason for alarm and a rationale for centralizing policy mandates or preemptions. An infrastructure of nationalized media, interest groups, and entrepreneurial national and state political leaders combines to accelerate the diffusion and nationalization of state policy innovations in a process that has probably accelerated in recent years. States provide niches for new policy ideas that later become nationalized through this political infrastructure, as states are increasingly linked to the federal government in what two observers referred to as a "positive feedback" process.[21]

Equally important, in a society whose economics, culture, and communications have increasingly becoming nationalized, state and local governments themselves have also become less insulated from national trends in both governance and programs.[22] As early as 1973, Douglas Rose argued, for example, that state laws and opinions agreed with national laws and opinion nearly 90 percent of the time. He asserted that state laws are largely the product of national policy trends, derived from the imposition of national norms or from intergovernmental competition and imitation among the states.[23]

Politically, as one observer said, state legislatures are becoming increasingly "congressionalized," as state political leaders rely less on party labels and gubernatorial coattails and become more like policy entrepreneurs running candidate-centered campaigns in search of visibility, campaign financing, and votes.[24] Governors too have had to establish candidate-centered campaigns independent of party, prompting them also to become more like policy entrepreneurs in search of new ideas to champion.[25] Interest groups have carried national ideas to the states by increasing their organizational presence in state capitols, and the kinds of groups represented in states have become more diverse and include public interest groups similar to those proliferating in Washington.[26] Over the years, federal grant programs have helped institutionalize national values and interests in state governments as bureaucracies and interest groups have coalesced around these programs in the states.

All of this suggests that policy problems increasingly are presented in similar ways at both national and state levels. And it means that state and local leaders are becoming every bit as vulnerable to the same publicly compelling causes and policy stampedes as are national leaders. In a nationalized media culture, state and national political communities and values have thus become more integrated, making it more difficult for state officials to define a mandate as a truly external constraint. States are still different in important ways, but what is argued here is a trend toward nationalization of political cultures that has made a difference for state and local officials' behavior on the national stage.

Viewed in this light, mandates are not only a tool of coercion applied by the federal government against protesting state and local officials. Rather, their increasing prevalence reflects the growing interdependence of national and state and local political cultures and political systems that redefines how state and local officials define their political interests in our federal system. Most important, state and local officials have become crosspressured by overlapping allegiances to nationally pervasive values. This has tended to temper, neutralize, or even subvert their expected defenses of their jurisdictional prerogatives. Programmatic values have frequently assumed the primary place in the debate at all levels, often rendering concerns over federalism and governmental process in general to the back burner.[27]

Cooperative Mandating?

This is not to say that state and local governments have not opposed certain mandates and achieved some success in modifying them. As discussed earlier, they were particularly successful in mounting vigorous assaults on existing mandates whose costs and frustrations are well known by their members. However, although they made mandates more cooperative and flexible, state and local governments, wittingly or unwittingly, helped legitimize mandates themselves.

Internally, it was often easier for state and local groups to obtain membership support for public positions seeking mandate modifications, flexibility, and federal reimbursement of costs than for positions in total opposition to the proposed mandate itself. Externally, modifications and funding were more readily accepted by the programmatic- and functionally based policy networks in command of policymaking in our system. Unlike federal grant funding issues, state and local governments and beneficiaries often had conflicting interests when it came to the creation of a mandate. Chapter 5 showed that state and local groups enjoyed their greatest influence on mandate issues when they were able to ally their interests with key beneficiary groups, and these alliances were most easily formed when seeking modifications of mandates and funding. Federal funding in particular served the interests of beneficiaries by promoting the greater likelihood of state and local interest and support of mandate implementation.

Modifications and funding to assuage state and local interests were also quite appealing to members of Congress pushing mandate legislation. A Congress averse to conflict will more likely embrace legislation that mollifies all significant interests. This type of legislation gives members the ability to claim credit for both the mandate benefits and for saving their states and localities from its worst effects.

From the federalism perspective, the successful modification of mandates helped blunt their state and local impact and surely made these seemingly coercive programs more cooperative in design and implementation. State and local success in achieving flexibility and funding of mandates confirms the relevance of the overlapping authority or cooperative model of federalism discussed in Chapter 2. This outcome suggests that state and local governments still have substantial political resources that limit the scope of the federal role when activated. Some observers conclude that this state and local influence over the design and implementation of federal programs is the most certain protector of their interests in a new federalism characterized by an ever-growing and increasingly pervasive national community.[28]

Ironically, the very success state and local governments enjoy in modifying mandates helped legitimize the federal regulatory presence itself.[29] Federal mandate programs were arguably strengthened and made more effective by promoting state and local cooperation in their implementation. State and local authority over the delivery of federally mandated programs were enhanced by it. However, the authority and autonomy of state and local governments over their own public services and values was ultimately undermined, as federal programs have grown to encumber a growing share of state and local resources and legal authority. This confirms the validity of the inclusive authority or coercive federalism model discussed in Chapter 2.

Participation in federal programs, although better than unilateral projection of federal power, does not protect the structural integrity of state and local governments from federal encroachment. The cooperative approach to mandates helped promote federalism values in choosing *how* to mandate, but it did not generally inform the decision about *whether* to mandate—a decision that may be best explained by the coercive model of federalism.

WHITHER FEDERALISM?

As the foregoing suggests, the stakes involved with federal mandate decisions are high. By the mid-1990s, the use of federal mandates had become both symbol and substance of a major shift in our federal system. The purported role of federalism as protector of state and local freedom and diversity from central control had been undermined by the growing influence of the national government on states and localities, first through extensive categorical grants and then through mandates. Far from checking and balancing, as theory suggests they should, actors in the federal system—federal, state, and local—engaged in what Martha Derthick calls "opportunistic cost shifting and benefit distribution in the context of a general obfuscation of responsibility."[30]

The political unwinding of federalism evolved against the backdrop of the continuing nationalization of the economy, communications media, and our political culture. Economists long argued that externalities associated with problems spilling over state or local boundaries justified a federal role. As the economy became more interdependent, it appeared that a growing number of public policy problems could not be contained within the boundaries of our intergovernmental system. States appeared to face collective action problems in addressing a range of these issues, whether it be acid rain, the regulation of brokers doing business in national securities markets, or the control of the sale of handguns. Some kind of national policy response in these areas might be viewed by many as functional for a national economy.

The nationalization of media and culture accentuated these trends by highlighting the need for national responses to problems and issues not characterized by externalities. It is indeed difficult to discern an economic rationale for federal mandates in such areas as asbestos in schools, handicapped education, or the release of convicted sex offenders into communities. Rather, one need go no further than to look at how national media and political infrastructures interact to nationalize sensibilities and convert problems that happen to occur within most states and communities into national issues warranting a federal response.

This is not the book to explore whether individual mandates or mandates in general are warranted or justified as public policy tools.

As the foregoing suggests, there appear to be strong economic grounds for some but not for others, and other national values commanding broad allegiance in a national community are also promoted by this policy too. This is the book, however, to reflect on how these nationalizing forces had become political variables that have served to accelerate and legitimize the reliance on mandates as tools of national action. It is also the place to point out that, even if justified in their particulars, mandates in general have had a cumulative impact on state and local governments, progressively eroding their discretionary resources to respond to unique state or local needs. However compelling each individual mandate and preemption is to the national community, their continued expansion at some point becomes incompatible with a healthy federal system. In fact, the consideration of mandates in isolation from their cumulative state and local impact has probably facilitated their adoption—an equation that mandate reform hopes to reverse.

Faced with this seemingly irrepressible nationalization of problems and solutions, our intergovernmental system withered as an effective constraint on national policy expansion during this period. In fact, our federal system, interacting with national media and political infrastructure, often served to stimulate expanded government at all levels. Paradoxically, the diversity traditionally protected and fostered in a federal system came to be a centralizing force. Innovations and differences among states, once the raison d'être for our federal system and a bulwark against centralization and standardization, had increasingly become catalysts for policy nationalization. Indeed, state and local leaders themselves sought the nationalization of their own policies, whether it be to protect against intergovernmental competition or to promote their own national policy ideas or political ambitions. As noted earlier, the increased nationalization of state and local political values and leaders have only served to further erode constraints on policy centralization.

As the foregoing suggests, the nationalization of political values and interests was accompanied by the ascendancy of an opportunistic view of federalism, as all partners in the federal system have attempted to use one another to achieve their own policy goals, regardless of the traditional boundaries implicit in a federal system. Federal officials ignored traditional constraints on national power by embracing mandates as a way to more directly and uniformly implement national objectives throughout an increasingly nationalized society. State and local officials have at times seemed unable to marshall the internal political resolve to protect their prerogatives against national encroachment and at times have quietly encouraged mandates to solve their own political governance problems. The prerogatives of states in our federal system came to be the ultimate victim of these trends.

The Sustainability of Mandate Reform

Do the changes ushered in with mandate reform in the mid-1990s offer the prospect of reversing these trends? Points of order and other changes in congressional procedure are not self-executing, but rather depend on supportive changes in the political environment.[31]

Many argue that we are, indeed, on the threshold of an unprecedented devolution of federal power, as reflected by the 1996 welfare reform block grant and UMRA's enactment itself. Bolstered by the institutional renewal of state and local governments and a decline in confidence in the federal government, a new Republican Congress came to power in 1995 dedicated to reducing the federal role in our system. Indeed, even before this party transition, the Congress began to show greater deference to state and local interests, as reflected by the bipartisan mandate reform legislation that nearly passed in 1994. The most important yet imponderable analytical question is whether these changes are short-term in nature, or whether they portend a shift in the more fundamental political variables that have prompted recent congressional reliance on mandates as a tool of government action.

Traditional sources of restraint—the Supreme Court, state and local governments, and congressional restrainors—may indeed have at least partially reasserted themselves in the mandate debate in the mid-1990s. Although restoring some of their past influence on the federalism debate, the impact of each of these actors on the mandate discussion remained decidedly mixed, as each actor continued to be crosspressured by other forces.

The Court has handed down rulings in the 1990s that reverse previous decisions by holding that the Constitution does provide protection against the direct commandeering of state and local governments through federal direct order mandates. Beginning with the 1992 New York case involving disposal of low-level radioactive waste[32] and culminating in the 1997 *Printz* case involving mandated local police background checks on prospective gun purchasers, the Court has overturned mandates on state or local governments that force them to regulate the private sector on behalf of federal policy goals and programs.[33]

These decisions have reinserted the Court as a constraint on federal mandates, a positive development from a federalism perspective. However, the implications of the Court's recent rulings are still unclear. Though direct order mandates that command state and local officials to enforce federal regulatory programs appear to be prohibited, the

Court's rulings do not apply to the mandate tools most commonly deployed at the federal level—grant conditions, crosscutting requirements, crossover sanctions, and partial preemptions. The Printz decision, in fact, suggests that these approaches do not violate federalism principles because the states' participation is voluntary, consistent with a long line of Court rulings.[34]

Moreover, these Court decisions do not address the legitimacy of total preemption as a tool of federal power. Thus, the Court has left Congress with tools should it wish to impose federal policies on states and localities.

As Chapters 8 and 9 document, state and local government interest groups themselves became more aroused on mandate issues, and their intensity reaped results in the congressional passage of mandate reform and the rollback of some existing mandates in 1996. In several cases, they succeeded in elevating the cost impacts of mandates to a valence status previously enjoyed only by mandate advocates. Once safe drinking water or highway mandates were defined in cost terms as opposed to benefit terms, for instance, it became more difficult to publicly oppose changing these mandates to reduce their costs. This is no small accomplishment, particularly when one examines the previous record of mandates by acclamation.

Although several mandates in 1996 still crosspressured state and local officials, their interest groups achieved some success in engaging mandate advocates in the conflict over defining the issue in cost rather than benefit terms. Redefining the terms of the debate in this way may enable them to challenge the creation of mandates at the outset. At minimum, the consensual style that characterized mandate policymaking in the past may give way to a more contested style on at least some proposed mandates if state and local governments succeed in sustaining their concern over mandate costs.

Nonetheless, state and local interest groups remained crosspressured and ambivalent on a number of important mandates and preemptions, as shown in Chapter 9. Whether it was family leave, welfare to work standards, gun control, federal health insurance standards, criminal justice, or the EPA's 1997 proposed air quality standards, state and local groups were too divided to take positions and mount the kind of concerted grassroots campaigns needed to overturn mandates and preemptions in these areas. Again, these kinds of mandates have deep roots in our political system and in our state and local communities as well. As with other actors, the fealty to federalism principles that motivated the effective state and local campaign for mandate reform can recede when other programmatic and policy goals emerge that tap stronger allegiances or internal conflicts among state and local officials.

The Congress itself showed renewed concern for our federal system during the mid-1990's. Democrats had already worked with Republicans to bring mandate reform to the agenda when the Republicans came to power in 1995 championing the revitalization of federalism as one of their main goals. Passage of mandate reform became one of their first legislative victories. The new Congressional leadership also sought to centralize policymaking in the House, and state elected officials gained more access to this new leadership-driven policymaking process. Republican Governors in particular were invited to play a major role in developing such devolution initiatives as the welfare reform block grant. This more collaborative relationship between state and national elected leaders offered the potential, at least for a time, for reviving traditional political linkages that reinforced federalism in the past. However, observers noted that the leadership had difficulties sustaining a centralized policy process over what remains an inherently locally based and fragmented political body.[35]

These initiatives indeed have borne fruit in specific legislation devolving authority to states for welfare and rolling back onerous mandates in safe drinking water and highways that had become intergovernmental flashpoints. The analysis in Chapter 9 showed that House Republicans in particular had lower mandate support scores across the board. As with the passage of mandates themselves, the tide of mandate reform swept over both parties to some extent, as manifest by joint sponsorship of mandate reform legislation by key Democrats such as Senator Glenn. Moreover, renewed caution exists in the Congress about the imposition of direct order mandates in particular covered by the mandate reform point of order, prompting forebearance in developing particular legislation. For instance, recent child health and child care initiatives championed by the Clinton Administration chose to emphasize the use of grants rather than mandates to improve access to health insurance and child care for low income families.

Clearly, important changes are in the works, but substantial continuities remain prompting continuing policy nationalization and centralization. Although direct order mandates may have fallen out of favor recently with both the Supreme Court and the Congress, pressures exist to use other mandating tools—preemptions and grant conditions most notably—to address compelling national problems and issues. As Chapter 9 showed, both parties continue to be pressed to address differing domestic goals that implicate state and local resources and authority, and various types of mandate tools are used to achieve these objectives.[36] David Walker has written that the more prescriptive a party becomes on how to achieve specific goals, the more likely it use mandates to achieve these objectives.[37]

Thus, despite the rising tide of interest in federalism principles, other national policy goals and values continue to offer competing and at times compelling lines of conflict in policy debates.

This gives rise to what David Walker has referred to as a period of "conflicted federalism," in which the national government seems to veer from an ad hoc and situational attachment to federalism to a continuing support for new national initiatives that impose new mandates and preemptions without any overall consistent strategy supporting devolution as one of the primary goals of public policy.[38] What underlies this phenomenon is the continuing nationalization of our politics. UMRA may have reflected a change in the political climate, but it remains to be seen whether it represents a sustainable shift in power and authority in our system. In fact, as long as the elements prompting and compelling national policy responses to problems persist, the resurgence of federalism will continue to compete with strong forces promoting policy nationalization.

It is widely acknowledged that Congressional incentives remain nationalized, as federal elected officials and their state and local counterparts remain entrepreneurial competitors rather than allies. Elected federal officials have strong incentives to champion national policy proposals, reinforced by a strong continuing national media and interest group presence in Washington. As discussed earlier, even state and local innovations and initiatives prompt policy centralization, as the diversity of our federal system ironically comes to promote federal expansion to limit the powers and resources of our states. The continuing strength of these incentives makes the federalism initiatives passed in recent years particularly noteworthy.

Prompted by political elites, the public comes to expect federal responses to public issues and problems. John Dilulio and Donald Kettl argue that Americans have not lost their appetite for national standards and federal programs to address a host of problems perceived as requiring a national solution. They assert:

> When cut-government push comes to address-problems shove, how many contemporary Americans really do not want government in general, or the national government in particular, to act on reducing crime, encouraging family values, and all the rest? Unless we have misplaced or completely misread the last half-century's worth of public opinion data, and unless the $3 trillion worth of government Americans have voted for themselves is a mirage, the only reasonable answer is a minority.[39]

If they are right, new mandate proposals are likely to continue to engender a compelling pull on politicians at all levels of government.

Fanned by an established national media and interest group presence in Washington, new waves of national policy impulses may very well continue to sweep over Washington in the form of mandates or other national policy tools.

The challenges to state and local governments' prerogatives will likely intensify over the coming years.[40] Deregulation of the telecommunications industry and new proposals for deregulation of electric utilities have major implications as state and local regulations, taxes, and fees come to be viewed as barriers to competition. National businesses continue to urge preemption, ranging from proposed legislation to preempt state and local taxation of the Internet, to renewed calls for federal product liability standards. The National Governors' Association itself has concluded that the internationalization of the economy will prompt calls for uniformity in business regulation, licenses, and taxes, which will often conflict with state sovereignty.[41]

The criminal justice area continues to be a focus of new proposed intergovernmental regulation, as leaders compete to find federal answers to public safety problems. Bipartisan pressures have also accelerated for further federal actions to regulate the provision of health care by health maintenance organizations and for extensions of health insurance to uncovered groups. The social and moral policy agenda continues to feature mandates and preemptions in the area of abortion, school prayer, expansion of family leave, and other family policy issues as well. Finally, bipartisan pressures to sustain a balanced budget, as well as the longer term federal budgetary pressures arising from the Baby Boom retirement, suggest that the reliance on regulation rather than on grants or other spending tools will continue, as will efforts to cap and devolve open-ended entitlement programs like Medicaid to the states.[42]

It remains to be seen whether these gathering forces will materialize in a new wave of nationalization of domestic policy, or whether state and local governments and their Congressional allies can build on mandate reform and pressures for a smaller federal role to forestall these initiatives and achieve further rollbacks of existing regulatory programs. Anthony Downs has observed how nonincremental policy change flows in predictable cycles, initiated by seemingly unstoppable bandwagons of enthusiasm and followed by periods of disillusionment and reconsideration, when it is realized belatedly that the new policy interferes with other priority values and concerns.[43]

Intergovernmental reform may also have a cyclical nature; David Beam has noted that brief episodes of federalism reform have typically been followed by longer periods of federal expansion.[44] This was the case in the Reagan era, when deregulation ushered in a new wave of regulation in the 1980s.

Block grants have been observed to have a similar cycle, as their passage seemingly heralds a new era of federalism, only to be followed by new restrictions and recategorization when it appears that state discretion may threaten other national goals. Even when state implementation of block grants appeared to support broad national goals, Congress nonetheless persisted in responding to an array of national groups who were seeking to use block grants as the occasion for the assertion of new national goals and interventions in state governance.[45] This episodic support for federalism is an expected result from a nationalized political system in which federalism is insufficiently institutionalized to provide a stable basis for national political choice.

It is difficult to predict turning points in these cyclical patterns. Ultimately, the sustainability of mandate reform will hinge on whether the desire to limit the scope of national government regulation becomes more politically compelling than the particular goals advanced by future mandate advocates. In other words, will the conflict over federalism displace the conflict over other social goals in our system?

As with other periods in our history, this cardinal question will never be answered one way for all time, nor one way in a given time. The outcome is critical, however, for much is at stake. The nation's ability to respond to emerging problems that can most effectively be addressed by the federal government on behalf of a national economy and community must be sustained. In so doing, however, the cumulative impact of such initiatives on state and local resources has to be watched closely, lest such initiatives undermine and encumber the capacity of state and local governments to respond to unique and diverse needs that is the benchmark for a vital federal system.

NOTES TO CHAPTER 10

1. Robert A. Dahl, *Democracy in the United States*, 2nd edition (Chicago: Rand McNally, 1972), p. 303.

2. Theodore Lowi, "American Business, Public Policy, Case-Studies and Political Theory," *World Politics*, 16 (July, 1964), pp. 677–715.

3. James Q. Wilson, *The Politics of Regulation* (New York: Basic Books, 1980).

4. The term mandate used in this chapter follows the six-fold definition in Chapter 1, so that mandates include both conditions of aid and preemptions, as well as direct order requirements.

5. David Mayhew, *Congress: The Electoral Connection* (New Haven: Yale University Press, 1978). Also, see Burton Loomis, *The American Politician: Ambition, Entrepreneurship, and the Changing Face of Political Life* (New York: Basic Books, 1988).

6. Some analysts suggest that grants are created by groups too weak to gain their goals at either level of government alone. See Thomas J. Anton, *American Federalism and Public Policy: How the System Works* (New York: Random House, 1989), pp. 82–84.

7. John Kincaid, "From Cooperative to Coercive Federalism," *Annals* 509 (May, 1990), pp. 139–152.

8. Frank R. Baumgartner and Bryan D. Jones, *Agendas and Instability in American Politics* (Chicago: University of Chicago Press, 1993).

9. *Ibid.,* p. 12.

10. Anthony Downs, "Up and Down with Ecology: The Issue Attention Cycle," *Public Interest,* 28 (Summer, 1972), pp. 38–50.

11. Frank R. Baumgartner and Bryan D. Jones, *Agendas and Instability in American Politics,* Chapter 5.

12. Anthony King, "The American Polity in the 1990's," in *The New American Political System,* 2nd edition, ed. Anthony King (Washington, D.C.: American Enterprise Institute, 1990), pp. 287–307.

13. Timothy Conlan, "Federalism and Competing Values in the Reagan Administration," *Publius: The Journal of Federalism* 16 (Winter, 1986), p. 45.

14. *Garcia v. San Antonio Metropolitan Transit Authority,* 105 S. Ct. 1005 (1985).

15. Advisory Commission on Intergovernmental Relations, *Regulatory Federalism: Policy, Process, Impact and Reform* (Washington, D.C.: ACIR, 1984), p. 117.

16. This classic pattern was viewed as a consequence of the politics of speculative augmentation, wherein Congress deliberately sets goals stretching current implementation capacity, with concessions made to reality over time should these goals prove to be impractical. See Charles Jones, *Clean Air: The Policies and Politics of Pollution Control* (Pittsburgh: University of Pittsburgh Press, 1975), p. 176.

17. Michael Reagan expresses the classic formulation when he observes that the reasons for federal preemption of states is that states are either not doing a good job or not doing the job at all. See his *Regulation: The Politics of Policy* (Boston: Little, Brown, 1987), p. 186.

18. For assessment of state modernization and capacity, see Advisory Commission on Intergovernmental Relations, *The Question of State Governmental Capacity* (Washington, D.C.: ACIR, 1985).

19. Paul L. Posner and Margaret T. Wrightson, "Block Grants: A Perennial, but Unstable, Tool of Government," *Publius: The Journal of Federalism* 26, No. 3 (Summer, 1996), p. 100.

20. David Rapp, "The Fifty-Headed Monster: Business Asks Washington to Save It from the States," *Governing* (October, 1990), p. 79.

21. Frank R. Baumgartner and Bryan D. Jones, *Agendas and Instability in American Politics,* p. 217.

22. States have been converging on per capita income, party competition, and voter participation at least since the early 1950s. For example, the coefficient of variation for party competition in gubernatorial elections declined from 42 to 18 percent between 1952 and 1984. Hofferbert reports steadily decreasing socioeconomic and policy variation among the states since 1890. See his "The Nationalization of State Politics," in Richard Hofferbert and Ira Sharkansky, ed., *State and Urban Politics* (Boston: Little, Brown, 1971).

23. See Douglas Rose, "National and Local Forces in State Politics: The Implications of Multi-Level Policy Analysis," *American Political Science Review* 67 (1973), pp. 1162–1173.

24. Stephen A. Salmore and Barbara G. Salmore, "The Transformation of State Electoral Politics," in Carl Van Horn, ed., *The State of the States*, 3rd edition (Washington, D.C.: Congressional Quarterly Press, 1996), pp. 51–76.

25. John F. Bibby and Thomas M. Holbrook, "Parties and Elections," in *Politics in the American States*, ed. Virginia Gray and Herbert Jacob (Washington, D.C.: Congressional Quarterly, 1996), pp. 78–121.

26. Clive S. Thomas and Ronald J. Hrebenar, "Interest Groups in the States," in *Politics in the American States*, pp. 122–158.

27. Edward W. Weidner, "Decision-Making in a Federal System," in *American Federalism in Perspective*, ed. Aaron Wildavsky (Boston: Little, Brown, 1967), p. 238.

28. Michael Reagan and John Sanzone, *The New Federalism*, 2nd edition (New York: Oxford University Press, 1981), p. 170.

29. American business also enjoyed success in modifying regulatory programs by accepting those programs only in principle. Richard A. Harris, "Politicized Management: The Changing Face of Business in American Politics," in *Remaking American Politics*, ed. Richard A. Harris and Sidney M. Milkis (Boulder, Co.: Westview Press, 1989), p. 275.

30. Martha Derthick, "Up-to-Date in Kansas City: Reflections on American Federalism," *PS: Political Science and Politics* (December, 1992), p. 675.

31. General Accounting Office, *Legislative Mandates: State Experiences Offer Insights for Federal Action* (Washington, D.C.: GAO, 1988).

32. *New York v. United States*, 505 U.S. 144 (1992).

33. Printz, Sheriff/Coroner, Ravalli County, *Montana v. United States* (1977).

34. On grant conditions, see *South Dakota v. Dole*, 483 U.S. 203 (1987); on partial preemptions, see *Hodel v. Virginia Surface Mining and Reclamation Association, Inc.*, 452 U.S. 264 (1981).

35. Lawrence C. Dodd and Bruce I. Oppenheimer, "Revolution in the House: Testing the Limits of Party Government," in *Congress Reconsidered*, 6th edition, ed. Lawrence C. Dodd and Bruce I. Oppenheimer (Washington, D.C.: Congressional Quarterly Press, 1997), p. 57.

36. Political scientists William F. Connelly Jr. and John J. Pitney Jr. commented that Gingrich seeks to supplant the traditional Republican language of dour austerity with a new language of hope and opportunity. See their *Congress' Permanent Minority? Republicans in the U.S. House* (Lanham, Md.: Rowman and Littlefield, 1994), p. 113.

37. David B. Walker, "Evolving Devolution, Continuing Centralization, and a Resulting Conflicted and Dysfunctional Federalism" (paper presented at USIS Germany-Sponsored Lectures, 13–20 June 1997).

38. David Walker, "Evolving Devolution, Continuing Centralization, and a Resulting Conflicted and Dysfunctional Federalism," p. 40.

39. John J. Dilulio Jr. and Donald F. Kettl, *Fine Print: The Contract with America, Devolution, and the Administrative Realities of American Federalism* (Washington, D.C.: Brookings Institution, 1 March 1995), p. 61.

40. See Frank Shafroth, "Local Rights, Authority Will Be Tested in '98," *Nation's Cities Weekly* 21, No. 1 (5 January 1998), p. 1.

41. National Governors' Association, "Legislative and Regulatory Pre-emptions Undermine Federalism," in *Issue Brief* (Washington, D.C.: National Governors' Association, 13 January 1998), p. 4.

42. Congressional Budget Office, *Long-Term Budgetary Pressures and Policy Options* (Washington, D.C.: CBO, March, 1997); U.S. General Accounting Office, *Long-Term Fiscal Policy: Implications for the Future* (Washington, D.C.: GAO, October, 1997).

43. Anthony Downs, "Up and Down with Ecology: The Issue Attention Cycle."

44. David R. Beam, "Federalism: Past, Present, and Future" (paper presented at the conference on federal mandates sponsored by the Advisory Commission on Intergovernmental Relations, Washington, D.C., 27 February 1996).

45. Paul L. Posner and Margaret T. Wrightson, "Block Grants: A Perennial, but Unstable, Tool of Government," p. 97.

Appendix 1

Major Mandate Legislation, 98th–101st Congresses

Mandate (Type[a])	Estimated five-year CBO cost/savings	Roll call
98th Congress		
Child Abuse Amendment of 1984, PL 98-457 (CO)—authorize "babydoe" regulations protecting handicapped newborns; require states to respond to medical neglect; federally defined	No estimate	Yes, H
Hazardous and Solid Waste Amendments of 1984, PL 98-616 (PP/DO)—establish partial preemption to regulate underground storage tanks; tighten federal regulation of land disposal practices and sites	$685 million[b]	No
Highway Safety Amendment of 1984, PL 98-363 (CO)—establish uniform national drinking age of twenty-one	No estimate	Yes, S
Social Security Amendment of 1983, PL 98-21 (DO)—prohibit state and local withdrawal from Social Security; increase and speed up their payments	$1.8–2.9 billion	Yes, S
Voting Accessibility for Elderly and Handicapped, PL 98-435 (DO)—mandate that polling places be accessible to elderly and handicapped	No estimate	No
Child Support Enforcement, PL 98-378 (CO)—mandate withholding of delinquent child support payments and state enforcement through liens; extend child support to nonwelfare families	$165 million in savings	No

Major Mandate Legislation, 98th–101st Congresses, *continued*

Mandate (Type[a])	Estimated five-year CBO cost/savings	Roll call
Cable Deregulation Act of 1984, PL 98-549 (TP)—limit local rate regulation; preempt local renewal standards	No estimate	Yes, S
Math and Science Education Act of 1984, PL 98-377 (DO)—require schools to allow student religious groups to meet in schools before and after classes	No estimate	Yes, H
99th Congress		
Age Discrimination in Employment Amendment of 1986, PL 99-592 (DO)—ban mandatory retirement with delay in coverage for police, firemen and college professors	No estimate	Yes, H
Asbestos Hazard Emergency Response Act of 1986, PL 99-519 (DO)—require schools to inspect and abate asbestos hazards	$500 million[b] ($3 billion/30 yrs)	No
Commercial Motor Vehicle Safety Act of 1986, PL 99-570 (CO)—direct states to administer national license and testing standards for commercial and school bus drivers	No estimate	No
Education of the Handicapped Amendments of 1986, PL 99-457 (CO/GC)—require coverage for disabled preschool children; establish early intervention program for infants at risk	$3.1 billion	No
Safe Drinking Water Amendments of 1986, PL 99-339 (DO)—mandate new national drinking water standards and new monitoring requirements for public water systems	$10 billion[b]	No
Handicapped Children's Protection Act of 1986, PL 99-372 (CO)—allow recovery of attorneys' fees for both administrative and court proceedings for parents challenging schools	No estimate	No

Major Mandate Legislation, 98th–101st Congresses, *continued*

Mandate (Type[a])	Estimated five-year CBO cost/savings	Roll call
Consolidated Omnibus Budget Reconciliation Act of 1985, PL 99-272 (DO)—extend Medicare payroll taxes to all new state and local employees; require Medicaid coverage for new categories and pregnant women	$800 million	Yes, S
Immigration Reform and Control Act of 1986, PL 99-603 (DO)—impose service mandates on state and local sector by granting legal status to illegal aliens	$2.3 billion in savings	Yes, S
Water Resources Development Act of 1986, PL 99-662 (GC)—require local cost sharing for federal water resources projects	$910 million	Yes, H
100th Congress		
Fair Housing Act Amendments of 1988, PL 100-430 (DO)—expand Civil Rights Act of 1968 to cover handicapped and children, with state and local enforcement that meets federal standards	No estimate	No
Drug-Free Workplace Act of 1988, PL 100-690 (CC)—require all federal aid recipients to certify to drug-free workplace; provide employee training and treatment	No estimate	No
Civil Rights Restoration Act of 1987, PL 100-259 (CC)—reverse Supreme Court's *Grove City* ruling to provide institutionwide coverage for nondiscrimination rules applying to grantees	No estimate	Yes, S
Nursing Home Regulation, PL 100-203 (PP)—states required to enforce federal quality and safety standards	No estimate	No
Ocean Dumping Ban Act of 1988, PL 100-688 (DO)—outlaw dumping of municipal sludge in seas	$1 billion[c]	No

Major Mandate Legislation, 98th–101st Congresses, *continued*

Mandate (Type[a])	Estimated five-year CBO cost/savings	Roll call
Water Quality Act of 1987, PL 100-4 (DO/PP)—new non–point source pollution program; new schedule for municipal storm sewer discharge; reduce federal sewage treatment grants and convert to state revolving loan funds	No estimate	No
Lead Contamination Control Act of 1988, PL 100-572 (DO)—require states to work with schools to replace lead-lined water coolers	No estimate	No
Family Support Act, PL 100-485 (GC)— overhaul the Aid to Families With Dependent Children program requiring state provision of jobs, child care, transitional Medicaid, and AFDC to unemployed parents, with additional federal funding and other mandates providing savings such as workfare requirements and new child support enforcement mandates	$99 million	Yes, S
Medicare Catastrophic Act, PL 100-105, and Medicare Catastrophic Act Repeal, PL 100-234 (GC)—mandate additional state Medicaid coverage for poor elderly Medicare premiums and new categories of children and pregnant mothers; prevent states from reducing other types of Medicaid or AFDC services; increase Medicaid nursing home coverage by liberalizing spousal impoverishment rules	$2.6 billion	No

101st Congress

Americans with Disabilities Act, PL 101-327 (DO)—prohibit discrimination against disabled; promote access to public facilities and transit	$1 billion	Yes, H

Major Mandate Legislation, 98th–101st Congresses, *continued*

Mandate (Type[a])	Estimated five-year CBO cost/savings	Roll call
Clean Air Act Amendments of 1990, PL 101-549 (PP)—new standards and deadlines for dealing with urban smog, acid rain, and municipal incinerators	$1.25 billion	Yes, S&H
Education of Handicapped Act Amendment of 1990, PL 101-476 (CO)—eliminate state immunity from parent suits seeking tuition reimbursement	No estimate	No
FY 1991 Budget Reconciliation Act, PL 101-508 (DO/GC)—extend Social Security coverage to all state and local employees not covered by pension system	$2.7 billion	No
FY 1991 Budget Reconciliation Act, PL 101-508 (GC)—extend Medicaid mandates to all poor children between ages of six and eighteen	$1.1 billion	No

[a] Mandate types: DO = direct order; PP = partial preemption; CO = crossover sanction; CC = crosscutting requirement; GC = major grant condition; TP = total preemption.
[b] Estimates derived from the EPA, not the CBO. Estimates include a capital expenditure component that has been divided by thirty years to approximate a normal timeframe for bond financing, and has then been increased to obtain a five-year estimate.
[c] CBO estimate used, assuming five years of fines paid by the nine jurisdictions subject to the ban.

Index

AASA. *See* American Association of
School Administrators
Abdnor, James, 101, 111
Abramson, Jerry, 168
Advisory Commission on Intergovernmental Relations (ACIR)
catalogue of mandates, 57–58
the Court and federal grants, 205
definition and typology of federal
mandates, 12–13, 175
demise of, 188, 202–3
federalism and pre-1970s regulatory
legislation, 22–23
mandate reform, 168, 170, 174, 187–88
Reagan's federalism initiative, xiii
state and local reaction, 75n3, 217
trends in intergovernmental relations,
4, 8, 10, 27, 62, 65, 165–66, 182
Age Discrimination in Employment
Amendment of 1986 (PL 99-592), 234
AHERA. *See* Asbestos Hazard
Emergency Response Act of 1986
Alabama, and unfunded mandates, 167
Allen, George, 167
American Association of School
Administrators (AASA), 102–3, 113,
146, 147, 148, 151
American Federation of Teachers, 87,
113, 149, 154
Americans With Disabilities Act (PL 101-
327), 236
Anaya, Toney, 83, 112
Anton, Thomas, 88
Armstrong, William, 45
Asbestos Hazard Emergency Response
Act of 1986 (AHERA, PL 99-519)
coalition politics, 102–6
consensual politics, 87, 107–11
in general, 60, 62, 234

heading off conflict, 83–84, 115–16
implementation, 117–18
incremental steps toward, 97–101
overview, 94–95, 118–20
policy entrepreneurs, 99, 105–6
reaction of the regulated, 111–15, 119
regulatory expansion, 96–97, 101–2
science and politics, 95–96, 110–11
Asbestos School Hazard Detection and
Control Act of 1980, 99
Asbestos Schools Hazard Abatement Act
of 1984, 101
Association of Retarded Citizens, 137–38
Association of Severely Handicapped,
151

Banfield, Edward, 21, 79
Bardach, Eugene, 26, 63, 66, 96
Bartlett, Steven, 71, 146, 148, 150, 151,
152, 154
Baucus, Max, 117
Baumgartner, Frank, 23, 163, 214
Beam, David, 7, 23, 163, 228
Beer, Samuel, 10, 22
Bennett, William, 143
Bereuter, Douglas, 118
Berry, Jeffrey, 78, 80
Biaggi, Mario, 145
Blackmun, Harry, 9, 78, 216
block grants, 180, 229
Bloom, Benjamin, 135
Brademas, John, 130
Brady Handgun Violence Prevention
Act, 28, 202
Budget Reconciliation Act FY 1991
(PL 101-508), 237
Bush, George, 7, 136, 161
Byrd, Robert, 173

Cable Deregulation Act of 1984 (PL 98-549), 234
Camden, New Jersey, asbestos regulation, 105
Camissa, Anne, 81, 82
Caraley, Demetrios, 37, 38, 40, 41
CBO. *See* Congressional Budget Office
Cheney, Richard, 41–42
Child Abuse Amendment of 1984 (PL 98-457), 233
Child Support Enforcement (PL 98-378), 58, 233
child support enforcement, and welfare reform, 189
Choper, Jesse, 22
Christian Coalition, 201
Chubb, John, 24, 30
Civil Rights Restoration Act of 1987 (PL 100-259), 235
Clausen, Aage, 41–42
Clean Air Act Amendments of 1990 (PL 101-549), 237
Clinton, Bill, 69, 168, 172, 174, 191
Columbus, Ohio, cost of unfunded mandates, 165, 167
Commercial Motor Vehicle Safety Act of 1986 (PL 99-570), 68, 85–86, 234
Congressional Budget Office (CBO)
    and UMRA, 181–84, 188, 208n8, 210n49
    expansion of intergovernmental responsibilities, 7, 160, 169, 203–4
    mandate cost estimates, 58, 75n2, 88, 143, 150, 174–75, 186
Congressional Task Force on Federal Mandates, 169
congressional voting. *See* roll call analysis
Conlan, Timothy, 7, 23, 26, 38, 43–44, 163, 166, 215
consensus on federal mandates
    achieved for asbestos. *See* Asbestos Hazard Emergency Response Act of 1986 (AHERA)
    denied for preschool programs for handicapped children, 150–53
    overview, 57–60
    in 99th Congress, 60–66
Consolidated Omnibus Budget Reconciliation Act of 1985 (PL99-272), 235

constrainers
    asbestos regulation, 110–11, 119
    disarming of, 66–70
    party affiliation, 70–74
    preschool programs for handicapped children, 143, 144–50
    See also governments, state and local
constraint models of policymaking. *See* models of policymaking, classical pluralist
Contract With America, 160, 172, 173, 198
coordinate authority model. *See* dual federalism
Council for Exceptional Children, 142, 151, 152–53
criminal justice mandates, 186–87

Department of Education, 136, 138, 150
Department of Labor, cost estimates of Fair Labor Standards compliance, 6
deregulation
    politics of, 92–92n21
    See also Reagan Administration, regulatory relief effort
Derthick, Martha, 23, 29, 30, 72, 91n21, 141, 222
devolution, of federal grants, xiii, 2, 17n1
Dilulio, John, 227
Dingell, John, 107–8, 110
District of Columbia, special education, 129
Dole, Robert, 173, 191
Domenici, Pete, 88, 162
Downs, Anthony, 148, 163, 214, 228
Drug-Free Workplace Act of 1988 (PL 100-690), 235
dual federalism, 28

Early Childhood Research Institutes, 137
education, special. *See* special education
Education Amendments of 1974, 130
Education for All Handicapped Children Act of 1975, 130–34, 136, 140, 142
Education of the Handicapped Act of 1970, 127
Education of the Handicapped Act Amendment of 1990, (PL 101-476), 237

Education of the Handicapped Amend-
    ments of 1986, (PL99-457), 234
Education Rights and Privacy Act of
    1974, 132–33
Elazar, Daniel, 22, 28, 201
Elementary and Secondary Education
    Act of 1965, 127
entrepreneurs, policy
    and asbestos regulation, 99–100,
        105–6
    emergence of, 24, 61–62, 212–13
    and the handicapped, 128, 138–39
    and mandate reform, 171–72
Environmental Defense Fund, 96, 98–100
Environmental Protection Agency (EPA)
    and asbestos, 6, 97–104, 106, 108–12,
        114–17, 121–22n24, 122n33, 217
    and safe drinking water, 84
explanations for federal mandates
    ambivalence of state and local
        government. See governments, state
        and local
    budgetary concerns, 65–66
    federalist policymaking models. See
        federalist policymaking models
    opponents constrained. See
        constrainers
    policy goals, 65–66
    regulatory expansion, 62–63
    state initiatives, 63–65
    valence politics, 190–91, 200–201,
        214–15
externality groups, 63

Fair Housing Act Amendments of 1988
    (PL 100-430), 235
Fair Labor Standards Act, 22
Fair Labor Standards Amendments of
    1986, 60, 62, 67, 75n3, 75n6, 88–89
Family and Medical Leave Act, 201
Family Support Act (PL 100-485), 236
federalism
    and congressional voting, See roll call
        analysis
    governmental roles within, 3–4
    after mandate reform, 211–29
    and mandate reform, 175–76, 284
    picket fence, 157n51
    reemergence of, 1–2

and Republican Party, 21, 27
    as a secondary value, 54, 74, 215
Federalist Papers, 21
federalist policymaking models
    dual federalism, 28, 31
    inclusive authority, 28–30, 31–32
    overlapping authority, 28–29, 31
federal mandate reform
    building support for, 163–68
    effectiveness through preventing,
        180–87, 18n25
    effectiveness through rollbacks,
        187–89
    in general, 2, 160–63, 175–76, 206–7
    legislative action, 171–74
    legislative options, 168–71
    post-legislation politics, 189–202
    reforming the reform, 204–6
    substantive details of legislation, 174–75
federal mandates
    asbestos. See Asbestos Hazard
        Emergency Response Act of 1986
    and congressional voting. See roll call
        analysis
    consensus on. See consensus on
        federal mandates
    criminal justice, 186–87
    defined, 4, 11–14, 229n4
    explanations for. See explanations for
        federal mandates
    and federalism, 2, 211–15
    and federalist policymaking models,
        30–32
    funding of, 68–69
    health care, 187
    minimum wage, 181, 183, 186
    overview of issues, 5–7
    pesticides, 187
    recent history of, 4–5, 7–8
    special education. See handicapped
        children, preschool programs;
        special education
    and the Supreme Court, 8–10
    See also titles of statutes (with PL
        number)
Federal Role Index, 25
fireman's theory of federal influence, 154
Florian, Lonnie, 135
Florida
    asbestos regulation, 98
    special education, 131

Florio, James, 71, 72, 105–13, 115–17
Ford, Gerald, 130
Fraas, Charlotte, 136
free-rider problem, 21

Gallagher, James, 134
Garcia v. San Antonio Metropolitan Transit Authority, 9, 22, 26, 62, 75n3, 78, 88, 119, 216
Garwood, S. Gray, 135, 151
General Accounting Office (GAO)
    and asbestos, 98, 102
    impact of UMRA, 204
    study of education for the handicapped, 131
General Revenue Sharing program, 163
Gingrich, Newt, 173, 231n36
Glenn, John, 172, 226
Gold, Steven, 176n9
Goodling, William, 101, 146, 151
Gorsuch, Ann, 106
governments, state and local
    continued ambivalence regarding mandates, 216–22, 225
    factors limiting influence, 86–89
    as interest groups in relation to mandates, 69, 78–81, 89–90
    positions taken during 99th Congress, 81–83
    reasons for ambivalence toward mandates, 83–86
Grace, Peter, 108
grant programs
    block, 8, 180, 229
    devolution of, xiii, 2, 17n1
    and overlapping authority model, 29
    v. mandates, 3–4, 86, 205
Grodzins, Morton, 21, 23–24, 28, 79
Guiliani, Rudolph, 189

Haider, Donald, 80–82, 86
handicapped children, preschool programs
    implementation of grant program and aftermath, 153–55
    legislation in the Senate, 82, 138–44, 159n91
    origins of political support, 133–38
    reaching consensus on denying mandate, 150–53
    resistance of regulated in the House, 68, 87, 144–50
    See also special education
Handicapped Children's Protection Act of 1986 (PL 99-372), 136, 139, 144, 234
Hanus, Jerome, 18n17
Harkin, Tom, 138
Hatch, Orrin, 141–43, 147
Hathaway, William, 133
Hawaii
    funds from Senate legislation for handicapped children, 143
    impact of mandates, 165
Hawkins, Augustus, 144
Hazardous and Solid Waste Amendments of 1984 (PL 98-616), 233
health care mandates, 187
Heclo, Hugh, 27
Hero, Rodney, 37, 38, 49
highway grants mandate rollback, 188, 200
Highway Safety Amendment of 1984 (PL 98-363), 233
Houston, Texas, asbestos regulation, 98
Hunt, J. McV., 135

ideology
    as explanatory variable in congressional voting, 37–38, 40–42, 51–53, 193–97
    and policy goals in congressional voting, 45–46
    shift from in policy debates, 26–27
immigration reform, and UMRA, 184, 185
Immigration Reform and Control Act of 1986 (PL99-603), 58, 60, 67–68, 235
inclusive authority model, 28–30
incremental model of policymaking, 98, 164
interest group model. *See* models of policymaking, classical pluralist
interest group politics
    asbestos regulation, 102–6
    by governments, state and local. *See* governments, state and local
    growth of, 25–26, 34n33
    post-mandate reform, 199–202
Iowa, costs of preschool program for handicapped children, 153

iron triangles, 23, 24, 164
issue-attention cycle, 148, 154, 163, 214

Javits, Jacob, 128, 133
Jones, Bryan, 23, 163, 214
Jones, Charles, 120
Journal of Childhood Special Education, 135

Kagan, Robert, 63, 66, 96
Kanka, Megan, 190
Katzman, Robert, 128
Kayden, Lewis, 30
Kean, Thomas, 106
Kempthorne, Dirk, 171
Kennedy, Edward, 133, 145
Kernell, Samuel, 26
Kerry, John, 136, 139
Kestnbaum Commission, 22
Kettl, Donald, 227
Kincaid, John, 4, 213
Kingdon, John, 23, 26, 95
Koch, Edward, 7

Lead Contamination Control Act of 1988
    (PL 100-572), 236
Lent, Norman, 71, 110–11
Lovell, Catherine, 5, 12
Lowi, Theodore, 11, 25, 43–44

Machiarrola, Frank, 148–49
Madigan, Edward, 73
Malaby, Michael, 37–38
mandate
    reform. *See* federal mandate reform
    reimbursement, 170–71
mandates. *See* federal mandates
Martin, James, 85
Maryland, costs of preschool program
    for handicapped children, 153
Massachusetts, asbestos in schools, 97
Math and Science Education Act of 1984
    (PL 98-377), 234
Mathias, Charles, 130
Mayhew, David, 24, 25, 59
McConnell, Grant, 103
McCubbins, Matthew, 154
media, and the breakdown of federalism,
    25–26

Medicaid, 6, 13, 84–85, 87–88, 162–63,
    176n9, 228
Medicare, 65, 66, 68, 87
Medicare Catastrophic Act (PL 100-105),
    236
Megan's Law, 186, 190
Melcher, John, 117
mental health parity mandate, 208n8
Miller, George, 99–100, 105
minimum wage, 181, 183, 186
Missouri, and unfunded mandates, 167
models of policymaking
    classical pluralist, 20–23, 78–79
    dynamic, 23–27
    federalist. *See* federalist policymaking
        models
    incremental, 98, 164
    punctuated equilibrium, 214
Murphy, Austin, 73

Nathan, Richard, 17n1, 29, 63, 80, 141
National Academy of Sciences, 95
National Association of Counties
    (NAACO), 5, 22, 80, 113, 114, 165
National Association of School Boards,
    117, 147, 149, 151
National Conference of State Legislatures
    (NCSL), 4, 22, 149, 200
National Education Association, 97, 102,
    106, 111, 113, 149
National Governors Association (NGA)
    opposition to mandating preschool
        program for handicapped children,
        149–50
    positions taken during 99th Congress,
        82
    and state officials, 83–84
    support for asbestos regulation,
        112–14
    support for mandates, 85, 89, 228
    as Washington lobby, 21–22, 80, 200
National League of Cities, 22, 132, 200,
    201, 202
National League of Cities v. Usery, 19n42
National Unfunded Mandates Day, 8,
    166
Neiman, Max, 127
New Jersey
    asbestos regulation, 64, 97, 98
    special education, 129
New Mexico, special education, 132

New York
  asbestos regulation, 98
  costs of preschool program for
    handicapped children, 153
New York City, spending on special
  education, 148
New York v. United States, 9
NGA. *See* National Governors
  Association
99th Congress, mandate activity in,
  60–74
Nixon, Richard, 25
Nixon Administration, and regulation of
  state and local governments, 24–25
Nursing Home Regulation (PL 100-203),
  235

Oates, Wallace, 65
Occupational Safety and Health Act of
  1970 (OSHA), 25, 95, 96, 120n4
Ocean Dumping Ban Act of 1988
  (PL 100-688), 235
O'Connor, Sandra Day, 169
Office of Management and Budget
  (OMB), 7, 104, 161
Olson, Mancur, 21, 25, 79
overlapping authority model, 28–29

Packwood, Robert, 72
Paperwork Reduction Act, 161
Parent-Teacher Association (PTA), 97,
  100, 102, 111, 113
party affiliation. *See* political party
  system
Pennsylvania, special education, 129
pesticides mandate, 187
Peterson, Paul, 30, 85, 133
Philadelphia, Pennsylvania, asbestos regulation, 102
Piaget, Jean, 135
picket fence federalism, 157n51
point of order strategy, 169, 171, 183,
  184–85
policy goals, as motivation for mandates,
  38–39, 42–47, 65–66, 192
policy entrepreneurs. *See* entrepreneurs,
  policy
policymaking process, models of. *See*
  models of policymaking

political party system
  breakdown of, 24–25
  as explanatory variable in
    congressional voting, 37–38, 40–42,
    49, 192–99
  mandate support/constraint, 70–74
  and policy goals in congressional
    voting, 43–46
  protection against federal intrusion,
    21
Portman, Rob, 171
Price Waterhouse, 5, 165
Printz v. United States, 9, 28, 202, 224
PTA. *See* Parent-Teacher Association
punctuated equilibrium model, 214

Quayle, Dan, 141
Quirk, Paul, 23, 72, 91n21

Rabe, Barry, 85, 133
RAND, cost of special education study,
  132
Reagan, Michael, 230n17
Reagan, Ronald
  federalism as a secondary value, 25,
    38, 43
  federalism initiatives, xiii, 28, 37, 61
Reagan Administration
  and asbestos regulation, 99, 104, 108,
    109, 118–19
  block grants, 8
  conservative social policy agenda, 25,
    43
  regulatory relief effort, 7, 161, 229.
    See also deregulation, politics of
  and special education, 133, 143,
    152–53
  state and local tax deductibility, 89
regionalism, as explanatory variable in
  congressional voting, 48–49, 51–53
regulation
  asbestos and the logic of expansion,
    96–97, 101–2
  expansion and federal mandates,
    62–63
  of state and local governments, 24–25
Regulatory Flexibility Act, 161
Rehabilitation Act, 68, 128
Rehnquist, William, 210n52
Republican Governors Association, 173

Resource Conservation and Recovery
Act, 109
revenue sharing, 89, 163, 167
Riggle, James, 166
roll call analysis
experience of officeholders as
explanatory variable, 49, 51, 195
ideology as explanatory variable,
37–38, 40–42, 48–49, 51–53, 193–97
influence of Administration position,
46–47
mandate votes in Congress, 40–53,
192–99
methodology, 14–15, 36, 39–40, 47–48,
54n1, 54–55n2, 55n11–12, 56n24
party affiliation as explanatory
variable, 37–38, 40–42, 49, 192–99
policy goals as explanatory variable,
38–39, 42–46, 54, 192
previous studies of congressional
decisions on federalism 37–39
region as explanatory variable, 48–49,
51–53, 195
Rose, Douglas, 219
Rose-Ackerman, Susan, 85

Safe Buildings Alliance, 103
Safe Drinking Water Amendments of
1986 (99-339), 60, 62, 63, 66, 69, 83, 84,
88, 234
safe drinking water mandate, 188, 191,
200
Salamon, Lester, 11
Salisbury, Robert, 63
Sayre, Wallace, 149
Schattschneider, Elmer Everett, 20, 100
Schecter, Stephen, 38
Schlussel, Yvette, 40
Schwartz, Donna, 166
Schweicker, Richard, 133
science, and politics over asbestos, 95–96,
110–11, 118
Scotch, Richard, 136
securities reform, and UMRA, 184–85
Selikoff, Irving, 96
Service Employees International Union
(SEIU), 97, 103–5, 106, 110, 112
Simpson, Alan, 113, 114, 143, 184
Small Business Regulatory Enforcement
Fairness Act, 204
Smith v. Robinson, 62

Social Security Amendment of 1983
(PL 98-21), 233
special education
background, 127–30
Education for All Handicapped
Children Act of 1975, 130–34
overview, 126–27
preschool programs for handicapped
children. *See* handicapped children,
preschool programs
speculative augmentation, politics of,
230n16
Stafford, Robert, 72, 97, 113–14, 116, 130,
133–34, 139, 142
Stanford Research Institute, study of
education for the handicapped, 131
state initiatives, and federal mandates,
63–65
Stone, Deborah, 164
Sundquist, James, 41, 65, 98
Supreme Court
and federal mandates, 8–10, 19n42,
22, 62, 210n52, 224–25
and model of dual federalism, 28

Task Force on Regulatory Relief, 161
Tax Reform Act of 1986, 101
telecommunications reform, and UMRA,
183–84, 185–86
Texas, handicapped infants, 138
topocrats, 22
Toxic Substances Control Act of 1976
(TSCA), 99, 104, 109
Truman, David, 20–21, 112

UMRA. *See* Unfunded Mandates Reform
Act of 1995
Unfunded Mandates Reform Act of 1995
(UMRA)
effectiveness of, 180–207, 227
enactment of, 2, 18n25, 160, 163,
167–76, 224
U.S. Conference of Mayors, 22, 165
United States v. Lopez, 9
Urban Institute, 5, 69
Utah, funds from Senate legislation for
handicapped children, 143

valence politics
asbestos regulation, 101

valence politics, *continued*
  and mandate benefits, 190–91,
    200–201, 214–15
  and mandate costs, 225
  and mandate reform, 176
Vile, M. J. C., 22
Virginia, and unfunded mandates, 167
Vogel, David, 23, 78, 80
Voting Accessibility for Elderly and
  Handicapped (PL 98-435), 233

Walker, David, 26, 30, 226–27
Water Quality Act of 1987 (PL 100-4),
  236
Water Resources Development Act of
  1986 (PL 99-662), 66, 187, 235
Webber, David, 37–38
Wechsler, Herbert, 22

Weicker, Lowell, 68, 72, 82, 135–43, 145,
  147, 152
welfare reform, 2, 188–89, 224
Wildavsky, Aaron, 100
Will, Madeline, 146
Williams, Pat, 138, 144–46, 148, 150, 151
Wilson, James Q., 21, 27, 79
Wilson, Pete, 167
Wilson, Woodrow, 3
Wong, Kenneth, 85, 133
Wright, Deil, 28, 29
Wrightson, Margaret, 23, 38–39
Wyoming Association of School Boards,
  113
Wyoming v. EEOC, 62

Zimmer, Richard, 190
Zimmerman, Joseph, 12–13